So Proudly We Taught

So Proudly We Taught

✿ Retired Tar Heel Teachers

by
NORTH CAROLINA RETIRED SCHOOL PERSONNEL
a division of
NORTH CAROLINA ASSOCIATION OF EDUCATORS

*A PRIDE IN AMERICA
BICENTENNIAL PROJECT OF THE
NATIONAL RETIRED TEACHERS ASSOCIATION*

edited by
AN EDITORIAL COMMITTEE OF
RETIRED NORTH CAROLINA EDUCATORS

directing editors
CLARINDA A. BRITT AND JAMES E. BRITT

1976

First Printing—Limited Edition

Library of Congress Cataloging in Publication Data
Main entry under title:
So proudly we taught.

    1. Education—North Carolina—History.   I. Britt,
Clarinda A.   II. Britt, James E.   III. North Carolina
Association of Educators. North Carolina Retired School
Personnel Division.
LA340.S65   370'.9756   76–6888

Printed in the United States of America by
Heritage Printers, Inc., Charlotte, N. C.

... "But I have promises to keep,
And miles to go before I sleep,
And miles to go before I sleep."
—ROBERT FROST

To those who have made and loyally
kept their promises;

Who have proudly and gallantly traveled
the miles toward a sublime purpose;

Who have "dreamed dreams and seen visions"—

To those who, in educating the children
and youth of this state and nation
not only to accept a great heritage
already theirs but to keep promises
yet unfulfilled—The Promise of America,
a promise almost too magnificent to
be envisioned—

To all Retired Teachers this volume is
gratefully and lovingly dedicated.

North Carolina Nickname—"Tar Heel"

When Carolina was divided in 1710, the southern part was called South Carolina and the northern or older settlement was called North Carolina, or the "Old North State." Historians had recorded that the principal products of this State were "tar, pitch and turpentine."

It was during one of the fiercest battles of the War Between the States, so the story goes, that the column supporting the North Carolina troops was driven from the field. After the battle, the North Carolinians, who had successfully fought it out alone, were greeted from the passing derelict regiment with the question: "Any more tar down in the Old North State, boys?"

Quick as a flash came the answer; "No; not a bit; old Jeff's bought it all up."

"Is that so; what is he going to do with it?"

"He is going to put it on you'ns heels to make you stick better in the next fight."

Creecy relates that General Lee, hearing of the incident, said: "God bless the Tar Heel boys," and from that they took the name.

—Adapted from *Grandfather Tales of North Carolina* by R. B. Creecy and *Histories of North Carolina Regiments*, Vol. III, by Walter Clark

❧ Contents

So Proudly We Taught—Retired Tar Heel Teachers is North Carolina's answer to a challenge by the National Retired Teachers Association to the retired school personnel of every state and territory of the United States to become recorders of the contributions which have been made. Since education of our youth is the foundation of our nation, it has molded us into a people who have just cause to celebrate the nation's Bicentennial Birthday in 1976.

Without the enthusiastic response and cooperative spirit of the members of the North Carolina Retired School Personnel Division of the North Carolina Association of Educators this book could not have been written. More than 625 retired Tar Heel teachers have contributed over 800 articles; however, over 1,000 retirees have been personally involved in the project. Some, who did not write, helped others to remember; some dug in attics for old pictures of early school days; and others helped friends recall incidents and urged them to record pertinent events which helped our schools contribute to North Carolina's greatness.

Financing for the project started with "seed money" from the National Retired Teachers Association, based on the number of members in the state. State financial support came from the fifteen districts, each contributing equally to the promotional and distribution expenses. The treasurer has received all monies and directed the distribution of the books.

The members of the state editing committee, who live from the eastern to the western sections of the state, met four times in

Newton to consult and plan the compilation of this volume from the material contributed. One of the primary concerns was that all the ideas expressed by contributors be used in the book. The artistic details of the dedication page were contributed by an editor.

The articles were sent to a central point where they were read, divided according to subject matter and sent to the member of the state editing committee who compiled the chapter to which the idea was pertinent.

In the last section of the book the names of the contributors are listed in alphabetical order.

Editing Committees at the local unit level and state level have spent many hours reading, writing, re-reading and re-writing in an attempt to show how our retired school personnel have lovingly and persistently guided the development of education for North Carolina's youth from the bare necessities of "readin', 'ritin' and 'rithmetic" to a more complex curriculum necessary to produce citizens living in the most technological age man has experienced.

A retired teacher has said: "The retired members of the teaching profession have been given a once-in-a-lifetime opportunity to combine efforts and, hopefully, to take a good look at the origins and development of education in our nation and thus to help lay the groundwork for a brighter future."

Two sisters, 84 and 86 years of age, spoke for all of us. Reflecting on a job well done, they declared, "We are proud of our contribution."

The earliest schools in America had as their main purpose the teaching of the 3 Rs so that the people might be able to read the scriptures for themselves, sign their names on legal documents and count their money.

Later, at the time of the Revolution and in the years thereafter when politics became a driving force, a democratic government demanded an enlightened people. "Finally as the process of industrialization, mechanization and technological improvements developed and grew, economics as a motivative purpose for education prevailed more and more. It became apparent that a capitalistic industrialized society cannot exist with an illiterate populace."

We believe this volume has historical value. It has been recorded "just as it was" by those who were there. In the one-room building with its lack of equipment, books, writing materials or laboratories, students did develop a desire to learn those things which would lead to real accomplishments and make life more worth while. Now our modern public school, with facilities of every kind, offers a curriculum which exceeds that of the college or university of yesteryear.

Under both circumstances, love and interest create a strong bond between student and teacher and *learning takes place*.

It is the hope of the editors that this volume will bring to mind other experiences, which will enrich the memories of all retired school personnel, and be a source of inspiration to all who follow.

AMERICAN BICENTENNIAL

A *Adapts opportunities for service to others*
M *Manifests pride of and hopes for our country*
E *Expands our horizons, encourages us to enlarge our knowledge of our Heritage*
R *Reaffirms the basic principles on which our nation was founded*
I *Implements the ideas clearly set forth 200 years ago*
C *Contributes to the building of a "More Perfect Union"*
A *Americans shall continue to make an ever greater America*

EDITING COMMITTEE

First Row (left to right): Mrs. Blanche Zimmerman, Miss Mozelle Causey, Mrs. Ruie Walker, Mrs. Clarinda Britt.

Second Row: Miss Thelma Laws, Mrs. Ethel Twiford, Dr. Elizabeth Welch.

Third Row: Mrs. Grace Brummitt, Miss Alma Browning.

Fourth Row: R. L. Rhyne, C. W. Twiford, H. S. Shepherd, James E. Britt, William E. Loftin (Printer), Fred G. Brummitt.

The following were not present when the picture was made: Ernest W. Morgan, Miss Maie Sanders, W. Amos Abrams, W. W. Howell, Eleanor Jamieson.

✑ State Editing Committee

Dr. W. Amos Abrams, Raleigh

Mrs. Clarinda A. Britt, Co-Chairperson, Newton

James E. Britt, Co-Chairperson, Newton

Miss Alma Browning, Lake Junaluska

Fred G. Brummitt, N. C. Director, NRTA, Bakersville

Mrs. Grace Brummitt, Bakersville

Miss Mozelle Causey, Greensboro

W. W. Howell, Greenville

Eleanor Jamieson, Greensboro

Miss Thelma Laws, Moravian Falls

Ernest W. Morgan, President NCRSP, Richlands

R. L. Rhyne, Treasurer, Newton

Miss Maie Sanders, Area III Vice-President, NRTA, Wilmington

H. S. Shepherd, Maiden

C. W. Twiford, Goldsboro

Mrs. Ethel Twiford, Goldsboro

Mrs. Ruie Walker, Vice-President NCRSP, Hickory

Dr. Elizabeth Welch, Winston-Salem

Mrs. Blanche Zimmerman, Winston-Salem

I ✒ A Glimpse of Education

At the Turn of the Century

Education in North Carolina has gone through considerable change as it has developed through the years. The earliest form of education outside the homes was sponsored by religious groups who felt keenly the need for teaching the three R's in addition to principles of right and wrong. There were old-field schools, subscription schools and boarding schools of various kinds. These were mostly for boys, although there were a few for girls as well as some co-ed schools. These were largely schools for the primary subjects. Schools for more advanced subjects were known as academies and were private institutions with no public or state support.

Support for these institutions came naturally from those who were concerned about education for their own children, children of their relatives and friends, or children of their church groups. There were those, however, who felt that education ought to be available for children of the poor as well as for those who could afford the private school. In fact, scattered voices were beginning to urge that schools ought to be free, with doors open to all youth.

The earliest attempt at free schools in North Carolina was recorded in 1744. It sprang from the will of James Winwright in Beaufort, North Carolina, providing for funds to set up a local free school. In 1759 James Innes in New Hanover provided funds in his will for a free school there; and in 1795 John Alexander of Bertie provided in his will that if his two daughters should predecease him, his remaining property should be converted to education of poor children of the counties of Hertford and Bertie. It must be said, however, that those first free schools existed for a short time. When funds were exhausted, support was gone.

Even so there persisted a disposition to provide free schools for the youth of the land. Certain provincial governors of North Carolina suggested statewide effort for public education. Among them were Governor Gabriel Johnson in 1736 and Governor Arthur Dobbs in 1775. These were followed by definite proposals by such men as Archibald D. Murphy. No doubt this concept accounts for the provision in our state constitution of 1776 "That a School or Schools shall be established by the Legislature for the convenient instruction of Youth, with such salaries to the Masters, paid by the Public, as may enable them to instruct at low prices; and all useful learning shall be duly encouraged and promoted in one or more Universities."

The first college in North Carolina was started by the Presbyterians in Mecklenburg County in 1771 and chartered as Queens College of Charlotte, no connection with the present Queens College. It was intended to be publicly supported, but was operated as a private institution until 1780 when it was discontinued because of conditions during the American Revolution.

The University of North Carolina, the first state-supported college in the state, incidentally in the nation, was chartered in 1789 providing for a building fund but with no appropriation for it. The only state support provided at that time was through escheats and arrears due the state.

The establishment of a university, though its existence was a struggle, had its effect as a reminder of the necessity for public education if the state was to prosper. Many propositions were made by some able leaders for the idea of education for "the rich and the poor, the dull and the sprightly." The Legislature, however, rejected every plan until 1825. That year it took the first step by inaugurating a Literary Fund for the support of common schools as proposed by Archibald D. Murphey. For the fund, various state receipts were set aside, such as dividends from state-owned bank and railroad stock, excise taxes and sales from certain state lands. The fund never grew as anticipated.

Times changed. The state came under the impact of Archibald D. Murphey. A state convention of 1835 brought about constitutional reforms. Since the report of the Literary Board and the legislature showed that the fund had experienced some growth and some federal surplus funds had become available, now something could be done toward establishing a state-wide public school system.

The legislature of 1839 passed a public school law which called for a special election on the issue of "school" or "no school." Sixty-one of the sixty-eight counties voted in favor of schools. Later the other seven counties voted in favor of schools. On January 20, 1840, the first state-sponsored public school was opened in Rockingham County. By 1850, some 2,657 schools were in operation.

Counties were divided into school districts. Any district which could furnish a building and raise $20.00 in taxes, to be levied by the county court, would receive $40.00 from the State Literary Fund for starting a school.

By 1860 about 3,500 school districts were operating schools. With a growing university, new denominational colleges and continued activity of academies and institutes, North Carolina was experiencing an intellectual awakening. It was being said that North Carolina had one of the best school systems in the country.

But with the intervention of the civil war, public education fell into the background so that by 1880 it was said that the schools were not as good as in 1840. Then with the help from two sources —the Peabody Fund and Federal Aid under the Blair Bill—various forces were laying the groundwork for educational advance.

Leaders like Walter Hines Page, Charles D. McIver, Kemp P. Battle, George T. Winston, L. L. Polk, and Edwin A. Alderman overcame the indifference toward education and overturned the political opposition, and in 1894 set up a fusion rule. In the election of 1896 Daniel L. Russell became the fusion Governor. Under the capable leadership of Superintendent of Public Instruction, Charles H. Mebane, a progressive program of public education was launched. By soliciting support of prominent persons, gathering endless supporting statistics, organizing the schools under the new township system, using organization aids, county supervisors' meetings, teacher examinations and other steps, a more thoroughly organized school system resulted.

Such was the school situation at the turn of the century when Charles B. Aycock was elected governor. Then came the groundswell which echoed through the state in the early 1900's. The battle cry became, "What we want this state to become must first be taught in school. No state can become great with a large percentage of illiterate citizens. If we can only educate one—just one—generation! We can! We *must!*"

MENTAL VERSUS MUSCULAR CONTROL

During an attempt at creative writing in second grade, Jack read aloud his exciting adventure story which began with a "terrybull storm."

His classmates listened spellbound and clapped loudly when he had finished.

Since we had planned to combine all the stories in a book for our library, I collected them. Jack's writing was never his easiest endeavor, but this particular time it was atrocious. I suggested he copy his story legibly enough for others to read.

"Please, Miss M, let Tom write it for me," he pleaded. He's my best friend and I know he'll do it and he's the best writer in this room. Besides, Miss M, it will be all right 'cause when I grow up, I'm going to have a secretary anyway."

II ✖ Preparing to Teach

From Examination to College Degree

We readily recognize that the first step in any action is to decide this is the thing we really want to do. Many factors enter into any decision, of course, and reports from those who began teaching during the first quarter of this century or earlier answer the question, "Why I chose to teach?"

In the early days of the twentieth century many young women went into teaching because it was the best profession for them and about the only one open to them. In many families the woman going into teaching was the first to earn a living outside the home.

Influences very frequently came from within the home circle itself, as illustrated by such answers to the question as these:

Many members of my family were teachers and I made up my mind early to follow the same profession, because their examples inspired me to do so—and, too, it was the expected thing to do in my family. My grandfather was a teacher in a one room school; my older sister was a teacher. I felt teaching was a preferred profession.

✓ ✓ ✓

I came from a long line of teachers and from the time I was four years old I rode my father "piggy back" as he walked to school. From then until I was in the tenth grade my teachers were my mother, my father, and my uncles; so I grew up expecting to teach. As I grew older that desire grew stronger.

✓ ✓ ✓

Parents and other relatives encouraged me to teach. My father realized the importance of regular school attendance, and often on bad days he would bundle my sister and me up and take us to school. Later a neighbor girl and I drove a mule to school, with warm bricks and a heavy laprobe in the buggy to keep us warm on cold days.

Play teaching often led to a deep desire to teach. Many recall teaching younger brothers, sisters, and playmates. Some even tried to cajole pet kittens and small dogs into becoming pupils. Others were inclined to follow examples of their teachers and lined up their dolls in rows in front of them as students, just as their teachers lined them up at school. These "play teachers" answered for both teacher and students.

In the days when there was no substitute list from which to draw when a teacher was out, an older student was often sent to take charge of one of the lower grades. Many report liking this experience so much that they decided to become teachers. Often these say, "I love children and enjoyed so much working with them." One of these reported:

> When I graduated from high school I took a six weeks teacher training course offered by our county. This work prepared me for my initial assignment to teach the first three grades in a two-teacher school. At the end of the first year I was started on my professional career which lasted forty-eight more years. I continued my education, in-service style, to a certificate in primary education and later a degree from college. Still later many summer schools, workshops, seminars and extension courses led to the achievement of an elementary Principal's Certificate.

One of the great influences in the decision to teach came from the examples of teachers from first grade through high school and college. One teacher reports,

> When I entered the first grade I fell in love with my teacher and told my parents I wanted to be a teacher just like Mrs. A. They encouraged the idea and being a teacher continued to be my dream. I held on to it in spite of many difficulties, and though the way was often rough, encouragement came from many sources.

A grammar grade teacher made her students feel they were a part of the classroom situation and that there was something each could contribute. From one of her students comes this:

The inspiration several teachers gave me in elementary school made me realize what a great profession teaching is. The idea of being a teacher came to me when I was in the first grade but credit is due to a fifth grade teacher, one of the kindest and most considerate of teachers, a teacher of children and not entirely of books.

Another teacher explains:

Being a teacher was a dream I held on to from play school to the real thing. When I entered my first classroom to teach grades four through seven and faced thirty-seven students, some larger and almost as old as I was, I did not know whether I would make it or not. I began the day by reading some verses of scripture, then usually a part of opening exercises. I asked if anyone would like to say a sentence prayer. One of the smaller girls said, "God bless Miss B." Believe it or not, most of the other thirty-six pupils followed with the same prayer—and I ended with a hearty *Amen*.

One teacher reports that she stumbled into teaching because a teacher was leaving a small school operating in an old cotton gin building. She was persuaded to finish the school year and liked working with boys and girls so much that she continued to teach for forty-one years, as she says,

I am very glad I chose to continue because of what children have added to my life. I have felt the responsibility to teach not only the three R's but also to help my pupils form good habits and develop desirable traits of character so as to become honest, respectable citizens.

One gives this reply as her reason,

My early education was in a wooded section with very poor access roads; thus it was difficult to get good teachers there. Very early I made up my mind that I was going to teach in a small rural school where the best teachers did not want to go. When I was ready to teach I went into such a situation and gave the very best that I had to the boys and girls there.

Who knows what may have influenced the student who came to her college professor and said, "Please give me a zero on that Shakespeare memorization I took two weeks ago but please give me a chance to take it over. I cheated the first time but I know those lines from *Hamlet* now. I've been miserable these two weeks." The request was granted and the student learned two lessons—the verses from Shakespeare and the value of honesty. She became a teacher and was an inspiration to students for more than thirty years.

More than one teacher says,

I pay tribute to the excellent teachers I had who went far beyond the call of duty to give special help and counsel to students when needed. To all of these I owe a special debt and say with Ulysses, "I am a part of all that I have met." Especially is tribute due to the wonderful teachers whose guidance, inspiration and examples have meant so much to me during my many years of attempting to guide, counsel and set examples for the many youths who have been in my classroom.

A former student of one of our teacher-training institutions pays this tribute to the first president of the college:

As an educator, he had great concern for the education of the youth of North Carolina and wanted his graduates to go into all sections of the state and give the very best kind of teaching service possible. When I left the college with the diploma and Bible he had handed me, I felt I had an abiding challenge facing me.

Because the teacher is the major factor in shaping the value system of our nation, the proper education of teachers has become a priority even though it has been a many-sided affair.

During the first quarter of this century obtaining even the lowest grade certificate was often a struggle for many who wanted to teach. Terms of most rural schools were not more than four to six months. Salaries were low. Some teachers reported they received only twenty dollars a month. Even so, they often saved enough out of the meager salary to pay expenses in the nearest teacher-training institution for perhaps a summer school of six weeks or a quarter after the short term closed in the spring. Thus over a period of years an "A" certificate or a degree was earned.

Today beginning teachers are university graduates and most of those who continue in the profession go on to higher degrees. Often scholarships are available both to graduate and undergraduate students. Frequently much in-service training is done in workshops underwritten by school funds, government subsidies, or foundation grants, while extension work offered by universities is brought to places convenient to teachers in a given area.

Teacher training done before the turn of the century was a local affair but good ground work was laid, though a very limited number had the advantage of the training. One retiree reports that in the summer of 1885, under the auspices of the first school board in the county, a six weeks normal school was held. The superintendent and other educators of note conducted the classes. In connection with the methods course a model primary school was conducted. At the night sessions, open to the public, distinguished school men, such as Colonel Bingham of the famous Bingham Military Academy, President Kemp Battle of the University of North Carolina, and the Honorable J.L.M. Curry, of the Peabody Fund, delivered addresses.

For the improvement of his teachers, in the school session of 1888–89, a superintendent instituted an intensive training course. At the close of school every Friday afternoon three classes were conducted. One was in Primary Methods, one in General Methods by the school principal, and one in School Administration by the superintendent—all forerunners of methods courses which came later with the teacher-training institutions which were often top-heavy with such courses.

Though the state legislature of 1899 had appropriated the sum of $100,000 to establish common schools throughout the state, many areas were still without schools. The next legislature was pledged to increase the school fund so as to provide at least a four month's term in every district of the state. Even then it was to be years before this plan was carried out. A teacher in one of these early schools tells her story:

> When a one-teacher school was opened in Chunn's Cove in 1905 or 1906, I was asked to teach there for six months at $30.00 a month. I taught there for eight years, averaging about fifty pupils in grades one through six. At that time no summer schools or teacher-training institutions were available in the area, but a two-weeks' institute, which teachers were required to attend, was held every two years in some central place. All the common branches were reviewed and we were given some thirteen different examinations.

Such examinations were held in local communities over the state and scheduled by race—black, white, and Indian. They were continued for many years as the means of obtaining a teaching certificate, even after teacher-training institutions were established in the state. One report reads:

> I was a first-year student in a recently-established two-year teacher-training institution when a notice of examinations for teachers appeared on the bulletin board. Not knowing whether I would have finances to continue in school for the second year, I signed up for the examinations. Separate essay type examinations were given in all the main subjects in the elementary school. These were long and required two full days to finish. One subject was state history which I had never studied. I got a history book from the library and read it through before time for examination in that subject. Papers were checked by someone in the superintendent's office. When reports were posted I was one to receive a first class certificate, which I never used, for I was able to finish the two-year normal course.

A diploma from a two-year normal school or a degree from the university entitled one to a blanket certificate, by virtue of which the holder was permitted—but not always qualified—to teach anything from first grade through high school. Many teachers held this certificate. Such teachers had a wide range of experiences, as noted,

> I was once in a two-teacher high school and was given any subject the principal did not want. Anyone holding a blanket certificate became the principal's goat or pet, depending on the point of view, and could solve any dilemma the principal might have in teacher placement. However, I kept the same kind of certificate each time of renewal, and in 1938 was granted one of the last blanket life certificates issued in the state.

✓ ✓ ✓

> For thirty-seven years I held a blanket certificate and became a general purpose teacher when I finished college in 1923. It was renewed in the thirties, but after it was raised to one of the first Master's Certificates in the state, it still noted permission to teach in any "public elementary or secondary school of the state." I first taught English in high school. I soon left teaching for the pulpit. When I returned to teaching during the depression, I taught sixth

grade, then history and English in the seventh grade. My next assignment was truly "all purpose" teacher with some history, a little business English, and a course in public speaking with emphasis on debating. During World War II came classes in science and history in grades seven and eight. During my last decade of teaching there were classes in general math, geometry, and typing. Along the line were health and physical education classes and coaching girls' basketball. I often felt that my most successful teaching came as I ploughed through a new subject and could impart to my students something of the thrill I was experiencing in learning a new subject.

An A.B. degree about 1920 initiated its holder into the class of the educated and gave proof of a sound moral character. If the proper courses in education had been taken, it entitled the holder to a teaching certificate in the elementary and high schools of North Carolina, subjects unlimited and unspecified. It meant the holder could teach "anything you want, and many things you don't."

During the 1920's several high schools in the state held one-year teaching-training courses for high school graduates. Students who completed this course satisfactorily were granted a temporary teaching certificate, good in elementary schools of the state. This certificate could be renewed with summer school attendance in any of the teacher-training institutions of the state.

Said one teacher,

> It was my privilege to teach in this program. Classes were limited to not less than fifteen and no more than twenty-five students. Courses included psychology and methods classes in the elementary school subjects. Most of the schools of that day were made up of grades one through eleven. The students observed in the elementary grades and often worked with the younger children. During the last six weeks of the school year, children who would be first graders the following year would be brought in for part of the day and the "training class" was responsible for starting them off.

> Though the certificate received was good in any state elementary school, the students usually began teaching in a one or two-teacher school in the county in which they lived. When these students entered one of the teacher-training institutions of the state, they were given credit for part of the year's work. Most of these students

were ambitious and hard working. Many continued to work during summer schools or part time when the short teaching year ended, until they had earned a college degree.

Those going into teaching often followed the route this teacher took:

After graduating from high school in 1925 I attended a twelve weeks' session at the nearest teacher-training institution and was issued an Elementary B Certificate. That fall I had no job when three committeemen came and asked me to teach in a nearby school. The school had had two teachers for several years but the superintendent said only one could be employed that year because the attendance had not averaged thirty-eight the year before. When I saw the superintendent he did not object to my lack of training but insisted that I was too young to teach. The committeemen gave me the job, however, and my enrollment averaged more than thirty-eight pupils for the first three months. I was not paid, though, until after Christmas when I received $60.00 a month for those three months. I felt very wealthy, for I was living at home and had no debts.

Another tells of the depression years.

In 1929 when the bottom was dropping out of the prosperity years of the twenties, I received a fifty-dollar college scholarship from _____. This stipend paid my entrance fees, and thus began my college career on sheer courage, stamina, and my mother's prayers. My sister, a teacher in a nearby county, paid $16.00 per month to meet my other financial obligations. I held a job as student worker at ten cents an hour for sixty hours a month.

As a worker I was assigned such various jobs as dining hall waitress, worker in the school laundry, cleaning offices after school until my junior year and senior years. Then I became an assistant to the librarian for three hours at night and on Sunday afternoons. This library work proved to be a great advantage, for there I read newspapers and periodicals and became familiar with many resources the library offered. Too, I learned basic information about the organization and operation of the library.

When the day of graduation came, my cup was filled when I learned that my mom had already secured a job for me in the high school about six blocks from home.

One tells of rigid discipline during her school days but praises the training she received:

In the first quarter of this century educational advantages for girls were not too good in most sections of the South. In 1887 the Presbyterian Board had opened a school on land donated for this purpose. This school had a wide influence on teacher training in the Carolinas and in Tennessee. In later years it became known as the Asheville Normal. At first it was only a two-year college but its graduates were rated as outstanding teachers and superintendents were glad to have them on their faculties. At first I graduated in 1922 with a B.E. certificate, taught for awhile, raised my son, then returned for further work, graduating in 1942 with an A Certificate. The school closed its doors in 1944 when it was thought to be no longer needed.

Young people of today would have trouble adjusting to the strict discipline and our work schedule but we really had a good time doing all that was required of us. The students did all of the work of the school—painting, cleaning, cooking. We were given duties for a period of nine weeks. Some of us made all the bread and our time was extended to eighteen weeks. These duties paid most of our expenses, for we paid very little cash.

As to discipline, we were expected to memorize certain Bible selections each week and we had a silent time from two to four o'clock on Sunday afternoons. A two-hour study hall was held each night. We had to leave our rooms in good order or we might be called out of class to take care of them. Chapel was held every day and students must attend that as well as church on Sunday. Lights were out at 9:30 P.M. and the rising bell rang at 6:00 A.M. with breakfast at 6:45. With high-buttoned shoes it was not easy to be on time for this meal.

Nobody read the Sunday paper. It was put away until Monday to be read. No visitors came on Sunday except for church and we could see them for a few minutes afterward. Visitors came only on Saturday afternoons, and if one had men visitors they had to be checked to see if the girls had permission to see them.

All the students wore uniforms of blue cotton dresses or white middy blouses and blue skirts on Wednesday evenings and on Saturdays. We wore blue coat suits for church and down town, with hat and gloves, of course, long black stockings and high top shoes. We had one white dress for special occasions and long white stockings to wear with it. Most of the rules we followed would not be tolerated today but we took them as a matter of course.

During the twenties, teacher training was done in Farm Life Schools of the state. In 1925–26 one of the training teachers in a Farm Life School reports that she was evaluated from A to Z on a demonstration lesson. Either standards were very high or there were some severe critics of her methods, presentation, materials used, and responses of students. Perhaps all of us remember such incidents! This teacher remembers that day full well, for she wore a long waisted white wool dress with Peter Pan collar and a colorful scarf which she had made.

It was during the "teen" years of the nineteen hundreds that my formal training as a teacher began in one of the state teacher-training institutions. Basic courses consisted of Mathematics, English, History, Biology, Psychology, and Methods on how to teach subjects in the elementary school. Students were also required to take courses in drawing and in music in preparation for teaching. In addition I elected to take Latin and French.

Most of us had come from poorly equipped high schools, though often with excellent teachers. I recall I was not required to take Mathematics because I had had in high school the courses listed for the first year. To most of us, a well-equipped library, for that day, was a well-spring of opportunity.

Relationships between staff members and students were warm and informal. Most of the instructors, and even the president, knew much of the backgrounds of the students and some of their problems.

A small practice school, grades one to six, was housed in one wing of the classroom building. From the beginning of the college career students had contacts with elementary pupils and teachers. These contacts and participation in grade-school activities culminated with Practice Teaching for an entire quarter. As one looks back and evaluates the situations in this elementary school, one finds them varying from rigid rows of desks from which children seldom moved except "en masse" through more informal situations to one of activity and considerable freedom. In the last-mentioned situation one might find children working individually or in small groups over the room, resulting in subdued but busy hub-bub sounds. Some of the other teachers considered this freedom heresy, but the children were happy and relaxed and many types of experiences led to much learning.

Both our teachers of Methods and those in the Practice School introduced us to the theories and philosophies of leaders and pioneers in education of that day as Charles McMurry, John Dewey, Francis Parker, W. H. Kilpatrick, William Bonser, and William Bagley. Then students bought their own textbooks and took them along when they went forth to teach. Dewey's *Democracy in Education* and Bagley's *Classroom Discipline* were my frequent references, and I might add, my comfort, during my early teaching years, for in those days no help was forthcoming from supervisors—or principals.

One reports her early experience:

After having finished college I came to teach in the Cherokee Indian School. At one time I had two classes, one in economics and one in American history, meeting in the same room at the same time, but on Wednesday I had to leave both classes for most of the period to go across the hall to the library for a library class with another group. One year at Christmas time I supervised three parties on three different floors at the same time for teachers who were victims of a flu epidemic.

Innovations in education came slowly but surely and new terms found their way into educational literature and in teacher-training programs. So Project Teaching had its day! A home economics teacher tells her story of her Project Teaching days:

To qualify as a home economics teacher one had to take a course in Project Training in that subject. Then she went into the field. After teaching all day in the classroom she was required to supervise the home projects carried out by students in cooperation with their parents, to teach adult classes and to participate in all community activities whose purpose was the betterment of family living. These vocational home economics programs were strictly supervised by district and state supervisors as well as by school principals and superintendents.

Because of the amount of out-of-school work, the vocational teacher was employed for ten months. The extra month was given to visits in the homes of students, supervising their projects, teaching adult classes, field trips, improvement of the department, and professional advancement.

Every four years the teacher was required to attend a six weeks summer session in a qualified college or university in order to keep up with trends in the field. Later the State Department of Public Instruction changed requirements for summer school study to once every five years and added a week of instruction in conferences each summer prior to the opening of school in the fall.

Qualifications of the teacher in a different era did not depend solely on the certificate held or the amount of college work done. One teacher remembers the letter her first principal wrote for her. He stated, "She neither dances nor smokes." Later during an interview with the principal to whom the letter was directed he pointed to that sentence and remarked, "I like that." She says she always felt that she was hired on the basis of that statement rather than anything the letter might have said about her teaching ability.

One teacher who lived in a teacherage with five other career women tells of coming in from a movie one Saturday night with a friend, when she was met at the door by the principal who asked, "Do you think your parents would approve of your coming in at this hour?" It was ten o'clock!

A contract to teach in one of the counties in the eastern part of the state spelled out conduct thought to be becoming of a teacher. It is given here:

> I have had _____ years of teaching experience. My N.C. Certificate expires July 1, 192__. I further agree that I will take a vital interest in church and Sunday School work and in community activities; that I will not entertain company until late hours at night and thus render my school work the next day inefficient; that I will not attend sorry moving pictures and vaudeville shows; that I will not fall in love or become familiar with high school pupils; that I will not attend card and dancing parties; that I will not fail to use good sense and discretion in the company I keep; that I will use my best endeavors during the year to improve my work as a teacher; and that I will do nothing to bring disrepute on the home in which I live or cause right thinking people to speak disparagingly of me and my work.

"Yes," says the teacher, "I signed such a contract and worked there for four years."

Often a marriage contract was a sure termination of the teacher's work. There was a day when bobbed hair was not to be tolerated nor were gym suits that did not blouse several inches over the knees. Leave of absence for pregnancy was unheard of.

These rules for teachers came from an earlier era:

RULES FOR TEACHERS—1872

1. Teachers each day will fill lamps, clean chimneys.
2. Each teacher will bring a bucket of water and a scuttle of coal for the day's session.
3. Make your pens carefully. You may whittle nibs to the individual taste of the pupils.
4. After ten hours in school, the teacher may spend the remaining time reading the Bible or other good books.
5. Men teachers may take one evening each week for courting purposes, or two evenings a week if they go to church regularly.
6. Women teachers who marry or engage in unseemly conduct will be dismissed.
7. Every teacher should lay aside from each pay a goodly sum of his earnings for his benefit during his declining years so that he will not become a burden on society.
8. Any teacher who smokes, uses liquor in any form, frequents pool or public halls, or gets shaved in a barber shop will give reason to suspect his worth, intention, integrity and honesty.
9. The teacher who performs his labor faithfully and without fault for five years will be given an increase of twenty-five cents in his pay, provided the Board of Education approves.

Little Ones

Shirttails hanging out, buttons lost,
Shoelaces untied, zippers unfastened,
Teacher puts back together!
What's a teacher for?

NEW DEFINITIONS

The opposite of "back" is stomach.
"Indent" means to scoot over.

III ❧ Teaching

From the One-Room School to Consolidation

From the beginning of our history as a nation, "we, the people of these United States," have realized, with Thomas Jefferson, that the success of our system of government depends upon educated leaders and an enlightened citizenry. Thus, the public school became our chief formal agent for perpetuating our unique values. Through the personal experiences of those who have taught during the past half century this chapter narrates part of the story of North Carolina education, beginning with the one-room school and conditions related to it. It is a story filled with drama—with humor, with pathos, defeats, victories, uncertainties, vision, imagination, determination, creativity, and most of all, with faith.

Teachers recall going through the "kerosene light, pine knot, and light bulb stages to reach the fluorescent age;" from "foot express" to cross-town-country bussing; from little outdoor "comfort stations" and bushes to modern indoor facilities; from cold bag lunches to lines of selection in a cafeteria. Throughout these changes, teachers remained committed to their profession and devoted to their students, caring about them and concerned for their welfare.

Three months is presumed to have been the typical length of school term prior to the Civil War, but it depended on how much tax was levied and collected by the sheriff of each county. The schools ran as long as the money lasted. If the teacher could collect some tuition, the school would run longer. Subscription schools operated for varying periods of time—from one month after the regular term ended up to a year, or, as one pupil put it, "after the corn was laid by until fodder pulling time in September."

A distinction was made by Governor Arthur Dobbs in 1759 "between free county schools which should be only for English scholars to learn to read, write, and account with some other branches of Mathematics" and the "one Public Provincial School for the languages and higher branches of learning." In 1776 it was decreed "That a School or Schools shall be established by the Legislature for the convenient instruction of Youth, with such salaries to the Masters paid by the Public as may enable them to instruct at low prices; and all useful learning shall be duly encouraged and promoted in one or more Universities."

What little education North Carolina enjoyed before the Revolution was controlled by the churches, especially the Church of England and the Presbyterian, and was to educate "gentlemen and those of professional classes." But the "Revolutionary political philosophy stressing the principles of religious equality, political democracy, and the right of the people to self-government meant—or should have meant—that the new nation needed an educated citizenry, and so these ideas broadened the concept of education as the function of the State."

In 1840 one-third of the adult whites in North Carolina were illiterate, and, if blacks and whites under twenty years of age were included, more than half the state's population was illiterate. But in spite of the efforts of Archibald Murphey and other staunch advocates of public education, the Legislature rejected every proposal to establish schools until 1825 when a "Literary Fund was created. However, without the teeth to enforce this provision, little happened, and in 1828 a "Legislative Committee threw the responsibility for the education of North Carolina children upon the Almighty by reporting its inability to discover any method of educational improvement except to unite in the prayer that a kind providence will hasten the time when literary, moral and religious instruction shall pervade our country."

In 1869 the Legislature passed the school law providing for separate schools for Whites and Blacks, a four-months term for all children, but, unfortunately, the administration of the school law was in the hands of a "carpetbagger from Massachusetts . . . and a lack of public confidence worked against success." But the state tax was entirely inadequate to provide a four-months term. "Public education in North Carolina was severely handicapped by religious poverty due to war and low income, to scattered population, to bad roads, to a large school population in comparison with the number of tax payers, and to the necessity of maintaining a dual system of schools. . . . Also the state's sterile political leadership and the colossal indifference to public education were responsible for educational backwardness in North Carolina."

One way to finance the schools is shown in the following order of January 2, 1886: To the Honorable Sherriff . . .

> Sir, we the undersigned as the Board of Education . . . do hereby notify you to proceed in due time to collect the taxes from all Public Distillers and Sellers of Spirituous liquors . . . and give us an itemized account as to the amount collected on the first Monday in June, 1888, also on the first Monday in December, 1888.

In the oldest statistical report on file in this county, in the year 1905–06, "sixty schools existed in the county, and fifty-three were one-teacher, seven were two-teacher, and none had more than two teachers. . . . The average teacher's salary was $28.95. The number of log school houses were eight white and five colored."

And so the vision and the challenge were here, and it was the *teacher* who brought the challenge into reality. Before leaving her teacher-training program, one beginning teacher was told by her critic teacher, "You have a good mind, but you've kept it so cleverly concealed no one ever discovered it." This teacher, motivated by the words, got busy uncovering her latent abilities to cope with a school where she had no desk, "only a discarded table with one short shelf under it. Nothing was ever furnished. The fifth, sixth, and seventh grades were told that if we raised $36.50 for a World Book Encyclopedia, the County would pay the rest. It took us two years to raise our amount."

The Early School

An account of the first free school in one community records that it was a one-room building with seats made of heavy unpainted slabs with legs fastened to the bottom side, no backs. There was one blackboard on legs, and the pupils used chalk similar to that used today. Slates were used for figuring, but copy books, pen and ink were for practicing penmanship. The children practiced penmanship at a special writing board, two inches thick. On one side of the room was a rock chimney with an open fireplace in which burned the wood cut by the students who also made the fires and cleaned the room. The teacher was hired by the school committeemen who relied on their own judgment in selecting the teacher, for there were no special requirements in that day.

The term consisted of three months of free school each year, with a fourth month paid for by subscription, the charge being about $1.00 per child. Those who could not pay stopped at the end of the third month. Pupils started to school at the age of five and had the privilege of attending until they were twenty-one, but most of them stopped to go to work before they were fifteen. Since there were no grades, pupils advanced as fast as they could learn in each subject.

The curriculum consisted of penmanship, arithmetic, spelling and reading. Pupils used the blue-back Speller for the reading and spelling textbook. The reading material was printed between the lists of words at the top and bottom of the page. It consisted of practical sentences and clever sayings. The only arithmetic textbook used was handed down from parent to child until it was entirely worn out.

To protect the pages of the book from wearing, students used "thumb papers," pieces of paper about the size of a dollar bill, folded and held so that the thumb would rest on it instead of on the book page. . . . Confederate money was used because paper was exceedingly scarce, and the family owned a bushel or two of Confederate bills.

School lasted from eight A.M. until four P.M. with one hour for dinner. Students brought lunches with them, and played games after eating. A favorite game of the boys was "Fox." One boy who was the fox would run and the others would chase him. Another favorite game was "Bull Pen," played with a soft wool yarn ball made by the students. The thrower tried to hit a boy by throwing the ball at him. The purpose was to avoid being hit.

To make way for a residence a citizen wished to build near the schoolhouse, the one-room structure was moved across the railroad track . . . near a good gum spring. A gum spring is one that is surrounded by four planks about two feet long, mailed together and placed so as to keep out trash."

Other schools had heaters instead of fireplaces, and the teacher and pupils had to keep warm by firing a dilapidated wood heater themselves. The desks which were double would "fall apart at any time, and we would have to stop lessons and nail the fallen desks back together. . . . It was an unusual day if at least one leg didn't fall from under the stove as well." One day, right in the midst of learning long division, the stove rolled over on the side and the door came open. Fire fell all over the floor, and the can of water kept on the stove spilled. "With the help of the principal, the fire was gathered up, and the pieces of pipe and stove were reassembled. No one was injured." In one room, when the large coals of fire fell through the opening at the front where ashes were emptied, the teacher saw how potatoes could be baked and onions cooked on the coals, and from this time on, "hot lunches" were enjoyed by all.

In another school the teacher had to hold an umbrella over her head and wear overshoes in the building when it rained. A one-room school where one teacher taught in 1899 had two windows and a door for light.

The benches were handmade with no backs. Nails on the wall held the wraps. The open fireplace was our heat. The enrollment that year was 36 . . . with all grades. The subjects were reading, grammar, spelling, writing, arithmetic, and geography. The schedule was from 8:00 to 12:00 with one hour for lunch, then from 1:00 to 4:00. At the end of the day it was the teacher's duty to see that wood was gathered for the next day, to clean the room, and lock up. Smaller children did not attend regularly because of the long distance they had to walk. Some of the students were older than the

EBENEZER ACADEMY — 1822 — IREDELL COUNTY

In the *Western Carolinian*, under the date of December 9, 1823 this advertisement appeared:

Ebenezer Academy was incorporated during the session of the General Assembly in 1822. It is now open to all who wish to pursue a course in liberal education or study English Grammar and Geography. All branches of Education required for college admission will be taught. We are happy in stating to the public that a new and commodious academy will be completed in a few days. The academy is in a rural situation, six miles from Statesville, so that the students will be measurably free from temptation to vice. It is convenient to a church, where there is preaching statedly.

Iredell County, N. C.
November 1823
s/Wm. A. Bell

Ebenezer Academy, Iredell County, was incorporated in 1822. Restored by Fourth Creek Chapter, Daughters of the American Revolution, in 1908, now used by the chapter as a meeting place. A retired teacher, Mrs. Sarah D. Parker, is pictured here raising the flag.

Teacher's *First* Grade Certificate.

I, County Superintendent of Public Instruction of ____ *Jones* ____
County, North Carolina, certify that I have, in accordance with Section 2566 of the School Law, and Section 41 of Chapter 199, Laws of 1889, thoroughly and fully examined ____ *W. H. Hammond* ____
an applicant for a Teacher's Certificate, on the several branches of study named below, and that ____
true grade of scholarship in each is indicated by the number annexed to it, 100 indicating the highest:

Spelling (Including sounds of letters),	96
Defining,	90
Reading,	95
Writing,	96
Arithmetic (Mental and Written),	98
English Grammar,	98
Geography,	95
Elementary Physiology and Hygiene,	95
History of North Carolina,	90
History of the United States,	88
Page's Theory and Practice,	90

The said applicant has also furnished satisfactory evidence of good moral character, and has certified that during the examination ____ *he* ____ has not received help from any source, and has given none to anyone else.

This Certificate will therefore authorize the said ____ *W. H. Hammond* ____
to teach in the Public Schools in ____ *Jones* ____ County during one year only from date thereof.

This ____ *8th* ____ day of ____ *October* ____ 18 *94*

C. H. Koonce

County Sup't Public Instruction.

The first public transportation for school children in North Carolina was at Thurman School, Craven County. Three leaders in the district, after investigation in other states, developed the horse-drawn or mule-drawn buses which were used in 1911.

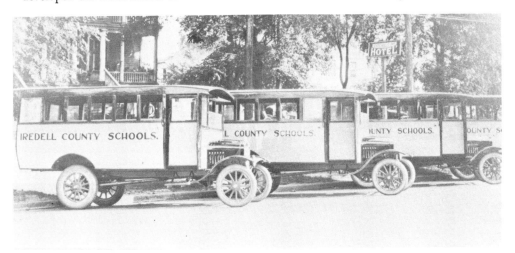

School buses operating in 1920.

Near the village of Ossipee, Stanley County, 1909. The lad holding the whip and sitting on the wagon rode it to school.

A typical one-room school building of the early 1900's. A yard stick and a blackboard were the most important tools and sometimes the only equipment.

WAYSIDE SCHOOL
When Charles Brantley Aycock became Governor in 1901, he called upon all patriotic citizens to aid in promoting "Free public schools, open to all." School buildings became larger to accommodate more students.

A nineteenth-century, one-room school building in Robeson County has been moved to the grounds of the County Board of Education Building and restored. It has been furnished with furniture of the period.

First and second grades, Martin Creek School, Cherokee County, 1921.

South Fork Institute, Maiden, sponsored by Baptist Association, opened September 2, 1903; closed when public high school was begun in 1917.

A summer session of Turner School, Wells Town, near the turn of the century.

Building used as dormitory for South Fork Institute students.

A "domestic science" class about 1920. Those not wearing caps wore hair nets.

Commencement Parade, Iredell County, 1915.

Flag Drill, Fairview College.

Atkinson Consolidated Union School. Larger buildings were needed as more students were bused to central schools and the curriculum was expanded.

Crossnore. Teacher Mary Logan used some native costumes of Holland in a program on windmills and tulips.

In 1947 the "Freedom Train" visited Greensboro. A second grade class of Lindley Elementary School planned and gave a program based on the contributions of varying cultures, leaderships and achievements. Mrs. Pattie S. Jackson, teacher.

Fourth Graders of Estes Hills School in Chapel Hill prepare for a concert of the North Carolina Symphony Orchestra. These students are dancing to a recording of a selection they are to hear.

Martha Mason, Lattimore, a victim of poliomyelitis as a child, earned a college degree while living in an iron lung. The cooperation of teachers with parents made this possible.

A bronze plaque, presented by the Iredell County Negro Parent-Teacher Association in 1945, bears a sculptored likeness of the head of Mrs. Charlton Holliday, outstanding leader in rural education. Mrs. Holliday, now deceased, served as Jeannes Supervisor of Negro schools from 1920 until ill health caused her to retire in 1956. Beneath the head is an open book on which is inscribed, "Our greatest hope for a better world is dependent upon the co-operation of parents and teachers in the right training of children."

Mrs. Oressa Hauser, Oak Grove School, with medals presented to her by Freedoms Foundation at Valley Forge for teaching the American Way of Life.

The 1975 Concert Choir of Northwood High School, Pittsboro, on the Capitol steps in Washington. Retired teacher Mrs. T. W. McBane, at the lower right, chaperoned the group. Congressman Ike Andrews and Dr. Charles Horton, director, are at the lower right. The choir performed at a Bicentennial Program during the national convention of the Daughters of the American Revolution in Constitution Hall.

Miss Janie Wilson, Balls Creek School, directed "Healthland," a play she wrote with her second grade students, 1957.

Ninth grade class, Morning Side High School, Statesville, 1930. Virgie Jones Davis, teacher, is second from left, front row.

Mrs. Virginia Little of Oxford School, 1951, inspects a squirrel box that has just been completed. Other students are carving, building a birdhouse, and weaving.

Conservation work is not confined to the classroom at Oxford school. Several students examine bundles of lespedeza, while one reads the directions for planting it.

A modern school plant, 1975. Alexander Central High School. Some of the courses in the curriculum prepare students to enter careers upon graduation.

Left, Mrs. Louise Collins plays pump organ about 100 years old. *Right,* Dr. Elizabeth Welch leading a children's literature workshop for public school teachers.

Left, above, Miss Louise Hood examines a blue-back speller as her first grade teacher, Mrs Lucille Hook McGumpsey, shows the school bell to her pastor. The oak split basket wa used as a school lunch basket 75 years ago. *Right, above,* Glenn Ward gardens for exercise. *Below, left,* Blanche Zimmerman made the banner and carried it in the "Plant a Tree" march. *Below right,* Mrs. Abbie S. Hildebrand demonstrates "fly-brush" used in days before screens.

teacher. Few days were lost because of bad weather. It was left to the teacher to decide whether there would be school. If "no school," the days were made up at the end of the term. The salary was $100.00. School terms were only five months . . . the position was continued as long as two of the committeemen agreed.

A general practice followed in several areas of the state was that the school term varied to provide for the needs of a particular community. "We had to get out in time for the children to pick strawberries," one teacher pointed out. Another commented that in those days there were "only seven months of school, six weeks summer school, then a harvest time for gathering the crops. School would begin with the first frost." In cotton-growing sections, "school began in July, ran for six weeks, closed for cotton-picking, began again in October, and closed in May."

The one-room log school with a chimney and woodburning fireplace in one end is well remembered by another teacher. "The school hired one teacher for about $30.00 a month. . . . The teacher's desk was a wooden affair with a top for writing. The children used slates on which to write and cipher. What few maps the school had were attached to the wall by tacks. The old blue-back *speller* was used . . . a series called Holmes' Readers was used by pupils as they progressed. Johnson's *arithmetic* was used for the more advanced pupils. The curriculum stressed the three R's and went from the ABC class through the 7th grade. Grading as such was unheard of."

One teacher recalled teaching in a mill village, surrounded by mill homes and families. This village supported a one-room, one-teacher school with grades one through four, and the teacher was "janitor, maid, nurse, and, hopefully, an inspiration to the community. Not only teaching the children their required assignments for the varying age groups, but organizing a sewing club for the mothers and teaching Sunday School class on Sunday afternoon" were part of the job.

In one classroom "one desk showed teeth marks all around it. I decided he must be hungry . . . and I went next door for some cornbread which he seemed to enjoy. I told him to let me know when he was hungry and I would try to supply better food than wood and varnish."

In her first job one teacher discovered that there were no inside toilets, and one day the girls asked her to do an inspection job for the sake of sanitation. "Boiling water, red devil lye, brooms, and manual labor preceded the discarding of their shoes which could not be used after the clean-up. Oil stoves used in the Home Economics room gave off so much soot that it was difficult to use them in the work." Thus, to raise money to get needed equipment, the students sold candy, cookies and popcorn which they made themselves, until, at last, an electric stove could be purchased.

In this same situation, some children came to school undernourished, without breakfast, some without any food at all during the day. The students began a study on foods, and invited these children to the Home Economics Department for a good bowl of soup and a sandwich. This innovation caused so much favorable reaction in teachers and students throughout the school that the Home Economics group took on as a project serving a light lunch to any who wished it. Later, this task had to be taken over by someone else because other projects occupied the full time of the Home Economics students. The money earned from the other projects bought draperies and other items for upgrading and beautifying their school and classroom environment.

Challenged by the vacant and dirty school, one teacher got the support of a fine school board, but found the superintendent resistant to changes—he didn't like change. "I changed him along with the community," she commented. She found running water, but it was running outside, as nearly everything else was—old spigot, broken-down toilets which, unlocked, were being used by families in the community. There was no lunchroom, and the desks fell over backward whenever a child stood up. The floors were old oiled floors, long ago ruled against by the state.

Many changes in the school environment were noted by teachers.

Fifty years ago one could find little one-teacher schools located in the center of a community or neighborhood, where children who lived within walking distance were taught, usually for six months each year. Later, these became two-or-three-teacher schools as children from greater distances were transported on unheated well-worn buses, if they lived near enough to roads on which buses could travel. Those who lived on poor roads inaccessible to buses had to walk long distances to school and often arrived late, wet, and cold. . . .

In verse one teacher shares some aspects of her first teaching experience:

> I had finished high school
> Had three months of college,
> And felt that I
> Was just loaded with knowledge.
>
> My ideals were high
> And I just yearned
> To teach all my students
> Everything I had learned.
>
> It was in a two-room shack
> By the side of the road,
> And I was assured
> I'd have a light load!
>
> In all kinds of weather
> Come rain, sleet, or snow,
> The more than two miles
> I knew I must go. . . .
>
> My assignment was teaching
> Grades one through four,
> And we all saw the cemetery
> As we walked in the door. . . .

And so, in its historical and educational significance, the one-room school, its conscientious and courageous teachers, its limited materials, and its many discouraging features became the first milepost on North Carolina's road to bringing about changes which would lead to an effective school program—changes so necessary to progress. And these very discouraging factors remain, as well, monuments to parental concern, community interest, teacher commitment, and pupil involvement in even the ordinary tasks of housekeeping. Who can doubt that one teacher and twenty-five students in five grades will, in one way or another, find ways to individualize instruction, encourage independent study, develop students into teacher aides, and perform miracles in constructing visual and other aids to learning? (One teacher's duplicator was a flat-topped biscuit pan, some gelatin and other ingredients, and it had to be carefully made in order not to have bubbles left to spoil the reproductions.) In one school "the only tools provided by the Board of Education were an ax, a water bucket, and a dipper." Indeed, in the one-teacher school with all of its frustrations and challenges, "the school was *ours*—we created it by *our* labor and effort. *We* made the place where we learned."

Living Conditions

Living conditions figure largely in the recollections of teachers. Often they had to live in the communities where, living with people who were tenants or sharecroppers, was an experience demanding extra qualities on the part of both parents and teachers, as well as those children who must either share their sleeping quarters with the teacher or give them up altogether. Many families were so large that they could scarcely take care of their own needs, much less provide for any privacy for the teacher who frequently found that a "potato-storing room" with a corn-husk mattress on the floor and washing facilities at the outside well were all that were available.

The great distance from the school made for transportation problems, also. Sometimes, the only way in to a school was by a footpath that wound several miles up a steep mountainside or through swampy land where the road or path ran between heavily overhanging trees that shut out the sunlight.

One recollection takes the teacher to a Sunday afternoon when her father, as he did every Sunday, took her in the buggy to the road's end, and she would carry her satchel and climb up to the little community where she taught. Each Friday he would be waiting for her at the end of the path to take her home for the weekend.

All the children at the school were close kinfolks and had the same surname. The school ran for two months and my salary was thirty dollars a month, out of which I paid five dollars a month board.

I boarded with "Old Tom" and "Miss Ellie" who lived in a three-room log house. There were two bedrooms and the "fireroom" which was a combination kitchen and sitting-room.

"Old Tom" always wore his black hat. He came out of his room in the morning with it on his head, and wore it all day, whether working inside the house, outdoors, or sitting by the fire at night. Even when he ate, that hat was on his head. When "Old Tom" died many years later, they buried him with his hat on his head.

"Miss Ellie" was a refined, gracious old lady and set a good table. There were tasty vegetables from the garden, either fresh or dried, as was the season. Her meats were wild game, hog meat and chicken. The hams and streaked fatback were preserved and dried with salt, pepper and saltpeter. The sausage was stuffed into a corn shuck or put into a cloth poke, and was cured by drying while hanging from the rafters in the smokehouse. The chickens, rabbits, squirrels, and 'possums were fresh killed and put into the pot. Pies and preserves were made from apples, berries and wild straw-berries or huckleberries. Often these fruits were dried in the sun and put in cloth bags to save for the winter.

"Miss Ellie" raised her hops and made her riffles so that she could have yeast-rising bread. The loaves of bread baking smelled so good and tasted even better. . . .

One fledgling teacher boarded and roomed at the teacherage whose owner was a member of the school board. One bathroom on the first floor had to serve everyone in the teacherage. The young teacher shared a room with two other teachers, and they took turns starting the fire in the mornings and also in sharing the one single and one double bed. Meals were served family style; the food was good, and included home-grown vegetables. Other teachers mention being given a lunch to take from their boardinghouses because there were no facilities at school.

All teachers did not experience conditions such as these—some had better, some had worse situations—but wherever they have taught, the teachers have been in and of their communities, visiting in the homes, working in and with the PTA, and extending the classroom beyond the four walls of the school into the lives of the people whose children the school was trying to serve.

The First Job

Getting that first job was a frequent recollection. The teachers viewed this experience as one of excitement, doubt, anticipation, fear. One teacher recalls how carefully she dressed in what seemed to her to be the most suitable attire in her limited wardrobe, only to be met by a disapproving look as her interviewer took in the "beautiful ruffled pink dress and the spike heels on the matching shoes." Uncomfortable at this bad beginning, the would-be teacher felt ill at ease and knew she had failed the interview. Taking a short-cut to her room in order to avoid meeting anyone she knew, she found a telephone call waiting to summon her back for another conference. She "retired" her ruffled dress and spike-heeled shoes, hat and gloves, and returned to hear these words, "You almost lost a job, but your academic achievement is sound, your training has been good—you just need to grow up. I think we'll give you the job."

Another teacher, with a hand full of applications and a list of qualities, launched a search for a position as a teacher of high school mathematics, only to be told by the chairman of the board, "We-e-ll, we've always had a man teacher, and I think we'll keep looking for one." She tried again in a small town near her home, and this time was told that one of the policies of the school board was that teachers must live at a certain boardinghouse (whose owner happened to be a relative of one of the board members). The board member admitted that the applicant seemed to be exactly what they needed in a high school mathematics teacher, but they didn't yet have a coach for the boys' basketball team, and when they found him, he would be given his choice of subject matter to teach. Discouraged but undaunted, she tried again, this time having the interview out in the hot sun in a plowed field in the presence of the farmer's sweating mule. This job required that she teach not only mathematics, but help in History and English as well. It meant going to summer school, but this she did and signed a contract for the regular state salary of $70 a month. "Once I was in the classroom and felt the joys and rewards of the student-teacher relationships, I never considered leaving it, ever, for any reason."

Another teacher found that, when she arrived at her first job and reported in to the county supervisor as instructed, she was greeted with the question, "What are you doing here? Didn't you get our letter?" It turned out that the teacher had come a month too early, for, due to the building of an addition to the school, the opening of school had been postponed one month, and the letter notifying her of this change had reached her home thirty minutes after she had left on the train. However, a place was found for her to live, and a job arranged in one of the county offices so that living expenses could be met. This experience worked to her advantage because she got to know the people, to become familiar with the school, to select her room in the teacherage, and to become oriented to her new teaching responsibilities.

Teacher D, frightened at facing her first job in a rather large high school, walked in to find a warm welcome from a gracious friendly teacher who was standing in the lobby to greet newcomers. This welcome put the new teacher at ease, and became the start of a long and treasured friendship.

Getting to a two-teacher school only thirty miles from their home took two teachers two days. The father of one of them took them in the buggy to the nearest railroad station to catch a train to a town where they would spend the night with friends. Early the next morning, these friends drove them the remaining twelve miles across the mountains to their school. "The road was steep, narrow, crooked, and full of rocks. The area was sparsely settled, and we were scared, because it was our first time to teach away from home. . . ." It was about eleven o'clock when they reached the house where they were to live, but no one was at home. The friends stayed as long as they could, unloading the bags and visiting on the porch, but they had to start back down the mountain so as to reach their home before dark, and they drove away, leaving the newcomers sitting there, alone.

Soon after the rumble of the wagon wheels died away, a well-dressed young man came up the road and stopped to talk with us. Since everyone in the community knew the new schoolma'ams were to get there that day, he was getting the jump on the rest by seeing us first. He passed the time of day with us, asked about our teaching experience, told about his recent trip to Kansas, and then gathered some apples from a near-by orchard for us to eat. After all this, he began to tell us about the local school. In vivid terms he described how the big mean rough boys had teased, played tricks on, and finally run off the man teacher who had been there the last term. He frightened us beyond words and then went his way.

Our friends were so far away by that time we couldn't reach them. . . . There was nothing to do but wait until our landlords arrived from church, but, if we could have left, we surely would have gone back home that day. Soon a surrey and some buggies full of people came over the hill and on up to the house. Mr. Al and Miss Sue soon put our minds at ease, showed us up to our rooms in the big old rambling white house with a banistered porch around it, and then set us down to a dinner we'll never forget. Afterwards, we found out that the dashing young man with his tales was just teasing, and was one of our pupils. Later, he helped us to enjoy teaching, and made us glad that we had stayed to learn how fine a community this was.

College friends sometimes met again in their teaching assignments, became roommates, and afforded security to each other. This coincidence happened in one instance where, after meeting each other again, the two college friends were told by the principal that a visiting evangelist had invited all of the teachers to the revival being held in the tent nearby. He advised them to attend.

This was my first introduction to "talking in tongues" and "faith healing." Several percussion instruments added to the shouting and loud singing. All this made me realize that I had much to learn about the beliefs, customs, and ideals of the people in the community. I thought many of them looked pale, but I was told that one of the denominational rules forbade use of make-up. . . . One parent told me he was disappointed in me because I "painted my face." Another parent told me to "leave off the extras," to just "learn" his child. I had the joy of "learning" them, with "extras" tucked in during the year.

Teachers have always had to be innovative, to make something from nothing. One teacher expressed it in verse:

Each day I was greeted
With eager faces,
And of course I tried
To step up their paces.

I had learned that flash cards
Was a very good way
To drill on Math facts
Day after day.

I made some with crayons
Shoeboxes and such,
And the students were learning
So very much.

But the parents asked students
When they got home from school,
"What did you learn today,
The Golden Rule?"

"No," said the children,
And laughed with glee,
"We played cards today
To learn two plus three."

"Played cards!" exclaimed Mother
And Daddy chimed in,
"Played cards at school?
Why that is a sin!"

The papas and mamas
Were all in a stew.
They went to the Superintendent
To tell him what to do.

"She must be fired,"
Yelled the angered mob.
"Hire someone else
To do this job!"

He kindly told me
The cards must go.
I must take them home
And use them "no mo."

I obeyed his orders
And then each day,
My students learned Math
In a brand new way.

We counted stones and nuts
Found in the yard,
And adding and subtracting
No longer was hard. . . .

Life was so interesting
And full of fun
We hardly knew
When the day was done.

I would not change
One bit of the whole,
Though I've never been able
To attain my goal. . . .

It is this "Unreachable Star" just beyond the grasp which seems to characterize the attitudes of the teachers in these days, and, in reaching out and beyond the immediate present brought them into conflict with changes which, at times, frustrated but never defeated them. "There is nothing so permanent as change" was accepted by most of them as normal, and they, themselves, became moving forces in the process of change.

Teaching Conditions

Changes caused teachers to re-examine their commitment to teaching and to decide that working with children and youth more than compensated for inconveniences and hardships. But teaching took its toll in physical energy.

> After a full day in the classroom without a break, the following duties were mine: readings and declamations had to be selected and taught; operettas had to be given; costumes to be made. Programs were presented; county fair booths were prepared; and often rooms had to have "spring cleaning" with woodwork and walls washed. But perhaps the most exhausting experience for me was taking care of the library in addition to my regular classroom work. There were books to be repaired, new books processed for circulation, all library books checked, and a final report made to the state. The hours after school days were just not long enough, and this work had to be finished during the wee hours of the morning.

In those days teachers were expected to teach a Sunday School class, sing in the choir, and engage in the general activities of the community, all of which many teachers tried to do. Furthermore, a teacher's morals were supposed to be above reproach, and an example of honesty and integrity had to be set, worthy of emulation. A teacher's social life was scrutinized, and one had to be very careful in choosing friends.

> One Sunday evening four of us younger teachers had dates. About 9:30 P.M. the board member (who operated the dormitory in which the teachers lived) knocked on the living room door and put his head inside to announce: "It's bedtime." One of the young men replied: "Don't let us keep you up, Mr. B___; just go right on to bed." The board member was so shocked that he could not reply. He went silently to bed.

In addition to classroom duties, another teacher recalls being assigned to coach basketball, drama, chorus, "elocution," all of which were to be done either at the noon recess or after school, and for no extra remuneration.

> Also, since many children walked to school, teachers frequently started the school day upon leaving home, accompanying their pupils to the school house, enjoying the world they all jointly shared together, feeling friendly and close, knowing more about one another each day. The teacher was made to feel important and respected, rendering a valued service to parents who were, in many cases, partners in the educational process.

It seems to be the consensus that, although the cost of teaching was high, the values received were higher.

In some school systems strict "Guidelines" for personal behavior *at all times* and *in all places* clarified the teacher's responsibility to the public which was paying for the service.

> On the twenty-mile ride to the country school and my future home, the teacherage, I was briefed by the principal on my many duties at school, and the rules at the teacherage: (1) All teachers in their bedrooms by 10:00 P.M.; (2) only soft-soled shoes in the hall at all times; (3) prompt attendance at meals after the principal had appeared.

One school board member would not allow the teacher to sign a contract until he knew that she did not dance and did not have bobbed hair. No Flapper was going to teach his son!

In many systems married women teachers were not considered for employment. "Jobs were so scarce that the rationale was that single teachers needed the positions, and husbands were to support wives. The rule also was that teachers living in the teacherage were to date only local fellows."

Another teacher was told to keep the fact of being a Baptist secret if she were to survive in a Methodist school district, and political affiliations were factors in employment and in holding a job. An entire school could be closed if a teacher did not "vote right," and was notified that the job was terminated, and, until another teacher could be found, the door to the school remained closed.

One teacher was fired because she got back late to her rooming house after a tire blew on her date's car, and no amount of explaining did any good. "Shades had to be drawn if any dancing or card playing went on in the teacherage."

In one system, if teachers missed a county-wide teachers' meeting, they had to write a long theme and deliver it to the County Superintendent. If they were sick, they had to bring a signed statement from their doctor. One teacher who was in bed with the measles, took the doctor's statement to the Superintendent *who still required her to sit down and write the theme before leaving the office.* Teachers in one town lived in a teacherage where they had to sign out and sign in with the principal by certain hours. They could not have dates except on week-ends, and then they had to double-date or stay at the teacherage!

Transportation—or lack of it—was a matter of importance. "Some farmers had horses for riding. Now and then I could catch a ride on a wagon. The only outside communication was by person or by mail; there was no telephone.

> To get from my home to my school, I walked to the railroad station and rode a train for several miles. Sometimes I walked the remaining miles to reach my boarding place. When the weather was bad, the road was muddy, and I would be met by a horse-drawn buggy driven by one of the women with whom I lived. . . ."
>
> ✦ ✦ ✦
>
> Through the years my biggest problem was transportation. . . . Sometimes I rode the school bus; at other times I rode the Greyhound Bus, and was often the only passenger. At other times I rode with a truck driver who would be going my way, but most interesting of all was riding with the mail carrier. Riding with him meant that I left home at 6:30 A.M. to walk to the post office near my home, and then walked from the post office at our destination to the school where I taught. This I did in reverse each afternoon. Sometimes there would be three or four passengers, the mail carrier and the mail. From this experience I came to know where people lived along the route and I helped to sort the mail and put it in the boxes.

High tides or storms meant that a teacher and students riding the bus would find themselves having to be pulled through the high water to higher ground. Once a storm arose and prevented the Buxton teachers from using the ferries to get home from a meeting held at Manteo. When they reached home the next day, they found that a tidal wave had crossed the island and the water was up to front porches.

Some incidents in the classrooms in these early days would be interesting today. "All the girls wore hats to school, and one of the struggles was to persuade them to remove hats during the day. Some refused." After asking if a certain boy was in school that day and being told that he was, the Superintendent ordered the teacher to send him out at once: "His father has smallpox!"

Working sometimes against hostile attitudes, teachers labored persistently and bravely for better conditions for their students. In one two-teacher school where no interest in the school was evidenced, the teachers had been accustomed to coming to school at any time. One teacher changed everything—including the attitude.

> The winter coal was being stored in the assistant teacher's classroom. The children were carrying water one-half mile from a house where eight other families used water. There were outside toilets without locks; there was no lunchroom, and the children went out to small stores to eat. . . . I had a basement under the building made to store the coal; I asked the Board of Education to build . . . pit toilets, and I locked them after school hours. I persuaded the Commissioners to put running water in our school if the school board would furnish the pipe. This was done. . . . With the surplus food from a federal program, I made sandwiches for the children, and gave them one-half pint of milk which they had at school for a few pennies a day . . .

There were good times and lots of wholesome fun as well as problems and frustrations. Where there had been no Christmas tree before, "we had one. You couldn't buy ornaments . . . so we made them. . . . Bags to hold candy were made of tarlatan of varied colors. Candles were purchased for the tree (by the teacher), and one man became interested and put a pencil on the tree for each pupil. Another gave oranges. . . . Popcorn strings made the decoration," and songs and speeches were taught to the pupils by rote since musical instruments and other materials were lacking. Parents came, and "it was hard to know who had the best time—parents, pupils, or teacher" who had made Christmas happen.

Corn huskings in the fall and wood choppings in the spring helped teachers get acquainted with the entire community, and tender hands became roughened as the inexperienced teacher determinedly undertook the shucking and the chopping.

Box suppers were high spots, socially, and, in one case, the entire group of local fellows pooled their money to outbid the "outsider" for the teacher's box—the unbelievable amount of $15.00! Silent movies, dancing, skating on the ice-covered river, sledding parties, group singing, parlor games, rabbit hunting and hiking were forms of entertainment. A county commencement became an annual event in one county. This event featured a grand parade, and a guest speaker, usually a well-known political figure; and large crowds of parents and interested citizens from all over the county socialized at this educational event.

The devastating flu epidemic of 1918 closed the schools, but many teachers stayed on in their communities to help out in nursing, in carrying food to entire families in bed with the disease, or, perhaps, in teaching one or two eager students on the porch in the open air. Once a bomb threat caused everyone to leave the school quickly, and, when the principal felt that the school should be searched, the teachers went back in, fearful and trembling, to look in every nook and cranny of their own rooms. It was only a hoax, but the fear was real. One teacher, sleeping in a room with all the children, felt the small house move. Thinking that it was an earthquake, she awakened the children urging them to escape. " 'Taint no earthquake," one child reassured her. "It's just old Mama Sow-Pig that sleeps under the house, and when she turns over, she lifts up the whole house." Another teacher, sleeping in a room made especially for her, heard rattlesnakes all night, and, later, engaged in a victorious duel with two huge rattlers, killing both with accurate shooting and sending their long bodies down the stream. Bravery, humor, determination, resourcefulness are outstanding characteristics of these teachers in the early schools who, in their commitment to their profession and to the children whom they loved and served, furnished the basis for the informed citizenry which this state needed—and still needs.

> In spite of the absence of a media center, a gymtorium, supplementary materials, modern teaching aids, para-professionals, and clerical help, the children in this old building got excited, motivated, and learned the basics, and many, many, went on to serve their community and themselves well.

To repeat another comment, made previously in this chapter, they all felt that the school was *theirs*, "they made it together." The challenge was there, and they summoned all of their resources to make the best of it.

In building strong PTA relationships, . . . "the parents were withdrawn at first, for they felt that teachers lived in a different world and were not real people as they were. I had each person attending the meetings to say just one word at the first meeting, and we began the 'icebreaking' in this manner. Before the year was over, I had officers who would speak out, would preside efficiently . . ."

> A teacher who became a principal and, later, an administrator learned that a sense of humor is more than essential. On one occasion a parent brought a "so-called" very nervous, retiring, sensitive youngster to be enrolled in one of the primary grades. . . . After explaining all of his eccentricities, she let me know in no uncertain terms that her youngster did not need "direct" discipline. . . . If her child should, for some unexpected and unusual reason, need any discipline at all, the only thing which would be necessary to bring the boy back in line would be to slap the child next to him.

Certain community-imposed rules created problems for teachers. Getting married was often banned by the ruling of some school systems, and one teacher was told, "Miss C., don't get married. You're a good teacher, and you'll fire yourself." Wearing lipstick (or makeup of any kind), belonging to the "wrong" religious denomination or political party, dancing, card-playing, dating under certain conditions—all were barriers to securing jobs in many communities where the mores were deeply embedded. Other examples have been cited in other parts of this chapter.

Situations arose frequently to challenge ingenuity and resourcefulness. One day several little boys came running back to tell the principal that there was a "dead man down there by our toilet." They kept insisting that the man was dead, not just drunk or fallen down. The principal went along with them and found that the man really was dead. The children were hastily guided into the schoolhouse, recess was temporarily called off, and the ambulance and police were summoned. "Soon, all evidence of the lovers' quarrel held on the school grounds on Sunday night was cleared away, and education calmly continued."

One teacher with eighty-five students, six other teachers, two lunchroom workers and the janitor were "marooned" at school in a heavy snow storm which caught them off guard. They ate bacon, eggs and toast from the lunchroom supplies, and slept on the tables and chairs until the next day about noon when horse-drawn wagons came to rescue them.

Discipline was, of course, a matter of interest to many teachers. "Every child over twenty-five (in number) is equal to two or three individuals when you have them daily." One record shows that the following action was taken by one school board. The Board went on record as "backing up Miss ———, teacher in ——— School until the disciplinary matter is finished, and if necessary to help defend Miss ——— in the trial she is to stand for whipping a boy in school." Another teacher heard an old lady say, as the young teacher passed her house on her way to school, "Oh, Lord, that child is too little; she can't do nothin' with those devils." Another teacher, challenged by the captain of the football team (and son of the chairman of the school board) found herself facing someone taller than she was by several inches, someone sure of himself and his ability to defy her and leave the study hall to go out early to the football field. She met him in the aisle, folded her arms, looked him in the eye, and, white as a sheet, said, "You'll only leave this room over my dead body." For seconds they stood while a dead silence held the rest of the students still in their seats, eager to see how this confrontation would turn out. He reached out his hands to lift her out of the way, and, then, his arms dropped, he looked away, turned and went back to his seat. She said that at that moment, she became a teacher, for she learned that, to teach, she must know how to have the respect of the student. The boy later said to his teammates, "When I saw her eyes flashing fire and her lips turn blue, I knew I'd better back off!" She had won a battle and had proved to herself that she could command respect.

Changes have been many through these years from the one-room school through the time of consolidation. "Throughout the years there have been varying methods: the traditional, the project, the progressive, the unification or correlation program. 'Learning by doing' filled the classroom with so much activity and projects that it was hard to move about in the room. Achievement tests became less frequent and . . . discipline was different . . . It was difficult to supervise the many activities."

Changes! Changes! Changes! From the day I went into a classroom with a pot-belly stove to the day of the radiator, central heating, air-conditioned room carpeted wall to wall or with scattered rugs—living in with a family, living in a teacherage, and then in a home of my own—from a group of committeemen to a Board of Education and its staff—segregated schools to integrated faculties and students going home to lunch or bringing their lunch, to the day of the cafeteria and hot meals—from a salary unequal because of race to equal salary based on educational requirements, and, in many school systems, supplements to this salary—from salary paid at the end of twenty teaching days to a set date each month—from a six-month or eight-month term to nine, and ten months for some personnel—from a teacher working with one class all day to departmental specialized instruction with teacher aides—from a teacher trying to make ends meet during the Depression years to a system set up by the state and government guaranteeing retirement income —these represent some of the contrasts which are a part of the memories of one teacher, and, probably of many others.

Changes in buildings throughout the years ranged from recollections of buildings of logs, of brick and plaster, two-or-three-story-high buildings to cinder blocks of one-story height. Some were air-conditioned; some were mobile units, and finally, by 1970, there were pre-fabricated buildings of one story, varying in shape, with moveable walls.

And what of the changes in the world served by the school, that world for which the school must be the testing ground for decision-making and for attitude-shaping, that school which is not only, in a democratic society, academic in nature but also social in its impact? Will these changes enable us to survive as a free people? Will it be our agency for re-discovery of our purposes and for a re-dedication to the founding of this nation?

Events of these fifty years have had a great impact on education. The Cold War, the Vietnam War, the struggle between the conflicting ideologies, the rapid advance of technology, the visible contrasting of affluence and poverty have singly or together, made many students feel that life is uncertain, and, therefore, must be lived to the hilt every day. Others have the feeling that life is futile, therefore meaningless in its context. . . .

The changing times have brought tremendous pressures upon the school: the guidelines from HEW, the decisions of the Supreme Court, the pressures for drastic and speedy changes in curricula and in methods of teaching from some persons in the field of Education. How the students and teachers act and react, how they interact under all these pressures, has had and will continue to have a profound effect upon the future of the United States.

"Some of the changes have been stimulating, thrilling, and enlightening. Others have been shocking, saddening, and personally provoking." Children outside the classroom see and hear so much that is "dramatic" and exciting that "they are not satisfied with regular classroom routine. . . . Much of the teaching-learning in the classroom lacks the glamor and drama" which the media have led the public to expect, and education has, at times, verged on entertainment rather than on challenge.

Many satisfying experiences, however, have made involvement in teaching worthwhile. The language of the child, for example, has offered exciting possibilities for understanding his world. As teacher and child walked together to school, the child asked, "Guess what I have for lunch today?" And his answer to his own question certainly has to be the earliest advertisement for peanut butter! "I'm having goober butter."

There was the demonstrated eagerness for learning by many students, "the good behavior and home training, the close cooperation between parents and teachers in communities where the church and school were centers and cohesive agents of activity."

> One thing we did was to cook a meal on the "two-eye" stove which was used to heat our room. We had wonderful cooperation from the parents. The children were asked to bring beans, meat for seasoning, a pot in which to cook; bowls, forks and spoons for serving themselves and the principal and teachers who were our guests. All these things came in on the appointed day, prepared and ready to cook, and, of course, the parents were responsible.
>
> Several learning experiences occurred, and surely, the school lunch was much more enjoyed. (This may well have been the forerunner of the school lunch program which was yet some years away.)

In a first-grade unit, *home*, the teacher and children went into the community visiting. After a trip to a farm, "cow" became so important to the class that a life-size cow was constructed.

> Strong wire was used for the body, wood for the legs and old newspapers for wrapping and stuffing the body. . . . Finally she was covered with many layers of paper and papier-mache, and painted. Horns were gotten from the market. During this eight-week unit, reading charts were used for spelling; phonetics, number work with "How many?" concepts, and many other related experiences took place with pleasant results. Butter was made in the classroom, and the class enjoyed a "cracker and butter party." *Cow* became a central figure later in an Art Exhibit in the school system.

A combination grade with pupils of all sizes and capabilities also meant, for one teacher, no textbooks furnished by the state, but each child bringing his own, in most cases, inherited from someone before him. Writing paper and art paper were not available unless the teacher provided them from personal funds, and pencil sharpeners were not a "normal" adjunct of the classroom. Some pupils had small pocket-size sharpeners, while others brought extra pencils. It was this teacher who experienced one of those intangible rewards which go far beyond financial remuneration.

> For two or three days Charles, who was very outgoing, said, "I'm going to save you a seat beside me in the lunchroom." I thanked him and sat in my reserved seat. This arrangement went on for several days, and one day, Bill, a buddy of Charles' and a bit timid, asked me, "Is Charles your pet?" Thinking fast, I said, "He is one of them, and you are one of them, and everybody in this room is one of them. Why did you ask?" He answered, "You eat beside him every day." I reminded him that he hadn't asked me to eat with him, and I promised to sit beside him that very day. From that time on, for as long as I taught, I rotated my "reserved" seat each day to sit beside a different child.

With the changes, then, teachers have "rolled with the punches," with one message coming through, loud and clear: the teachers, with their commitment to their profession, with their earnest and persistent search for ways to help their students, have been the basic factor in promoting the growth of this state. The enlightened citizens, both men and women, coming from the classrooms, have translated into action the lessons they have learned, and, in their own lives, have demonstrated that, for many, the impact of the teacher has been a strongly motivating force for their own contributions to our local, state, and national heritage.

> There have been changes in buildings and in methods, too—
> Parents, teachers, and students—just to name a few.
> Books are not bought but are rented by the State,
> And are sometimes free as are the lunches by the plate.
> There's more to be taught, so you get in the swing
> And try to let each pupil continue to do his thing.
> We've roamed the land, the sea, and the sky,
> Man's need for knowledge has never risen so high.

Yes, the kids are wiser—why shouldn't they be?
They've had more to learn than was taught you and me.

Students today can see history as it's being made,
And view the world's sports as they're being played.

The moon, it seems, is just arm's length away.
And you can travel almost anywhere in just one day.

So much for the pupils and what they have learned.
For all of us teachers, too, the pages have turned.

As we've grown older and kept up with the pace,
Many have been the problems we've had to face.

The going was rough back in the year '35,
We did well to eat, sleep, teach, and stay alive.

Conveniences were few and the pay was small;
Once, even, the checks were delayed until fall.

The chores were many and responsibilities great,
We knew we had to do them, and we couldn't wait.

Rooms had to be cleaned and the fires kept,
Errands to be run and halls to be swept.

Custodians, hot lunches and modern plumbing
Were things we hoped would soon be coming.

Now salaries are higher and benefits better;
A teacher can do wonders . . . if the Public will let her!

We have seen changes come about gradually, "a change in our thinking from a time when men met four times a year and spent four or five thousand dollars for the education of the children (in one county) to the time when the Board of Education spent many thousands of dollars and uprooted schools and radically changed the Old Order. The Period of Consolidation had begun, and a new era in North Carolina lay ahead.

ASTOUNDING

A little boy in the second grade came up to me, the teacher, sitting in a reading circle, and tapping me on the shoulder whispered, "Don't be astounded, but it is snowing."

43

IV ⤞ Teaching

Tarheelia Schools Move into Consolidation

Consolidation of schools was destined to move rather slowly; however, by the 1920's North Carolina began to plan for better schools for its children. In 1923 a law was passed saying that all the 100 counties should prepare for the consolidation of one and two-teacher schools.

During this period, 1923–1928, there was much bitterness and fussing over consolidation of schools. Churches took sides; neighbors disagreed; and the children were in between. Some parents insisted that the one-teacher schools with forty to seventy pupils in grades 1–7 should stay where they were, as they had been for almost a hundred years. Others insisted they wanted better schoolhouses, more teachers, and a better chance for their children.

One problem of immense proportions emerged, largely because of the manner in which Reconstruction was imposed. This refers, of course, to the dual school system: One system for whites; another for blacks and Indians. Our state could not hope to cope successfully with two distinct and separate systems of public schools. The United States Supreme Court decision, 1954, was the beginning of the end for this practice. But adjustments and compliance with court-ordered reforms, which often included quotas or ratios of whites and blacks according to numbers of the two races in the administrative unit, were expensive and usually difficult to administer. In the process frequently good school facilities were discarded and a type of consolidation appeared in the process, as completely new structures in locations that had not previously been anticipated became more or less mandatory. As a matter of fact, another element injected into the scheme—"cross-bussing"—was expensive, inconvenient, and tended to make this type of consolidation questionable. North Carolina had long boasted of operating the largest fleet of school buses in the world.

The great "Depression" during the 1930's hit the state a hard blow just at the time when it was gaining real status in the consolidation movement. Those who experienced that misfortune probably would agree that it was somewhat difficult even to "buy a job," let alone consolidate schools.

North Carolina, fairly early, became interested in good roads, an absolute necessity for consolidation of educational facilities. Indications of concern in this endeavor may be pointed out as one reads about the plank road, from east to west, about the middle of the 1700's. But significant progress in search of excellence for public highways had to wait, for the most part, until after the beginning of the present century. Soon after that the Old North State vied with more advanced states in the nation as a leading contender in the drive for good roads.

Another reason sometimes advanced, which resulted in slowing the consolidation movement, was the charge by smaller school units that larger schools tended to "gobble up" all of large areas of the less affluent schools. This was done under the guise of offering better educational opportunities. Actually, the real purpose was athletic in nature: The larger consolidated schools could field stronger athletic teams! This charge was often hard to refute.

Finally, following consolidation of a number of schools, pride in the "little red schoolhouse" was shaken. No longer could a mother stand in her own yard and see the one or two-teacher schoolhouse where her children might be observed actually playing or engaging in some outside activity. Thus pride in the neighborhood school consequently diminished. The close rapport between teachers and pupils that existed in the one or two-teacher schools was modified. In the larger consolidated high school, the pupil might very likely be bussed several miles and be taught by a number of different teachers. As a result, he ran a risk of becoming a statistic or number rather than the energetic school child he actually was.

Knowledgeable proponents for consolidation of schools were able to advance certain rather convincing arguments for this movement. Indeed, they usually countered fairly successfully many of the objections cited by their opponents. Students in the larger units could be grouped according to interests, ability and desired subjects. They were given choices often impossible in smaller units. New departments, such as vocational home economics, industrial arts, agriculture, and commercial work became attractive to youth heretofore deprived of those special advantages. Academic subjects, especially foreign language, mathematics, science, history and English could now blossom under teachers who specialized in those subjects. Art, music, and band catered to many who were talented and interested. Dramatics occupied a welcomed role. And there was a central library, the pride of the school, with thousands of volumes representing the different required areas of reference and study.

Finally, to counter the charge that one might become a statistic rather than a real person, the position of a full-time certified counselor came into existence. Such an advisor had adequate facilities necessary to cope with a host of student questions and problems. Each student could talk with this counselor in confidence and receive information desired in making later decisions about school and life.

Not to be overlooked was the Physical Education Department and the competitive athletic sports, the latter being extracurricular but frequently exerting more than its justified share of influence on both school and community.

Along with all these apparent virtues of the consolidated school went the tremendous dispersal of instructional supplies, made available through Federal Aid, and through the efforts of the local administrative Board and the State Department of Instructional Service. Every teacher had access to many supplies for his students. Science laboratories rivaled those of a small college. Audio and visual aids made their appearance—and the list of services rendered remained far from complete. Those who favored consolidation usually contended that, whatever the price required it was not a penny too much!

Superintendent Calvin Wiley, the Horace Mann of the South, had tried to bring a type of consolidation closer by the 1860's, but the effort faded.

Then, during the term of Governor Charles B. Aycock, this champion of education went almost everywhere in the state proclaiming the right of every person to have a better education than the State then afforded. The minimum school term advocated was four months. Aycock influenced the citizens to act. This he could not do single-handed; instead, he attracted men of action who were educationally minded to support his effort. At this time, it seems, an important step toward consolidation on a gradual scale began to be taken. A few representative counties selected at random will serve to authenticate the trend throughout the state.

Sometime about 1910, with the one-room, one-or-two-teacher school giving way to more elaborately designed buildings, area citizens were proudly admiring split-level structures capable of accommodating four teachers, and a curriculum embracing seven grades, the extent of grades in the elementary schools for several years to come. And there were specific provisions, too, for certain needs of the boys and girls: an outside rest room with toilet facilities for boys; outside rest room with toilet facilities for girls. Lunch was brought in lunch baskets or paper bags. Water came from someone's well, drawn the old fashioned way with buckets, and shared from a common drinking dipper, unless a pupil possessed his own folding drinking cup.

The teachers were surprisingly good, and the administration through the principal and his school board amazed many by the efficient manner in which it operated. But now a good look around the area revealed a startling fact. Another village, a bitter rival, located near the banks of a second stream which was known as a river, "also was the happy recipient of a split-level school as appealing in design as ours! They envied, perhaps hated, not only the building, but also the students who attended it as well. The rivalry was keen indeed, and a lot of prejudice existed on the side of each school community."

Following World War I, or about 1920, an unbelievable event took place. Citizens of the two villages and the immediate areas surrounding them, met in a called session in a hall of one of the mill village-owned facilities. A representative from the county administrative office attended, spoke about consolidation of the two schools, answered questions, and departed, claiming almost unanimous support for the merger idea. Citizens were not only willing that their children attend a larger and more progressive school which would also embrace grades 1 through 11, first grade through high school, but they went on record as favoring a bond issue so that facilities might be made available at the earliest possible moment. They would be enabled to have a fine high school or a "Union School." Previously students fortunate enough to complete seventh grade could get no further training unless they went to boarding schools, institutes, or academies. Most students were financially unable to do this. In the meantime, those who were graduating that spring would attend high school in the large room over a store building standing on a knoll between the two rivers.

A number of students attending other high schools now came back to their own communities. Consequently, in the year 1921, in one upper room under a single qualified principal-teacher, with a student body representing grades 8–10, a new high school was born. The school year 1922–23 favored us with two high school teachers, an increase of 100% in the teaching force! But events moved along so rapidly that before the school year was over the student body was moved into the improved facilities of the new consolidated union school! Then next year, a bussing program began with one school bus operating. Others would be added year by year as the consolidated school expanded and began bursting at the seams due to the influx of students. The citizens in the two villages, who had been envious of each other, now joined hands in such a way that this modern school came to be a force for educational and moral strength in the respective communities as well as in the entire county. It is worthy to note that of the many high schools and union schools existing in the county by the beginning of the 1920's, consolidation proceeded at such a rapid clip that, by 1967, only five high schools existed in the entire county, including rural and city systems. All were accredited not only by the State of North Carolina but also by the Southern Association of Colleges and Secondary Schools.

Thus the small high school was wiped out in its entirety, being replaced by elaborately-constructed facilities containing special departments, lunchrooms, and additional subjects which students might *elect*. The elementary schools frequently remained untouched. Pupils used the vacant rooms for constructive activities. Massive-scale bussing came into existence.

Beginning with the small log school house, about 1900, then to the larger two-teacher frame building, 1905, on to a more spacious split-level four-teacher setup, around 1910, culminating in the excellent Union Schools in 1921, the story of consolidation in one county is summarized.

Another typical county was created in 1842 by the General Assembly. The first public schools were opened in 1845–46 and ran for about 3½ months, the perennial custom in those days. Again, education started with the one-room, one-teacher school, all of the instructors being males. Substantial progress had been made, however, before the Civil War interrupted and all but closed school doors. The 1866–67 legislature came to the aid by passing acts which authorized the establishment of school systems, and provided for taxes to be collected for cooperative purposes.

Charles H. Mebane, State Superintendent of Public Instruction, has been credited with beginning a real revival in education during his term of office, 1896–1900. Then Governor Aycock took up the torch, 1901–1905. Later, from 1907 and for the next eighteen years, another native son, the late Reverend George Edward Long, a county superintendent, worked to combine or consolidate the inefficient, expensive, and deplorable one- and two-teacher schools. He compiled information and put it in booklet form, pointing up the shortcomings of the small school. Among the reasons cited were small taxable area, school officers who opposed progress, few pupils, limited number of teachers, inefficient teachers, impossibility of grading and classifying pupils, brief school term, lack of vocational training, no provision for those who wish to attend high school and excessive per pupil cost.

Later actions determined a more nearly complete consolidation in the early 1950's. County citizens voted a 3¾ million dollar bond issue and built five consolidated high schools which, according to some reports, were the most modern and best equipped in the state.

In fact, one of these high schools is at this date in the process of constructing an observatory, one of the very few high schools in this state so favored. The progress in this county, from log-structured or slab-siding schools, near 1900, to multi-million dollar super structures with all facilities imaginable, 1975, sounds like the "from pennies to riches" story. And it is!

The account of growth in another county school system serves as a reminder of how North Carolina struggled to develop its system of schools. This county system, formed in 1777, began the usual program of constructing one- and two-teacher buildings, in vogue during that period. The population was scattered, so by 1881, 77 school structures for white students and 18 buildings for black students were in existence. Annual teacher salary, usually less than four months, was whites, $50; blacks, $44.

Moving to combine and upgrade educational opportunities, in 1900, the county began the effort to consolidate certain schools, out of which, 56 schools appeared for white students and 10 for black students. This reduced the number of schools by 21 for whites, and 8 for blacks. The annual school term became just over twelve weeks for whites, eleven weeks for blacks.

However, an ambitious consolidation program had been begun, some of which was successfully carried out—some of which was unable to be achieved at that time. At that stage, this county, rated 33rd economically and fifth on the local effort, was doing an outstanding job in meeting its educational challenge.

For example, a 1960 survey will show that, of the 75 or so schools existing in 1924, consolidation had reduced the number to 17, but the undertaking had not paid off fully, and more problems were soon to follow. Today, 1975, there are two senior high schools for this entire county; five junior high schools; and 15 elementary schools, a grand total of only 22. Contrast this figure with the 1881 total, white and black, 95 schools. At that time, there was a sparse population; in 1975, the county is well populated. It would appear that a bit of a miracle has happened in a span of about 95 years.

The coming of all-weather roads hastened the consolidation effort, making it possible for fleets of school buses to operate. There had been a question earlier whether this county might have consolidated too much, too soon, since the necessary good roads had not kept pace with the consolidation effort. But, eventually, most factors involved were resolved so that the county could proudly point to one of the finest consolidated school systems in the state.

One extremely important item—money—may be cited, indicating one reason why such progress was possible. Property evaluation tends to tell a large part of the story. In 1889 the property evaluation in the county was about $1,200,000; in 1975, it stood at approximately $400,000,000. A 400% increase in property evaluation is certainly indicative of real economic progress, a fact which made the consolidation of schools much easier to realize.

In many cases the federally-ordered cross-bussing to achieve racial balance was met head on, and acceptable compliance was achieved.

Another interesting development working to the definite advantage of the more prosperous and larger cities and counties is the state-allowed supplementary tax the local citizens have been allowed to vote for school purposes. A school system may use the proceeds from such taxes for a variety of school needs, including additional teachers or teacher aids and teacher salaries. Thus, better teachers often were attracted to the larger consolidated school systems. From the teacher's standpoint this extra money frequently became a great drawing card. Consider what this might mean to a teacher in 1918 with an average monthly salary of $56.83, or an instructor of 1970 with an average salary per month of well over $700. A supplement of several hundred dollars a year is usually very attractive. While the less prosperous counties and cities were accorded the same privilege of voting a supplementary tax for their own school needs, many never got around to doing much about it. Thus the city and larger consolidated units were able to draw off some of the better teachers from the less fortunate school systems. An acceptable and fair answer to this problem may not come immediately.

Where do we stand today on the education ladder? Not so high, really, as one might have reason to expect. The Tar Heel State has never regained, at any time, the high ranking it held, *relative to other states*, than that in the early 1860's—over a hundred years ago. Our state has made giant strides, usually in spurts, during those years, but most other states have gone forward also, usually managing to forge ahead at a more accelerated rate. Many educators, however, predict that, with the big consolidation-integration issues mostly behind, North Carolina is destined to attain a more commanding or commendable position among our sister states in the not-too-distant future.

TEACHING IS NOT ALL FROM BOOKS

As a first-grade teacher, I have tied shoestrings by the dozens, rebraided pigtails and tied ribbons, tied sashes which I could never arrange like mothers had tied them before school, painted knees and stuck on band-aids, dried tears, and sometimes washed faces; but if I had my life to live over, I would not want any day changed.

V ✑ Developing the Curriculum

From the Blue-Back Speller to the Metric System

The curriculum of the public schools during the early part of the century centered largely around the textbooks available at that time. In fact, public schools as such were few. It was not until 1899 that the state legislature appropriated the sum of $100,000 to set up common schools for the state, thus committing itself to the democratic principle of public education. For those attending the public schools in existence in 1900 educational opportunities were exceedingly limited.

The first step on the educational ladder was usually the learning of the ABC's. Many teachers recount their experiences with the ABC's either in their early school days or in their first years of teaching. These three paragraphs are typical reports:

> I remember in our small one-teacher school there was a little red headed girl in pigtails. She was from a very deprived family and had great trouble in learning her ABC's. Some of us felt sorry for her when she was made to stand in the corner because she did not know them.
>
> ✓ ✓ ✓
>
> Punishment was seldom needed but I can remember very clearly an experience I had in the first grade. Our teacher, who was a man, called us to the front of the room to stand in line and, one by one, read the ABC's from the top to the bottom of the page. All of us were stumped by the letter G. We were told to stand on one foot until we knew it. I went home feeling very much disgraced and told my father about it. He said, "If he does that again get your bonnet and come home." Fortunately, we were not punished in that way again.

At the turn of the century my mother taught in a one-room school house with eighteen pupils, ages five to seventeen. On the first day the pupils brought their own books and her first task was to find out which reader each pupil was in and if he knew his ABC's. She approached a husky six year old whose hair hung in his eyes and whose clothes were evidently hand-me-downs. He had no book, slate or pencil. She asked, "Son, do you know your ABC's?" He gave her a defiant look and answered, "Naw, but I can cuss awright."

Much of the learning was more or less by rote and grade placement was according to the reader the child had. Teaching materials were limited to a painted board for the chalk board and a few pieces of chalk. There may have been an eraser but, if not, a piece of sheepskin was used for erasing the board. Pupils brought their own slates and pencils with a small piece of sponge or a piece of cloth for cleaning the slate. Rare was the child who could own a pencil and tablet.

Absent was any kind of visual aids we depend on today. Mimeographing and duplicating machines were unheard of; even the gelatin hectograph came later. What paper and pencils were available were not to be wasted on questionable projects. Assignments were made by the next so many pages.

The *McGuffey Readers* had been published in the nineteenth century and were a mainstay of public education for more than half a century. One teacher says, "As I look back over my forty years of experience I remember when I started teaching that the first grade curriculum consisted of one book and, for a time, that was *McGuffey's First Reader*."

The *McGuffey Readers* contained collections of stories, poems, proverbs, mottoes and drawings, all illustrating moral truths and such values as thrift, courage, honesty, and obedience. The short selections were used for memorization and were frequently recited in the Friday afternoon exercises. One recalls the elderly man who, not too long ago, was still entertaining friends and club members by reciting longer selections he had memorized for those Friday afternoon exercises in the early part of this century.

Noah Webster's *The American Spelling Book* had appeared even earlier. Commonly known as the blue-back speller, it was used in public and private schools for more than a century. This text contained page-long columns of words, each word divided into syllables with each syllable pronounced as it was spelled. One teacher recalls the spelling matches using words from the blue-back speller:

> On Friday afternoons we chose sides with all the children who studied spelling taking part in the match. We lined up along two sides of the room facing each other. The teacher called the words and when any of us misspelled a word that child went to his desk. This continued until only the winner was left standing.

Arithmetic began with learning to count—up to 100 finally. Then came the intricacies of the four fundamental processes and the memorizing and reciting of the tables. In many cases little attention was given to any understanding of what it was all about. Younger children often learned the "tables" from hearing the older ones recite them.

Some teachers recall mathematics as they taught it:

> When I began teaching the teacher was left to her own initiative to tie the subject matter in with everyday life. A project we worked out one year in arithmetic was to measure the school ground and determine how many acres and fractional parts it contained.

✓ ✓ ✓

> One rule I continued to break. I kept a pocket knife in my bag because there were oranges for holes to be cut, apples and pears to be divided. These were brought from home. Yes, we learned fractions and shapes in the cutting.

✓ ✓ ✓

> Though the metric system may be considered something new today, I recall the arithmetic text I used early in my teaching career. It contained tables of the metric system which students memorized, and such topics as papering, carpeting, finding volumes of wells, and other cylindrical objects.

Maxwell's *Grammar* also appeared early in the century and soon easier texts appeared for younger children. These texts contained poems to be memorized, stories to read and discuss, and pictures to study. It still included some formal grammar as one teacher states:

> In grammar we began early to learn the parts of speech, how to parse and to analyze sentences. As early as the second grade, children were expected to write their own compositions, and since spelling was a "must," little help was given as they struggled with such assignments.

> I recall quite well my early experiences with "grammar" in our little one room school. With an excellent teacher I felt that I had become quite expert in recognizing the parts of speech, parsing, and analyzing sentences. When we moved to a small village in order that we might have advantages of a larger school, I was placed in the fourth grade. All students from the fourth grade and up sat in a large room and went to smaller rooms for classes. I did very well until I went to the "grammar" class. There we were sent to the blackboard to diagram sentences. Never having heard of diagramming I did not know what to do with my sentence. I looked around and saw other children drawing lines so I did the same. The teacher was very understanding in not criticizing my efforts but nobody could have interpreted my sentence from the way I had filled my lines with words from the sentence. An aunt, who had been a teacher, was in our home that night and soon set me straight on how to fill the lines properly.

Geography was introduced some time after the appearance of Matthew Fontaine Maury's *Elementary Geography* and became a part of the elementary curriculum. For some of its concepts teachers were sometimes faced with criticism, as illustrated by these stories:

> One father wrote me a note asking me to read my Bible, especially *Revelation* 7:1, about the angels standing on the four corners of the earth, and stop teaching that the earth is round. Of course there could be no argument in such a case but we continued to teach according to the geography book.

> ✓ ✓ ✓

> One fourth grade teacher was faced with a group of children one morning as they came trouping into the room saying, "Miss A, R. W. says she doesn't believe the earth is round." We had been studying

the globe the day before, and tried to illustrate the roundness of it. R. W. quite excitedly said, "Show me a ball that has four corners, like the Bible says, and I'll believe the earth is round."

✓ ✓ ✓

We were studying the United States. We began in the northeast corner and followed a "down up" pattern to the west coast. I thought I had done a grand job teaching the New England States. A question on a test was, "Locate the New England States." One boy's response was, "You will find the New England States on page 48." Along with this pattern we also did much drawing and memorizing of state capitals.

All textbooks were bought by the children and at the beginning of the school year business was brisk in the buying, selling, or exchanging second-hand texts. Especially was this true after the state began the policy of adopting books for state-wide use, and the original price and that for exchange as well were stamped on the back binding of the text. One teacher quotes the price of *The Elementary Geography* as forty cents and the exchange price as twenty. If a book was "third hand" it might be bought for as little as ten cents. Even at so low a price many families who had several children in school had difficulty in supplying all of them with books.

Many teachers recall the order of the day in schools during the first quarter of the century:

The school day began with the reading from the Bible, a prayer, usually the "Lord's Prayer," the singing of a hymn or *America*, and roll call from the ledger. In some schools children answered the roll call with a verse of scripture, usually short and easily remembered ones, such as "Jesus wept," "Honor thy father and mother."

✓ ✓ ✓

Arts and crafts of the 1923 vintage found the supply cabinets and bookshelves empty (when there were any), unless filled by the teacher. All materials for any arts and crafts had to be purchased by the teacher, sometimes with the help of the children, and we made use of many bits of material the children brought from home or that the teacher might beg or buy out of her own meager salary. Teaching first grade made handwork a necessity for seat work, or busy work as the case might be.

There was need for pencils, crayons, scissors, paper, paste and imagination. On one occasion after sending home a request by a pupil, I saw his father accompanying him to school the next morning, bringing a new speller, paper and pencil. No art supplies! The father very politely told me his son did not need crayons and scissors, that he did not have time for these things. He said, "Please teach him an extra lesson while the others are playing with such things."

One teacher in a two room school describes her situation thus:

I did not know it at the time but the program in my classroom was about thirty years before its time. You would recognize many things that took place: multi-age grouping with first, second, and third grades together; student aides—with forty-three children in the group they needed all the help they could get; peer teaching with the older ones helping the little ones; learning centers of which the teacher had to have many; materials, mostly teacher-made of anything available. This was truly an "open classroom," primitive style, but in spite of it all, the children learned.

Changes came slowly for a time but some forward-looking teachers and administrators had courage to move out into new fields. More than one teacher refers to the present-day physical education program with stories of their earlier years in the classroom.

We had not heard the term *"physical education,"* but there was ample time and space for such games as "hide and seek," "anty over," "fox and hounds," "drop the handkerchief." There were foot races and ball games with homemade balls made with yarn or cut up strips of cloth and perhaps covered with a piece of heavy woolen cloth sewed on the ball by a mother. The bat was a paddle shaped out of a board.

✦ ✦ ✦

Physical education was stressed in our school through systematic drilling in marching to the music of the piano in the wide hall as we went into the assembly room, and to the stirring beat of the drum outside at recess time and at the close of school. So soul-stirring was the marching of the children down the front steps and on to the street when they were dismissed in the afternoon that parents would often line up across the street to watch the spectacle as the children marched, not a foot out of step, not a head turned, and not a word spoken!

It amazes me now when I think of the activities in health and physical education we were able to carry on and enjoy so much in so small a space. On rainy days physical education was held in a small classroom. I would cringe every time a ball was hit, close my eyes, and expect to hear a window crash. Believe it or not, it never happened!

Science in the elementary school, as such, was not taught, though as high schools developed, general science was first taught, later followed by physics and chemistry. Teachers in the grades had little or no training for teaching the nature study through which most science teaching was first done there, but many found sources and used opportunities to teach about the world around them. This approach was often choice by chance with no systematic program. They often did well in arousing interest and stimulating curiosity in such experiences as these:

One day a very frightening thing happened in our classroom. One of the boys came in with a garter snake coiled in his pocket. The boys and girls followed him around wanting to see the snake. The snake dropped out of his pocket and to the floor. Then there was really a scuffle. Some were chasing the snake; others climbed upon their desks to get away from it. Finally one of the boys caught it and we put it in a glass jar so that all might be able to see it. This was a good beginning for nature study and was my first "show and tell."

One day as the children started from play a boy found what he thought was a dead bird on the ground under a tree. He took it into the room and put it in the insect cage where all might see it. With the help of the *Bird Guide* (bought at the ten cent store for just ten cents) the bird was identified as the ruby-crowned kinglet. Not even the teacher had ever seen one before, and as we were trying to learn more about the kinglet all eyes were on the cage on a table in the front of the room. Suddenly there was a flutter in the cage and the children almost as one rose in their seats in surprise. We proceeded to give him water and some bread crumbs. The bird survived and when it was time to go home we took the cage outside, placed the bird on a low limb as all the children watched silently, almost breathlessly, to see what would happen. After a few seconds on the limb he took wing and flew away while the children breathed again!

✓ ✓ ✓

We took an annual field trip into the woods surrounding our school to find and learn about the wild flowers in the area. We made collections of some of these and pressed them for a scrapbook, learning to identify and classify them as we put them in the book.

✓ ✓ ✓

We tried but sometimes our attempts went astray as it did for one child as we were studying *The Universe*. I had asked the children to go out into the yard one night after dark and see if they could locate the planet Mars. The next morning I asked how many had seen Mars. All hands went up except for one little girl. When I asked her if she forgot to look, she replied, "No, Mrs. W., we don't have plants in our yard, we just have cement." Perhaps it was a little over her head!

Commonly used nature study projects mentioned by elementary teachers included:

Collecting and identifying leaves in the fall as they change color.
Watching seeds germinate and grow in boxes or jars on the window sill.
Watching a cocoon as the moth emerged in the spring, commonly mentioned are the cecropia and luna moths.
Watching a praying mantis get its food.
Studying evaporation with a pan and a jar of water on the window sill.
Examination of snow flakes during a snow storm.
Looking at a rainbow during a shower.

There was no attempt to arrange a curriculum of any kind, and several grades in the same school might be found collecting leaves in the fall, making collections of seeds, or studying birds, all more or less on the same level. I remember my chief sources of information were Comstock's *Handbook of Nature Study* and small inexpensive editions of books about birds, trees, and wild flowers.

Near the beginning of the second quarter of the century individual school systems and the State Department of Public Instruction began to look at the curriculum, and teachers were relieved when textbooks in science were adopted for use in the elementary grades. Teachers attended science workshops and summer schools to become more knowledgeable in the teaching of science. Then came World War II with the atomic bomb which "gave a nudge" to science teaching at all levels. It was not until Sputnik, however, that we began, as one teacher said, "trying to get an instant science education by reading scientific material, taking all sorts of courses, and attending workshops held everywhere." Others reported:

> We were flooded with scientific materials and equipment that we often did not know how to use properly and some of which gathered dust on the shelves or in a store room. The Federal Government poured more money into the schools than we sometimes knew what to do with, both at the elementary and high school levels. High school science programs underwent a complete revolution. After a time we began to find ourselves, with still more changes!

✓ ✓ ✓

> On the heels of so rapid changes we were confronted with the magnitude of John Glenn's feat of orbiting the earth. My students and I were very much excited that day as we had prayers in our class for the success of that mission. Yes, we still had prayers in our schools in those days!

It was during the twenties and early thirties that many new terms began to appear in connection with the curriculum, such as correlation, the project method, unit of study, activity program, child-centered experience curriculum, to name a few. These additions were in connection with the "Progressive Education" movement which countered the role of the so-called lock-step methods of teaching. Good teachers had developed their own methods involving some of the principles that had been evolved. As one teacher said, "We had developed methods of our own which seemed to work. Then as we went back to school we found these being developed more fully in the *Methods Courses* we were taking."

Many larger school systems began evaluations of their own courses of study and often teams from these administrative units would spend a summer in an educational institution, in our own state or in one of the prestigious teacher-training institutions out of the state, that had a curriculum study program. There that team would set up the curriculum for certain areas to be used in their schools.

And so, we went from the three R's to the three R's plus as new methods and new materials came into use. For a time the idea of correlation through units of study came to be the order of the day in the elementary school. One teacher said, "I found the social studies offered the best possibility for correlating most areas of the curriculum." Numerous reports indicate the same.

One of the highlights of our third grade unit on "Food and Clothing," was cooking breakfast at school one morning. We kept "petty cash" for several weeks and it accumulated amazingly fast. We bought bacon, eggs, apple sauce, and day old bread. One of the mothers sent jelly. Each child had two slices of bacon, a serving of apple sauce and at least two pieces of toast. All enjoyed the meal. The many loaves of bread were nearing the last heel when I asked if everyone had had two pieces of toast. D raised his hand and I said, "Haven't you had two pieces of toast?" He hung his head and sheepishly answered, "Yes ma'am, I've had seven."

✓ ✓ ✓

Happiness was a train ride for many first-graders. Hours were spent in planning and in making all preparations for the trip. We looked forward with anticipation to the bus trip to the town where we would take the train and to a picnic along the way. When we reached the station we bought our tickets, waited to hear the whistle, and to see the train come slowly around the curve. We climbed aboard when the train stopped in front of the station. Happy laughter and calls of joy continued as we proceeded to our destination. What happy experiences for the children, most of whom had never been on a train before. But that was not the end. Back at school there were books and poems about trains to be read, charts and booklets about our trip, pictures to draw or paint, and many happy memories for those involved.

✓ ✓ ✓

Since social studies were defined as how we live, work and play our program centered around the study of our community. We would make plans in detail for visiting the post office, the dairy, the fire station, the public library. We read library books, talked about what we would look for and how we should behave on the trip. With the help of the mothers, if the distance was too far for us to walk, the second-graders would set out on an "educational adventure." On the return to the classroom we drew murals, wrote charts, or made booklets about our trips. Yes, we read poetry, often making up some of our own, and wrote "thank you" letters to those who had helped us during the trip.

✓ ✓ ✓

A favorite unit of study in the third grade was how people of the Netherlands (Holland) lived. From time to time these units were introduced in various ways. As with most units all possible areas of the curriculum were involved. One year a local nurseryman proved a valuable resource person since he had transactions with the Dutch in buying their famous bulbs. He had agreed to talk to the class when an unexpected turn of events took place. On the morning he was to come we had a surprise development. Instead of the scheduled speaker, a Dutch bulb salesman was in town and would talk to us. Imagine how thrilled we were! He seemed pleased that we were studying about his country.

✓ ✓ ✓

I realize now that I was teaching during dramatic moments in history, moments that marked great social, economic, and political changes after which things were never quite the same. I was teaching in 1932, the year that marked the depths of the "Great Depression," in 1942 when the United States first became involved in World War II; in 1945 the year of the first use of the atomic bomb; in 1957 came Sputnik; in 1962 John Glenn orbited the earth; then in 1969 came total integration in our schools. These world-shaking events were truly history-making years.

Specialists in reading, mathematics, science, even music and art were rather remote ideas in most schools twenty-five years ago, but such specialists now play important roles in developing the curriculum. The teaching of reading had received priority during the last few years. When the book, *Why Johnny Can't Read*, was published, there was an immediate rush to do something about reading. Money was poured into reading programs; all kinds of devices and programs designed to give Johnny instant reading ability appeared. New series of reading texts were published. Whole communities began to look at the problem; educators tried to find out why pupils could not read as well as they should. Some teachers say:

We had gone from the ABC and the "read around" methods to the word method, then "look and say;" we tried phonics and the individualized reading program, back to phonics and around and around we went.

✓ ✓ ✓

I tried many methods of teaching children to read. What would work with one would not work with another. I kept trying, though, until I found some way to reach most of them. What a joy it was when a child would look into my face and say, "Teacher, I can read."

✓ ✓ ✓

There are many methods of teaching and learning. From observation, I have been unable to discover very few really new techniques. The good teacher has always looked on each child as an individual, has used grouping, trying to find the right level of learning for each one, searched for enrichment material or that suited the individual child, though such material was quite limited until the past few years.

We are still looking for answers to reading problems and are making progress. Even now North Carolina is in the midst of projects not only to help Johnny read better but also to help his father and mother, even his grandparents, to become more effective readers. Task Forces over the state are working on such a program. Yes, more of our people are reading but we still reach for the stars, hoping eventually all of our people will be the educated citizens whom Thomas Jefferson envisioned.

Reports indicate that when many of us began teaching no such thing as a school library existed. In rural areas few books were found in the homes except the school books of the children, and usually a Bible. As years passed, parents were asked to contribute to the school any books they might have that children could read. Few on the child's level came in. Teachers give interesting accounts of these early libraries.

In one of our libraries contributed by the parents there were a few of the Horatio Algier books written for boys but avidly read by both boys and girls. Their one theme stressed "from rags to riches" with such titles as *The Rolling Stone* and *Luck and Pluck*. Another was a copy of *St. Elmo* which the older girls found interesting.

After a time we were able to get reference books. These were often of the one volume variety and frequently bought by the teacher. Later PTA's were organized and one of their first projects was to raise money to buy books for the library. Those bought by the PTA were the first books we had in our library. Bless the members of the PTA!

✓ ✓ ✓

Perhaps the most worthwhile educational project of the year, about 1930, was my obtaining a section of traveling library. From some source I had learned that the state department had traveling libraries and that I could borrow a box of books to be used by the pupils as a lending library. Eventually the box came and, amid great excitement, we opened it and put our "library" to good use.

✓ ✓ ✓

One lasting contribution of the WPA days during the depression was the establishment of a library in our school for grades one through twelve. A very competent and intelligent woman served as librarian. She had been trained under the guidance of a library supervisor and took pride in organizing the library as it should be. Books were housed in a small classroom with a cloakroom at the back for storage and work space. This librarian enjoyed thoroughly working with the books but most of all with the children who checked them out. We were very proud of our library!

WPA days passed and there was no money to pay librarians; so many teachers were asked to serve as librarians in addition to teaching a full load. Among those who served in this capacity was one who says,

I served as a teacher-librarian for years and in the meantime began working for a library certificate. When I received it, I was full-time librarian for eleven years. During that time I saw the library develop into the "Resource Center" with all kinds of non-book materials and equipment and offering all kinds of services. After Sputnik our libraries became rich when federal funds became available. More funds came our way during the sixties and science films were made so rapidly that we often wondered if their facts were really scientifically correct. All of this assistance did more, though, to increase the enthusiasm of dedicated teachers than anything that had happened during their years of teaching.

When magazines became a part of the school library one teacher writes:

> In years past my husband, principal of schools for many years, would censor all magazines and papers for alcoholic advertisements. He then removed all pages containing such items before allowing them to be placed in the school library.

On a morning in 1973 one librarian tells of turning on TV for the news and was shocked to see the school in which she served going up in smoke. With the shock came the thought, "Now I will be unemployed!" Not so! School was immediately reorganized and she tells her story:

> This time will always be one of the most satisfying of my school memories. My time was spent making up book orders and in helping students and teachers in every way possible. The loyalty of the student body, over 50% black, was an inspiration to the faculty. Out of chaos we reassembled a school that fire could not destroy. There were few complaints about the noise, cramped space, cold rooms, bag lunches, and other undreamed of inconveniences. Everyone shared everything! Students cheerfully did their part. When graduating time came, they wanted to have their exercises on the steps of the old building, the only part that remained. The loyalty inspired in everyone by the unfortunate disaster taught us all a lesson we will remember long after we have forgotten the lessons learned in books.
>
> During the past few years drastic changes have been made in the entire curriculum. To meet the needs of students and teachers, extensive materials centers (libraries) have been set up. In these centers are found materials and helps unheard of a few short years ago. These aides have prompted students to find and develop study patterns that coincide with basic subject matter. Keeping this possibility in mind, groups or individual projects are set up according to the child's interest and achievement.

The state set standards for qualifications of teachers early, then began to require that certain subjects be taught in the schools. In the high schools certain units were required for graduation. One can predict, with certainty, that the schools of tomorrow will still be different from those of today. The schools are still evolving with more and more public interest and participation. People are still asking the question, "What should be taught?"

As I look back over my forty-two years in the teaching profession, I can truthfully say that we have come a long way. Yet the soul of the child has ever remained the same. As Dr. William Bagley once said, "All children are the same, alike in some respects and different in others." Yes, we have come a long way since the day of the one-room school and teacher, though dedicated to their task, with barely a high school education or less. The overall objective has remained the same. We have attempted to educate the whole child in order to improve a whole society.

TARDY AGAIN

"Bill, you will have to remain after school for being tardy again."
Bill replied, "Yes ma'm, I knew I would, so I brought two boxes of candy, I thought we might as well enjoy it."

SEX

A pupil came in the first day of school and said, "Are you Miss C____?" I answered, "Yes."
"My Mother doesn't want me in your room," he said.
"Why?" I asked.
"Because, she says you teach about sex."
"Oh, she does? Are you a boy or a girl?"
"I'm a boy," he replied.
"Dear me! Tell your Mother that you already know about sex."

A MEMORY

The following is a quote from a student's note at the close of school long ago. "I will never forget you. You are the best teacher I've ever had. I am going to give you a nickle because I love you." (The nickle is still attached to the note with tape.)

VI 🦎 Increasing the Range

From Kindergarten to University

In the course of educational events there came a time when those in charge decided that children should get a "head start;" thus the kindergarten program was born. Very few of our state retirees can add enlightenment to this subject, but from their reports the majority have approved of the event, as stated in the words of one who has had forty-one years of rich experiences:

> What a wonderful dream has come true. With the modern conveniences and advantages, young people are able to reach to the sky for their learning. Our government has played an important part in making this dream come true. The world has grown closer together through the international events. With the modern programs and planning for the kindergarten through twelfth grade a child begins earlier his training for his total development of life.

From the one-room school to regular neighborhood schools to special classes for individual students, retired teachers have seen much progress take place in teacher certification, in curriculum and even in the day's schedule. It is interesting to note the reflection of a ninety-four-year-old retired teacher:

> I was ten years old when I started to school in 1891 in the two-room building that the people of the community built. The girls were in one room, and the boys were in the other.
>
> We began the morning with worship and a song service. The teacher read the Bible and talked about the words of the song; then we prayed the "Lord's Prayer."
>
> After devotions we took our seats from which we were not allowed to move without permission.

68

But even with the strictness of the early days, children of every generation have similar characteristics as seen in the continued episode of this same teacher as she recorded:

> I sat next to the wall in the girls' room. Beside my crude, home-made desk there was a knot hole in the wall between our room and the boys' room. Sometimes I would glance at the knot hole, and there would be an eye peeping in that hole. How hard it was to keep a straight face so that the teacher would not see the eye too.
>
> At recess we played "Tap Hand," "Draw Base," and other running games or sat under the big trees and chatted.

The change from the project method of years past, unit teaching, and present-day methods are different, but the basic concept has been to try the method by which the child could learn best. However, to some, "rote teaching is still very much needed even though they want the child to enjoy the learning process."

From the old program of "readin', 'ritin', and 'rithmetic" have come special classes designed to give broader and more up-to-date learning in the field of education. Some of these methods have died a natural death; others have developed and changed over the years.

Certainly, changes in the make-up of text books, as well as in the subject-matter used in the books, can be noted. For example, one retired first grade teacher can remember "those series of *Dick and Jane* and even *Baby Ray*. Now, those subjects have changed to *Tigers, Lions*, and *Dinosaurs!*"

When the state began to make a standard list for schools to achieve, many schools did not reach the goal due "to the neglect of some principals who did not keep the proper equipment on hand." New courses, especially agriculture and home economics, were added not only in the rural school but also to those in the city.

The increase in the range often came as a result of "new laws." After the Child Labor Law was passed, there was a need for courses of instruction in cooking and sewing. When these courses were first added to the school curriculum, they were called "Domestic Science Courses."

Then later "a course in 'Family Living' planned for both boys and girls in the senior year was directed toward preparation for marriage and homemaking for those who had little or no home economics in prior years." In the development of Domestic Science, "more homemaking areas were included in the program and the name was changed to home economics." It took a number of years to educate the public to the fact that home economics classes included much more than cooking and sewing.

The majority of the retired teachers have lived through and taught school during at least two war periods—maybe three. And these circumstances helped to widen the teaching of mathematics —and brought the study of aeronautics into view.

Of course, a little humor could be inserted here, for often the teacher asked to include aeronautics in her course was no more prepared than the students. As one teacher said:

> I was asked to teach a course in aeronautics. An airplane engine was placed in an elementary school basement. I was told to take my class there and dismount the engine. A carpenter's hammer and a cold chisel were made available to the class. For two weeks the students hammered away on that engine and never made a dent in it. Then they were told that the engine was intended for an adult class.

From the "Friday afternoon Literary clubs" at which the students were taught to "elocute" by extending their arms in great gestures in declaiming such masterpieces as *The Gettysburg Address* and oftentimes, the emotional pieces such as *The Last Leaf*—to the formal Debating Societies—came the need for "public speaking" classes. This trend could be the result of "Show and Tell" which originated in the primary grades.

In time "the child became a more specialized individual" (to the classroom teacher); therefore, "special classes for the slow learner" began to materialize. It became quite fashionable to declare that the "individual should progress at his own speed." Also, the academically-talented student needed attention in "classes set up" to challenge that individual into more learning which included "starting foreign languages at an earlier age and giving him a chance to read for more research."

Naturally, this alteration brought about a change in the scheduling of subjects to be taught. Almost all schools throughout the state had "stuck to" the basics such as English courses, history, mathematics and one foreign language—sometimes "Latin was cited as the latter." These subjects were "geared to the college-bound student."

A seemingly dramatic change, however, began to take place in the offerings of public schools that show quite an increase in the range of subjects to be provided—

> In North Carolina a few schools began to offer courses in industrial arts, commerce (shorthand and typewriting), household arts, and agriculture in the early part of the century. However, very little progress was made until after the passage of the Smith-Hughes Act in 1917. Federal funds appropriated in this Act provided impetus to develop programs in agriculture, industry, and home economics. Such programs grew slowly until the depression era of the thirties.

According to a retiree of the beginning of vocational education "the ideal was to offer for all youth vocational education along with the English, social studies, mathematics, and science which made up most of the curriculum." This plan would have united general and vocational education. But according to the same retiree:

> A schism developed between so-called "vocational" and "general" educators. This rivalry resulted in the dichotomy of either "vocational" or "academic" education for students. Only in recent years has this jealousy to a great extent been overcome so that academic and vocational teachers are working together as teams in the design of patterns to develop more creative learning for each person according to his unique needs.

During the depression years of the thirties, much emphasis was given to the concept of cooperative work experience programs in North Carolina. Cooperative programs called "diversified occupations" were expanded to approximately 80 high schools in the state. In a decade more specialized cooperative programs were developed as a result of expansion in distributive education. Subsequently, each type of cooperative program became much more specialized and more effective so that between 1960 and 1970 cooperative programs were developed in all vocational areas. Industrial cooperative training has taken the place of the catch-all "diversified occupations." Cooperative programs now exist in "distributive education, home economics for gainful employment, agricultural education in off-farm work, office education, and health occupations."

Therefore, the increase in range of the cooperative work experience caught the imagination of teachers, students, and leaders from business and industry. For the student, the cooperative job provided opportunities to apply the skills and technical know-how he/she studies in school. But as the small high schools were consolidated into larger secondary schools which could offer comprehensive programs, the curricular offerings in occupational preparation became more realistic and more specialized to meet student needs as well as the needs of business and industry. Active local and state advisory committees helped to make the curriculum more realistic and responsive to community needs and also helped to secure financing for improved instruction.

Wisely, the planners of the initial Federal Vocational Education Act saw the need for specialized preparation of vocational teachers. The first Act mandated the use of Federal funds for such specialized teacher education; subsequent acts have permitted the use of Federal funds for full vocational teacher education. This encouragement has provided leadership for the many students dropping out of school before being exposed to opportunities to explore various occupations. Vocational educators have provided the leadership to develop the extended day programs. This is another opportunity for students who for various reasons do not remain in the regular high school to continue learning in the late afternoon and evening to acquire an occupational skill and to achieve graduation from high school.

And as the students turned to view "the more related jobs

around them," they began to ask for courses in Radio and Television. At least two schools in the state owned and operated their radio stations. Even if these stations operated on a "Ten Watt" system, they gave the students a "chance to work out time schedules and to broadcast school programs that originated in the classrooms of those cities." One retiree who taught the radio class stated, "When I turn on my radio, I hear the voices of former students, and when I turn to two of the state TV Channels and see former students, I am truly proud."

Early in 1953 the General Assembly established the North Carolina Educational Radio and Television Commission and directed it to investigate possible uses of assigned reserved channels. At this time, the University of North Carolina officials took prompt action to secure a license and to activate the station. The first state Educational Radio and Television Commission "followed the development of the consolidated University of North Carolina's educational television station with interest and close scrutiny, since it became apparent the WUNC-TV would be the first educational station on the air in North Carolina and, more than likely, the only educational station on the air during 1953–1955." The Commission decided "to deal with Channel 4 as an educational television pilot station," and recommended that "key programs of WUNC-TV be made available to all the people of North Carolina through the cooperation of commercial television stations."

In 1957 the University entered into an experiment for the "Advancement of education in several North Carolina public school systems." For the next four years WUNC-TV produced and broadcast for the North Carolina "In-School" television experiment four daily programs for use in the public schools. The subjects were United States History, Physical Science, World History, and Mathematics. The studio teacher and the classroom teachers planned the television lessons and the classroom preliminary and follow-up lessons to complement each other. With the cooperation and substantial contribution in broadcast time of a number of commercial stations, two of the lessons were seen not only in the University Channel area, but also in many other areas of the state. It has been estimated by those teachers who were pioneers in the program that "30,000 North Carolina students in 314 schools participated in the 'In-school Programs'."

It can also be said with pride that retired teachers are seeing the results of such groups as the North Carolina Council of International Reading Association—and are continuing to help as teachers and consultants. This group "strongly supports the national effort to eliminate illiteracy in the United States by 1980. The 'Right to Read' effort works to unite all segments of society, both public and private, toward this common goal. This rapidly growing organization is determined to improve educational opportunities for parents, pupils, and teachers.

From recent retirees, who can look backward with pleasure and pride and also look forward to a growing profession, come most interesting stories showing the development of community colleges and technical schools. With their beginnings, the state has indeed increased its range from the one-room school. Extending from the east to the west, these "new institutions have made it possible to further universal educational opportunity beyond the high school."

The first institution of this type to develop in North Carolina opened as a public junior college in Asheville in 1928. Under the local public school system, "after hours" tenant of a high school building, emphasizing the first two years of college studies with occupational courses limited, it operated with no state aid or supervision.

"The next development came about twenty years later." Stimulated by returning veterans with GI Bill benefits who flooded existing college campuses with applications, a number of off-campus temporary centers were sponsored by the North Carolina College Conference. Due primarily to local school superintendents, two of these became permanent—at Charlotte and Wilmington. They were, however, called Community Colleges rather than junior colleges and offered more occupational courses.

"The 1957 General Assembly recognized the need for state

coordination and more substantial aid for community colleges by passing the first Community College Act. It set up for these institutions independent trustees and joint state-local aid, as well as state supervision by the State Board of Higher Education."

This new community college system has been so well received by the people in North Carolina that it has undergone rapid expansion. As of the fall of 1975 there were in the community college system in North Carolina 57 institutions; 18 community colleges and 39 technical institutes. They are so located that it is said 97% of the population lives within 20 miles of one of these schools.

Together with the public schools and higher education, means to achieve educational aspirations are now available "to all of the people to promote political participation, social mobility and economic self-sufficiency."

As an example of continued growth in the state's community colleges, Wilmington College, by an Act of the General Assembly in 1963 "became a senior college with a four-year curriculum, authorized to offer the bachelor's degree." The first degrees were granted in 1965. On July 1, 1969, by a vote of the Board of Trustees of the University of North Carolina, approved by the North Carolina Board of Higher Education and by an Act of the General Assembly, Wilmington College was taken into the University of North Carolina system." At the present time, there are 16 units included in the State University System.

Therefore, when one takes a long look at the educational opportunities provided to the children of North Carolina—and at the picture of the "retired teachers from the turn of the century, who taught the alphabet and to the ones who have seen the expansion of the curriculum in language arts, music, teacher education programs, and even in a computerized program, it can be truly said that the range has been greatly increased from kindergarten to university."

TEACHING is perhaps one profession which has a bit of immortality in it.

VII ⚡ Battling for Public Education

From a Job to a Profession

Within the professional lifetime of recently retired school personnel of North Carolina, a miracle has been wrought in the area of financial support of public schools. The retired editor of *North Carolina Education* wrote:

> Long-range objectives have been attained, and legislative goals once eagerly sought and won, though valiantly opposed, are now taken for granted by those not present when battles were being waged at close quarters.

The retired teachers of today were the active teachers when these advances were being made. They helped to bring them about. They worked singly and collectively for good schools. They can be proud of their accomplishments, and North Carolina can be proud of these teachers. I am proud to have been one of them.

Articles written for this book tell about changes so great in the areas of financial support and conditions of work for teachers and students that one is forced to ask, "Why?" and "What brought about these changes?" The scope of this particular topic is so extensive that this volume can but touch upon the answers to these questions.

To begin with, real progress resulted from the coordinated efforts made possible by a strong professional organization. True, the professionals enjoyed the help of lay groups of concerned citizens and many committed public officials who knew what public schools had done for them, who wanted improved education for their children and for every child in the state, and who joined together to work toward common goals. Literally fighting against immeasurable odds, they have sought to bring the teacher and the child together under the most favorable conditions. The welfare of teachers has unquestionably been a legitimate concern but the educational welfare of children has loomed even larger in commitments of both teachers and lay persons. The ideal which has motivated the development of financial support for public schools in North Carolina has been the equality of educational opportunities for *all* the children of all the people, whatever their place or circumstance of birth.

By what means has this state secured ten-month school terms with some days for teachers to work without the presence of children—higher standards of certification—improved retirement benefits—tenure—better school buildings—free textbooks—increased salaries for school personnel along with fringe benefits valued at 21¢ for each dollar of income (such as disability and health insurance, sick leave, personal leave, death benefits, etc.)—more progressive school consolidation—special services for children—help for handicapped children—orderly desegregation of the school system—an expanded curriculum—kindergartens, twelve grades, and community colleges—adequate teaching supplies and materials—and more clerical help, even teachers' assistants in some instances? Just how were these and many more accomplishments gained? . . . . They were sculptured by the joint efforts of dedicated teachers working cooperatively with other known friends of education. A retired teacher, formerly the state president of the Classroom Teachers Association, said it thus: "*Together* is the magic word—*together*, hand in hand, heart and heart, shoulder to shoulder to provide a richer and fuller life for all."

A retired superintendent expressed it this way: "The taxpayers of North Carolina have furnished the financial support for these improvements and have provided an excellent school system for the children of North Carolina, but it has been the dedicated teacher who has shown educational statesmanship in keeping ahead of the times and demanding the best for the children even though it sometimes meant less financial support for themselves."

The North Carolina Education Association with its various divisions and the North Carolina Teachers Association, now the North Carolina Association of Educators by virtue of their merger have been the state's most influential spokesmen for educational progress. The NCEA had its beginnings in Warrenton in 1857 and the NCTA in Raleigh in 1881. Both organizations, beginning primarily as "conventions" or "assemblies" which edited educational journals, evolved into working organizations at state, district, and local levels. Each has been served by strong elected leaders and an able and hard-working Central Staff. Much committee work and local unit participation have involved the membership in effective legislative activity largely responsible for the spectacular progress made by schools since World War II.

It must be said, too, that the divisions have been especially important, although harmony has not always prevailed. The Classroom Teachers Association was organized in 1932. "An infant organization then, but mighty in its leadership, in vision, in zeal for professional growth, and afire with the desire for improved education for youth," wrote a retired teacher. The following article tells of the struggle for a unified legislative effort:

> There was a time when some classroom teachers believed the Classroom Teachers Association should have a legislative program separate and apart from the North Carolina Education Association Legislative Program, no matter how different it might be.
>
> At a state CTA fall conference held at the Sir Walter Hotel in Raleigh, the idea of having a CTA Legislative Program was brought before the group by a teacher who had a program she wanted presented to the upcoming General Assembly. This, I believed, was the wrong way to go about gaining legislative goals and so stated in the meeting. In short, sometimes there was fiery debate between the two of us.
>
> The majority of those present thought as I did, so we did not have a separate CTA Legislative Program that year or any other year. The opposing forces did not give up the idea for several years, but the majority prevailed. The NCCTA has always supported the NCEA Legislative Program, though there have been a few scattered individuals who preferred to 'go it alone.'

Objectives of
The North Carolina Education Association

*The professional advancement of its members
and the advancement of the cause of education
in North Carolina*

"We the undersigned, in order to promote the cause of Education among the people of North Carolina, by maintaining a regular and frequent personal intercourse with each other, by concentrating our energies and efforts and by collecting and diffusing among our neighbors important information concerning our labors, do hereby form an association to be called "The Educational Association of North Carolina," and having the following Constitution.

CONSTITUTION.

ARTICLE I. The officers of this Association shall consist of a President, six vice Presidents, a corresponding secretary, and a Recording Secretary, to be elected at the regular annual meeting and to serve for one year, or until their successors be chosen.

ART. II. It shall be the duty of the President to preside and preserve order at the meetings of the Association. But in the absence or inability of the President, either one of the vice Presidents shall perform his duties.

ART. III. The corresponding Secretary shall conduct the correspondence of the Association. He shall also act as Treasurer, and discharge all such duties as may be devolved on him by law.

ART. IV. The Recording secretary shall keep a faithful record of the Constitution, By-Laws, and proceedings of this Association; he shall preserve such papers as may be committed to his care, and he shall superintend the publication of such documents as the Association may designate.

ART. V. The Association shall meet regularly on the first Wednesday of July, in each and every year, at such place as it may select. But the President, with the consent of four vice Presidents, shall have power to call a special meeting at such other time and place as they may appoint.

ART. VI. Twelve members from four different counties shall be a quorum to transact business at any meeting of the Association.

ART. VII. The members of this Association pledge themselves, each to the other, to contribute such funds as from time to time may be necessary to meet the contingent expenses of the Association.

ART. VIII. Teachers of Schools and Colleges in North Carolina and other residents of the State, who may desire to cooperate with us, may be elected members of this Association by a majority of the members present at any regular annual meeting.

ART. IX. No article of this constitution shall be altered except by a vote of two-thirds of the members present at a regular annual meeting.

ART. X. The Secretaries of this Association with the general superintendent of Common Schools in North Carolina shall be an Executive Committee to attend to the general interests of the Association during the intervals between meetings.

The members then came forward, and thus signed the constitution and thus organized "The Educational Association of North Carolina." The term "Convention" will hereafter be supplanted by the name ASSOCIATION.

**THE FIRST CONSTITUTION OF THE ORGANIZED
TEACHING PROFESSION IN NORTH CAROLINA**
Adopted in Warrenton in 1857

Cooperation, united effort, and support of the NCEA, now the NCAE, have made it possible for the advancement of legislation favorable to schools and to educators.

Now, the State Board of Education and the Superintendent of Public Instruction sometimes agree and support the NCAE Legislative Program.

Lest the NCAE and its divisions be mistakenly thought of as simply being welfare groups concerned only with selfish interests, it should be noted that the organization has always had a rounded program of professional activities, including, among other things, the promotion of a Code of Ethics and the improvement of instruction in all areas of the curriculum. In a recent survey, 67% of the teachers responded that the reason they join NCAE is that they want to be a professional and they believe the NCAE to be a truly professional organization.

Proof that there has been a strong belief in the value of education and in the public school system has been the support of the lay people in North Carolina. Without this help and support, the legislative goals of the association could not have been attained.

Most effective among lay groups promoting good schools was the United Forces for Education (UFE). Organized in the late forties, this group, both on a state and on a local level during the fifties and the sixties, helped identify and validate needs, set priorities, create favorable public opinion, and work with legislators before, during, and after the sessions of the General Assembly. Quoting from one local unit NCEA president, now retired:

Our leader—chosen by the group—was a prominent lawyer, Lion's Club Governor, and former legislator who devoted much of his time and effort to the activities.

The Advisory Study Commission Report on Education had recently been published. The job of acquainting the public with its contents was our main project.

You may recall that there was a *Summary Report* and a filmstrip which graphically told the story. This program was presented to every PTA in the city and county, to every civic club, women's group, and to anyone else who would listen and permit us to present it. Over 350 copies of the *Summary Report* were distributed at these meetings.

Close contact was maintained by me with the NCEA Staff. Anytime letters to our legislators or visits to them in Raleigh by lay persons might prove beneficial a very effective Calling Committee was set in motion. Even a delegation (mostly lay persons) was dispatched to call on the Governor to seek his support.

All of this was done, now mind you, by lay persons who were kept informed.

Among the members of the United Forces for Education were the following: North Carolina Congress of Colored Parents and Teachers, North Carolina Congress of Parents and Teachers, North Carolina Division of American Association of University Women, North Carolina Education Association, North Carolina Federation of Women's Clubs, North Carolina Junior Chamber of Commerce, North Carolina Junior Woman's Clubs, North Carolina State Grange, North Carolina State School Boards Association, North Carolina Teachers Association.

In addition to the United Forces organization on the state level, in many communities local UFE units often included organizations and agencies other than those listed above. A United Forces for Education filmstrip, complete with sound tape and script, was produced which described the history, structure, organization, and objectives of the UFE. The United Forces for Education was a most effective avenue through which lay citizens made their influence felt as they sought to provide better schools for North Carolina.

This report of public school progress would not be accurate and complete without acknowledging the work of the many friends of education who have served in the legislature and the governors who have contributed immeasurable help. The names of two governors loom especially large: Charles Brantley Aycock, who at the turn of the century campaigned for and built a school house each day during his four-year term; and Terry Sanford, who in 1960 set education as his first priority, endorsing the entire legislative program of the UFE and carrying out his campaign pledge of "Quality education is the rock upon which I will build the house of my administration." Historical perspective will doubtlessly add the names of still others.

When teachers banded together in professional organizations to work for better educational opportunities for the children of the state, there was sometimes a lack of understanding by some of the general public. They have been accused of always asking for salary raises, more buildings, and lower class loads *for themselves.* By like token, teachers have felt that the public was demanding more and more but wanting to pay as little as possible.

Legislators, struggling to meet the total needs of the state, see school finance in terms of hundreds of millions of dollars; the teacher sees it as a single salary, small because of the tiny base from which it began. Teachers have found themselves (in the words of Governor J.C.B. Ehringhaus) "saving the credit of the state" during the depression. Time and again, they have seen the state budget brought into balance at the expense of teachers' salaries. Even with the improved salary schedule of today, teachers resent the misplaced values of a society which pays a high school graduate who becomes a rock and roll musician or a professional athlete a half million dollars a year. They feel that "teachers also deserve some of the finer things of life—travel, homes, fishing trips, decent automobiles, good clothes—perhaps on a little better than average scale" because they have had a part in making these things possible for others.

Throughout the country, teachers have become militant and are beginning to use the strike to gain financial support for schools. Retired educators have worked hard to keep off the strike in North Carolina. They are now saying, "Look how much has been gained by using the professional route of seeking public school support!" They have seen these methods pay off, and they hope that cooperation will continue to be the North Carolina way. Gains came because of public respect. Public concern can be killed by pressure tactics.

Retired teachers repeatedly point out the fantastic salary gains which have been made. From a *maximum* of $740 for eight months of work in 1933–34 to an estimated *average* of $10,950 for ten months in 1975–76, today's teacher has a salary which is fifteen times that of the depression salary. It is true, of course, that the purchasing power of the dollar has been eroded by inflation; but nothing like the amount that salaries have been increased.

A recent study made by the NCAE estimates that one 1933 dollar would buy $4.19 worth of goods and services at 1975 prices. If salaries had increased at the same rate as that of the cost of living, the top salary for the teacher with the bachelor's degree would be only about $3,000! True, the teacher works two months longer for his salary now, and his take-home pay is reduced by deductions not made in earlier years; but the greatest difference in the financial status of today's teacher is that things which were considered luxuries in 1933 are now considered, and sometimes are, necessities.

NORTH CAROLINA STATE SALARY SCHEDULES FOR TEACHERS
(dollars)

| | | "A" Certificate | | | | "G" Certificate | | | |
| | | Beginning | | Maximum | | Beginning | | Maximum | |
Year	Term	Mon.	Ann.	Mon.	Ann.	Mon.	Ann.	Mon.	Ann.
1920–1921	6	100	600	133	798				
1933–1934	8	70	560	90	720				
1941–1942	8	96	768	133	1,064	114	912	150	1,200
1943–1944	9	111	1,001	155	1,395	136	1,224	172	1,548
1965–1966	9¼	436	4,033	603	5,577	489	4,523	663	6,132
1973–1974	10	780	7,800	1,071	10,710	853	8,530	1,168	11,680
1975–1976	10	813	8,130	1,151	11,510	917	9,170	1,256	12,560

Among the greatest benefits won by teachers has been adequate retirement pay. A quote from a retiree expresses the feelings of most of today's retired teachers:

On the day the county staff members had my retirement luncheon, I made a few remarks. One thing I said was, "Now, don't worry about my financial standing, for I will be taking home more pay in one month than I did for the first two years I taught." One wise supervisor said, "Yes, but you were not making anything then, and you won't have anything now." For a while, my bubble burst; but I am very grateful to the Retirement System and Social Security for making my retirement days secure. Along the way, *we* worked hard to make the two systems what they are. Thanks to everyone who helped.

Some people feel that material gains have been won at the expense of public respect for the teacher. A retired teacher who is now "up to her ears" in community involvement wrote, "There is one area in which teachers then stood higher than now: in the eyes of patrons and children, we were examples of sobriety, good manners, high morals, and generally persons to whom youth and parents could look for inspiration and high ideals." Do you agree that teachers have lost the respect of society? If so, why? Should the teacher occupy this exalted position? If so, how can it be maintained?

In order to comprehend the magnitude of the changes in financial support and conditions of work which have occurred during the past forty years, let us now do two things:

1. Look at the signposts along the road over which public education has traveled in North Carolina.
2. Listen to experiences and observations as related by retired teachers who fought the battles for better schools along that road.

SIGNPOSTS ALONG THE ROAD TO GOOD PUBLIC SCHOOLS IN NORTH CAROLINA

Early Days

- Slow recovery from Civil War and Reconstruction
- Beginning of professional organizations
- Great diversity among counties in resources and initiative
- Some excellent schools; most rural were minimal or nonexistent

Consolidation in the Twenties

- Long, painful process; some teachers lost their jobs
- Broke up friendships
- Moved teachers and students out of schools near their homes
- Brought strangers into the community who were not trusted
- Better buildings constructed, transportation system begun
- Broader curricular offerings, extra-curricular activities promoted

- School term of six months; some were 7, 8, and a few 9
- Teachers raised money for school supplies
- Some counties ran out of money and could not pay salaries the whole year

The Great Depression

- Teachers paid in script; sometimes kept school open with no pay
- Sales tax instigated to operate a uniform state system of eight months
- All local supplements eliminated by legislature
- Teachers' salaries cut 40 to 50 percent
- Groundwork laid for 9th month and 12th grade

The War Years in the Forties

- Shortages of materials and manpower
- Ninth month and twelfth grade added
- Free textbooks
- Salaries equalized for white and black teachers
- Holding pattern for other improvements

Fears, Blame, Then Renewed Interest in Quality Education in the Fifties

- UFE legislative programs laying groundwork for progress
- Newer and better buildings from state bond issue
- Supreme Court decision of 1954
- Fear that public schools in south would close
- Sputnik and America's reaction of blame for the schools
- NDEA funds for science, library books, and guidance
- Technical schools and community colleges

Great Gains in the Sixties

- Civil Rights Act of 1964
- Court orders and HEW guidelines
- Desegregation and federal money for disadvantaged students
- Salary gains—paid by calendar month instead of 20 days taught
- Sick leave and other fringe benefits

- Written personnel policies
- Groundwork laid for kindergarten and tenth month

Political Involvement of Teachers in the Seventies

- Political Action Committee of Educators (PACE) and political clinics for teachers
- Reduced class size
- Kindergartens
- Salary gains
- Improved retirement benefits
- Ten-month school term
- Tenure

Bicentennial Year in 1975–1976 and Unsolved Problems

- Inflation and recession
- Fuel and power shortages
- Crime and drugs
- Disintegration of traditional institutions
- Teacher strikes and student rebellion
- Gulf between teachers and administrators
- Less respect for the teacher

EXPERIENCES IN BATTLING FOR PUBLIC SCHOOLS OF THE STATE

Articles written for the "Pride in America Project" by North Carolina retired teachers would fill several volumes. Since this material has never before been available, it was a painful process for the editing committee to reduce the material to one small volume. It is hoped that the items included will both convey some degree of the pride felt by retired teachers in their services to the youth of the state and also give to present and future members of the profession some knowledge of the heritage which is theirs.

Education—1935 and 1975 . . . . .

When I began my teaching career in 1935, I found these: Small classrooms with thirty or more children seated in desks arranged in straight orderly rows; rooms so quiet the fall of a pin could be heard; home-packed lunches with little thought given to nutrition; a mid-morning and mid-afternoon recess to afford the opportunity to visit the outhouses located on each side of the building; play periods with little "store-bought" equipment; one set of textbooks bought by the children or no books if the cost was too much; a sick child on a makeshift bed in the corner of the room; school buses of ancient vintage on almost impassable muddy back roads; art, drama, music, library books, magazines, and audio-visual materials almost unknown; no coffee breaks, sick leave, workshops, teacher aides, or work days without the children; attendance at all church services and participation in community affairs compulsory; decorum in dress and behavior a must, and no married women teachers; pay for an A certificate less than $100 per month paid at the end of twenty teaching days; small schools as the center of the community; support of officials and parents if paddle used; children of all types and classes together in one room.

In 1975, when I retired, the scene had changed to the following: Spacious suites or rooms given to team teaching; cafeterias serving well-balanced meals at a reasonable cost and in some instances free; play periods supervised by trained aides using all kinds of equipment furnished by the school system; multi-choice of free textbooks suited to the individual needs of each child; well-equipped sickrooms manned by volunteers trained by Red Cross; modern school buses making runs over well paved secondary roads; materials for art, music, drama, library books, magazines, and audio-visuals in abundance; teacher aides, coffee breaks, sick leave, maternity leave, workshops, and work days for teachers taken for granted; large consolidated schools combining the pupils of all races from the smaller communities now the order of the day; to embarrass a child before his peers is a cardinal sin, and a paddling must be witnessed; separate classrooms with specially trained teachers and aides with selected materials for children with learning problems.

1935 to 1975 . . . Forty years of change, but one I would not exchange!

Building a School System . . . . .

The story of the emergence of any school system is long and involved. A superintendent told his Board: "We are going to have the best school system in the state. What is the best way to establish a great school system? Use every opportunity to beg the community for all needed facilities." This was done for nineteen years, and a number of new buildings were eventually erected. For instance, by 1944 the old high school building was sinking at one end. By dint of unrelenting effort, a replacement school was erected five years later.

The superintendent continued: "But supposing classroom needs are finally met? What then? Why then, the thing to do is to search the state over for the finest teachers who can be found. Sell them on the system's fine spirit. Support and encourage them. Give them materials and equipment. Urge them to love the children and give them encouragement." So, the school system set up one of the best corps of teachers to be found anywhere and progress was assured. An unusually large percentage of male teachers wanted to join our faculty, and, through the years, have added to the distinctiveness of the school staff.

Patience and Wisdom Were Necessary . . . . .

It was no easy task confronting these pioneer school commissioners of our town: lots had to be chosen and purchased, buildings erected and equipped, courses of study mapped out and textbooks selected, broad principles for the conduct of the new and untried system laid down, teachers wisely chosen, public interest aroused and maintained in the project.

The far-reaching policies of the pioneer commissioners of this town . . . have borne fruit . . . in the constant expansion of our school plant, in the ever-increasing opportunities for the youth of the community not only in the preparation for life in the business, industrial, and cultural world through the varied courses offered in the schools, but also in the living of life through ever-widening avenues leading to mental growth and satisfying use of leisure time.

Special School Tax . . . . .

A school term was six months. In order to get better teachers and an extra school month, a special school tax was levied for the district and collected and paid out by the county.

Tuition Charges . . . . .

Students coming from outside the township will pay a tuition of $2.50 a month.

Financial Recognition of Teachers' Service
Was Slow in Coming . . . . .

Through the years it seemed that trying to gain any suitable income for teachers in recognition of the service they gave was a slow and disappointing procedure. Followers of other professions set their fees; teachers took what was decided upon by those slow to realize the value of their services.

Interest and Dedication of Many Citizens
Brought Improvements . . . . .

Schools were hit hard during the depression days following the 1929 financial crisis. Probably the low point was reached about 1932 or 1933, when local support of North Carolina's public schools almost collapsed in many places and actually did so in others.

This situation was gradually improved over the years due to the interest and dedication of many citizens.

Community Groups Worked Together for the School Needs . . . . .

What a challenge! I knew each member of the Board. One was a banker. All of the others were executives in the mill. I asked the superintendent first what help he would give. He had many excuses. The Junior Woman's Club came out to see what they could do. Members of the Lions Club came, the Kiwanis Club came, the Woman's Club came. The members of the Board came. Everyone wanted to help. The Junior Woman's Club took over, helping to set up the kitchen as their project. The Lions Club painted the building inside. Many citizens of both races gave vessels to help in the lunchroom.

The Board of Education put the water inside, and put a restroom in each classroom, sanded and waxed the floors. We had a combination dining room and library. We had all new desks put in the building. We also had new blackboards and bulletin boards.

Some civic organizations paid for lunches. The owner of the Mill paid for some as long as he lived. After the first year, Mrs. R. H. sent a check to pay a lady to wash dishes.

Support of Administration Helped Teachers . . . . .

The administration backed the teachers. I found them to be well trained, conscientious, and dedicated. I figured my job was to get people out of their way so they could teach, and they did.

Three students didn't make the honor society. The superintendent was asked to fire those responsible. Powers in the community wanted students to get good grades and be in the honor society. The superintendent threatened to resign if the teacher was dismissed.

The family of a ball player called the superintendent to their home where they demanded their son play on the varsity team. The superintendent refused to make the coach do it. One week later, the son had surgery for a ruptured appendix.

The Year's Supply of Teaching Materials . . . . .

On the appointed date I went to the teachers meeting with Reverend J. G. M. and his daughter, both of whom were teachers, riding high in a Model T Ford. We spent the day being instructed in the proper way to operate a school. We left the meeting with our materials to use during the entire school year in the back seat of the car. My materials consisted of one broom, one eraser, one box of blackboard chalk, and a ledger to be used as a roll book.

Not Enough Seats . . . . .

Several students walked four or more miles to school. Transportation was not provided for them. Each teacher had an enrollment of fifty or more pupils, and the number of seats was based on the average daily attendance. Parents who were handy with carpenter's tools made seats for children and teachers, since the average daily attendance was less than one half the enrollment. Teachers were first janitors and maids, then teachers.

World War I Inflation . . . . .

This small town had a nine months term and a salary supplement. I received $50.00 per month. Room and board was $30.00. I taught there six years. During World War I, inflation raised everything but salaries.

Raising Money for Teaching Materials . . . . .

One of my most enjoyable events in my early days of teaching was playing a part in numerous plays to raise money for the school.

Usually, a comedy was selected and the principal and I would take the roles of the comical characters.

I remember one in particular, *Aunt Samantha Rules the Roost*, in which I was Aunt Samantha, the mother of a large family who was the head of the household instead of the lazy husband, who was played by the principal.

Needless to say, all the students, parents, aunts, uncles, and grandparents came to the performances, and we raised a sizable sum of money for the school.

On other occasions, we had box suppers, cake walks, fiddler's conventions, oyster suppers, and sold popcorn, parched peanuts, and homemade candies at the ball games. We also operated a school store where students could buy pencils, pens, notebooks, and paper. All the profits were used to buy needed materials for the school.

Teaching Equipment Was Hard to Get . . . . .

Now that large amounts of money are spent on modern school buildings and equipment of every sort, I am reminded that equipment was not easily acquired during most of my teaching days.

In promoting our athletic program we raised money for basket-ball suits, our hockey sticks, and our trips. Once, in order to make money for our expenses, we assembled one afternoon in the domestic science kitchen to make pineapple layer cakes for a sale. The layers must have been too spongy and light, or the pine-apple filling was too heavy. Just as we completed smoothing beautiful frosting on the last layer of the last cake, the cakes began splitting, slipping and falling apart. Discouraged in our efforts to hold them together, we looked up to discover a waiting, small sister writing on the blackboard, "Whoever heard of a cake splitting?" Anyone can guess what became of the cakes.

Teachers Bought Their Own Instructional Supplies . . . . .

My superintendent knew I was spending my own money for desperately needed supplies. Whenever I needed glue, red or colored pencils, pipe cleaners, ink, etc., I purchased these supplies with my money. So, Mr. W. asked me to keep an accurate record of everything I spent money for to use in my classroom. This I did very conscientiously for one year. If I remember correctly, the amount was approximately $48. (The PTA was buying scissors, crayons, and some paper.) In those days, $48 represented a major portion of a monthly pay check. I was one of the happiest teachers in the state when the state provided for instructional supplies. In addition to supplying some of the materials I needed, this assistance helped me to eliminate two awful ugly statements I had been hearing for so long: "Teacher, I ain't got 'nary pencil," and "Teacher, I hain't got no paper." This instructional supply money helped me keep a continuous supply of pencils and ruled paper for the pupils to use.

"God works in mysterious ways, His wonders to perform" . . . . .

My students had caused a history teacher to resign at the end of the second week and were working on a science teacher next. I have always thought I was to have been their third victim.

It was during the first month of school and I was on duty during recess. The building had been renovated during the summer and all of the material had not been picked up on the school yard. I saw a board with three nails sticking up and I thought how much harm could come from it if it were left there. I picked the board up intending to take it in and put it in the trash basket in my room. As the students were being seated, I placed the board on my desk, nails up, and started calling the roll of that high school English class. Eyes flitted here and there from the desk to one another and back to the desk. No questions.

At the close of the period one boy lingered long enough to ask me why the board was on my desk. He said: "You wouldn't use that board with the nails still in it, would you?" I assured him that I would if I thought it necessary. News got around that I might be young but that I was tough. Intentionally, I left that board on my desk, and now and then during a lecture I would pick it up and finger the nails and talk right on. They never asked me for what I would use the board, and I never told them.

I taught there seven years and I have never had more love and respect from students in any school than there, nor have I loved students any more. God does indeed work in mysterious ways, His wonders to perform.

Class Size No New Problem . . . . .

Mrs. A——: "Oh. I do hope I escape catching mumps. I've never had the disease and what would I do if I should take it now—this near to the closing of school!

Angela (in a crowded classroom): "No, Mrs. ——, you won't catch mumps. There are so many children in here there's not enough germs to go around."

School Holidays . . . . . *with Pay* . . . . .

Holidays were at the discretion of the principal; at Thanksgiving, a half-day or a whole day was observed. If a person died in the community, it was left up to the principal and school committee of three, as to how much time was observed. The salary was not cut because of these events.

Paved Highways Helped . . . . .

It is hard to believe all the changes that took place during the years I taught. When I began teaching, the roads were unpaved, narrow, and rough. Even a little rain or snow made chains necessary. My first school term was six months at a salary of $55 a month. Forty-four years later, paved highways made access to the schools much faster and easier; the school term was nine months at $739 per month.

Tenure Was Needed . . . . .

It is entirely understandable to teachers who have been in the profession for a long time why teachers now are so vitally concerned with tenure. In the twenties and thirties, it was not at all unusual for a complete faculty to be refused a new contract. The members of school boards had complete authority over the hiring and firing of teachers and could do either without giving any reason. This misfortune happened to me after I had taught for seven years in the same school. The school seemed to be fulfilling its responsibility, but we were all released. In the end, however, this dismissal was the spur that sent me on to further training and better positions.

Criteria for Teacher-Selection . . . . .

During the very late twenties and early thirties, the depression was hitting hard at the teaching profession. I was trying to find a position. Since I had no experience, the job was doubly difficult. I applied in a public boarding school (at this time there was very little consolidation). While I was being interviewed, the superintendent said that he was impressed with my qualifications, but he would have to know my church affiliation before he could give me a definite answer. I wondered just what answer I should give him, since I saw no reason for such a request. I decided I knew nothing better than telling the truth, so I said, "I am an Episcopalian," and held my breath.

He said, "Oh, that is fine. You are an 'off' brand and I can hire you. You see in this hamlet we have two religions—Baptist and Methodist. I have to hire a Baptist and then a Methodist, but you can fill in as either."

Equipping the New High School . . . . .

The sparsely-populated community was proud of its new high school department and enjoyed the monthly PTA meetings that they religiously supported with 10¢ per person plus "box suppers" at which members brought gaudily-wrapped boxes of "custard" pie and cake to be auctioned off to the highest bidders.

Salary Supplements Were Eliminated
When State Took Over the Schools . . . . .

When the state took over the schools, in order to bring the poorer ones up, the better were brought down. This change affected the length of the term as well as salaries. Around the state many school units began to supplement the state salary— but not ours at first. During those lean years, the teachers remained professional and loyal in their performance. Recognizing the perseverance and loyalty of the teachers in those difficult years, our county called for an election to vote on a special school tax. When the election was coming up for vote, the teachers, as well as others, worked hard to get it. We even *marched* all over town in support of it. That parade had little in common with today's "marches," for there was no protesting nor demanding anything, but simply soliciting the support of all voters to vote for the school tax to bring our schools to a creditable standard. When the votes were canvassed, the election was declared in favor of the local tax by a 509 majority.

Early Salaries Were Hard to Collect . . . . .

Until the state took over the operation of the schools, our salary scale was very good and even a retirement fund was paid entirely by the county. The misfortune was that while we worked only nine months, we were paid on a twelve-month basis. When the county funds ran low, they said that plan was not legal. We had

94

to sue and wait two or three years, but we finally got the money with interest. However, the lawyer's fee more than ate up the interest!

Teachers Chose to Work for Half Pay . . . . .

Once there was only money enough to pay one extra month. The teachers were allowed to decide, one month with full pay or two months with half pay. The teachers voted to take two months with half pay!

Children Learned that Teachers Received Money for Their Work . . . . .

The last minutes of the day, after all activities were over and book sacks packed, ready for bus time, was usually a time I read stories until the bell rang. It happened that one day, during this quiet period, the principal came to my chair, handed me a voucher, and quietly left. The room was perfectly silent for a moment—then the questions began: "Was that money he gave you?" "Do you get money for teaching?" "Was that a check?"

There was again thoughtful silence when I answered, "Yes, and it's more than a hundred dollars, and if you grow up and go to college, you can make money."

Script . . . . . Script . . . . . Script . . . . .

The close of the gay twenties saw me receive the teaching certificate which I had wanted since I was a small child. Over the years my interest in subject matter had changed many times, but my desire to teach had never wavered. I did not expect to get rich—just earn a good living—but I did hope to help make life happier for those whom I would be privileged to instruct.

Salaries were low in the early thirties, but when that first check for $100 came, I felt richer than I've ever felt since. The second year my salary was $105 per month. That meant $40 more per year than the year before because schools operated for only eight months then.

Imagine the shock the next year when I received $80 per

month or $640 per year. The depression was here, but—I did have a job.

Six of us lived in a teacherage, hired our cook, took turns buying groceries and supervising the kitchen, and dared any one to miss a meal without announcing it beforehand. In this way, we were able to keep our grocery bill to a minimum. Eggs—we were able to buy these delectable morsels for eight cents a dozen. Because of this low price, we were sometimes on an egg diet. (Remember the novel, *The Egg and I*?) We paid three dollars per month for room and utilities.

We were doing very well keeping our debts paid until the middle of the year when we were told that there was no more money. It would be necessary for us to complete the year's work without any more pay; however, there was a slim chance that money would be available at the end of the year. Alas and alack— we were paid—paid in script! Who would or could cash this? No one. There was no money! But who needed money? According to some of the women of the town, teachers were far overpaid and should consider it a privilege to teach for script. (I can hear them now, "What *is* script?")

During the following summer, I learned that there was one store in the county which would take script in trade. This was a clothing store which could clothe men, women, and children from top to toe. Here was the chance to trade my script, so I gathered my parents, brother, sister, and script and went shopping. My brother still says his $12.50 suit was one of his best buys. It was purchased with my precious script.

Those of us who lived through those days know that we can get along on much less than we sometimes think we can. In spite of our many obstacles, when we left school that year, all of our debts had been paid, and we still had *script.*

Citizens Helped Teachers During Their Depression Plight . . . . .

"In the early thirties we were paid in script, a paper that could hopefully be redeemed in money later. The man with whom we boarded gave me money for my script. I hope he got it back later, but I never knew. One takes so much for granted when he is carefree."

"We had to take script for the last month. I used mine to pay taxes for my family and two neighbors, so I got my money."

"Through the bank failures during the depression, the school funds were all spent before the end of the year. Those of us who lived in the county were given credit on taxes for the two months work. This was good for our parents financially, but we did not like it ourselves."

"Some of the parents of our students bought our script at the end of the year, paying us in real money."

"Mrs. I. agreed to board the teachers and let them repay her if and when they received the remainder of their salaries. She said they all repaid her the next year."

"Several businesses—a department store, a ready-to-wear store, a drug store, and a few others gave teachers a ten per cent discount on purchases. Many others were very considerate and did favors for teachers."

"We received help from our own parents: we went home to spend the summers with them, and we put up fruits and vegetables from their farm on which to eat the following winter."

"The president of the Woman's Club, introducing a teacher who was to speak on the subject of teachers' salaries, said: "You all know about our poor teachers (!)""

The Teacher Gets a New Dress . . . . .

A mother coming to see a teacher, knocked on the classroom door and motioned her to come out into the hall. Holding the teacher at arm's length, looking her over, she said, "I'm sorry to interrupt you, but my son insisted that I come to see you. At home during lunch today he carried on about how good you looked today. He said, 'My teacher's wearing the prettiest orange satin blouse and new brown suit. You've just got to go and see her in it.' "

Having had to do with few new clothes during the depression college years, with the first month's pay of $72, the teacher had gone on a shopping spree to get a new outfit for a trip to the Chicago World's Fair, but she couldn't resist showing the other teachers that at last she had something new. It had not occurred to her how much children notice such things.

Teachers Helped with War Effort . . . . .

During the World War II years, teachers helped with the rationing programs for sugar, gasoline, and shoes; served on selective service boards; sold Savings Stamps and bought War Bonds; and still improved the schools.

"Good Old Days Not So Good" . . . . .

In 1943 I took a position as principal of a six hundred student high school. I also taught government, coached varsity football and baseball and boys and girls basketball. There was no truant officer or guidance counselor, and I had to pinch hit in these capacities, too. To make matters worse, it was war time and all the men teachers had been drafted. I was the only man left on the faculty.

Those were the "good old days."

Good Old Days Not So Bad After All . . . . .

Recently, I came across my Income Tax Return for the year 1943. Needless to say that I was surprised when I realized I had taught an entire school year for just $1,234.

But, on reflection, I had to admit I had more money then than I do now—it was worth more then. Guess the good old days were not so bad, after all.

She Taught 37 Years . . . . .

My starting salary was $65.00 a month. The check I received just before I retired was for $996.60. Quite a difference!

Notable Examples of Progress . . . . .

Certification procedures for teachers and principals have been initiated, upgraded, and refined. Individual rights for teachers

98

and students have been spelled out. Codes of ethics, hiring-firing-and-hearing procedures, fringe benefits, in-service training are notable examples of a better day for education in North Carolina.

Financial Security for Retired Teachers . . . . .

Retired teachers in our state recently received an eight per cent increase in their checks (July 1, 1975)—to counteract to some extent the inflation rate.

A little more than twenty years ago, an aunt of mine who had for twenty-six years been principal of a large school in one of our cities, drew one of the two highest retirement pensions in our educational system. Her monthly check was for $29.00!

Improvements Should Be Recognized . . . . .

Many teachers feel that their salaries are inadequate now. Perhaps they are. However, this writer started with a salary of $78. Out of this, she paid room and board and bought a car during the eight months school year! We have seen continuous improvement in the salaries over the years.

HEALTH EXAMINATION

Early in the fall, I had to check the immunization of each first grade child. This I had done. As the children stood in line, one little girl had no health slip, so I said, "Sally, where is your slip?" She very carefully lifted a corner of her pretty plaid skirt and said, "I didn't wear one today."

FIANCÉ BOUGHT HER WEDDING CLOTHES

My husband's favorite story was telling that he had to buy my wedding clothes before we could get married. That was in 1932 when I had been paid my teacher's salary in script. He had been paid in money for his commercial job. He owed taxes for which script was acceptable. So he paid for my wedding clothes with his money and took my script and paid his taxes.

VIII ✦ Journeying Toward Unity

From Separate Schools to a Single System

Perhaps our greatest challenge for public schools of the South resulted from the Supreme Court decision in 1954, which rejected the "separate but equal" doctrine. In the *Brown v. Board of Education* decision, the court found that segregated education is inherently unequal education and, therefore, unconstitutional. The passage of the 1964 Civil Rights Act, ten years later, which authorized the federal government to withhold funds from any segregated schools, followed by the Department of Health, Education and Welfare guidelines that required compliance evidenced by an acceptable degree of racial balance, brought about years of negotiation and litigation between HEW, parents and civil rights groups, and local school boards. These efforts culminated in drastic reorganization of local school systems, accompanied by massive busing of students of both races.

Prior to the Civil Rights Act, boards of education were accepting requests of individual students for transfer to formerly segregated schools. "Freedom of choice" was a policy which was instituted, permitting parents to send their children to the school of their choice. This policy was a continuation of dual systems and was eliminated by the Civil Rights Act.

School boards were then faced with immediate desegregation, and they needed help from the whole community. Complete involvement of citizens was the best overall plan for successfully realizing a unitary system. Parent advisory committees, faculty groups, student committees, school department heads, and citizens at large met regularly to form an organizational plan. Classes in human relations for teachers, principals, and school patrons were organized, and college psychology professors were appointed as teachers of these classes.

A giant step was made. Superintendents, principals, and teachers made a gallant effort to satisfy the demands of HEW. The law of the land was upon the state. To do or not to do was the question. Some parents could not take it and patronized the private schools. Some moved their families where the concentration of whites was greater. Today, many problems have been solved, but not all. Busing is still a concern nationwide. Blacks moving into towns and cities and whites moving to the rural areas are causing resegregation. The merger of county and city schools would help the racial balance in the schools; however, a constitutional amendment could provide for a uniform, nationwide pupil-assignment policy which would solve many more problems.

Teachers who have recently retired tell of the challenges brought about by desegregation. When deprived children were bused into affluent areas, many teachers who had been teaching successfully for years suddenly found that their methods no longer worked. Teachers with little knowledge of a cultural background different from their own were often frustrated. Some who were approaching retirement age found the changes too difficult to cope with and retired early. Today, thousands of these retired teachers now return to the school to serve as volunteers or go to other community agencies where their skills continue to help people. However, by far the greater number of school personnel have made the tremendously great adjustments that were necessary and have brought an increased degree of integration of students into the unitary system.

As a result of desegregation, a wealth of teaching methods and knowledge has come to the front to help the low I.Q. child to achieve greater learning. Federal monies have helped to place books in the library; and improved teaching materials are now found in most classrooms throughout the state. Teachers constantly attend workshops to learn how to use the new methods and materials. Individualized instruction has become a necessity, and the disadvantaged students are catching up while other students continue to progress at their normal rate. Once again, North Carolina teachers have met the challenge and are providing better education for more children than ever before.

The following paragraphs were written by retired teachers. Seemingly, the easiest of their teaching days are not recorded, but the highlights they describe relate to the adversities in their experiences during the dual system of schools or during the days following desegregation. As one reads these contributions, it is apparent that desegregation is now seen in many different ways. Even persons of the same race have expressed a variety of feelings. Conditions varied from teacher to teacher, school to school, and community to community. Most contributors, however, feel that North Carolina is successfully integrating its schools. As one person expressed it, "Not only do I have Pride in America, but also pride in my professional colleagues who have brought us closer to the brotherhood of man."

A Tolerable Transition

In the late fifties when I joined the County Staff as Director of Instruction, white and Negro (referred to as quaint vernacular) schools were two different worlds. Principals' meetings and teacher's workshops were held separately.

A reading workshop was scheduled in the afternoon for white teachers and in the evening for black teachers. The consultant directing the workshops was told by her boss not to go to a Negro school without a white man along. Reluctantly, she agreed to go. After the workshop was over, this consultant agreed that she now had the same feeling as I did toward this Negro school. I must admit that that night gave me one small ray of understanding, and hope was cast on the social change to come.

"This is KKK Country" was a sign which I had to pass by on my way to visit a school. One day a white man in an old model Chevrolet tried to force me off the road. As I was memorizing the license number and locking my doors while trying not to hit the ditch, we rounded a curve in a wooded area where two State Highway employees were repairing a hole. I was then allowed to speed away with a pounding heart. A complimentary copy of *The Firey Cross*, a KKK newspaper published in Alabama, was left one morning at my doorstep. I have often wondered if it were a threat or an invitation.

While there was no violence, it seemed an opportune time to take a look at our values at this critical time. A proposal was submitted to the Department of Public Instruction's Experimentation in Educational Development Project on Value Systems. The project was funded.

Mine was a lonely assignment as I shared the joys and sorrows and the horseflies of education. Extra problems and pressures arose and bruised feelings were tender. The professionals learned to cope with the situation and accepted each other for their own worth and dignity.

The home and the church did not always accept the new social order as well as the educators. I felt the pain of their prejudice and tried to be sensitive to their pain of change.

Successful Student Achievement

Elimination of black and white schools created serious problems for white teachers. Changes were so great that many white teachers left the classroom or went to schools where there were fewer blacks. For those of us who stayed on, teaching became so difficult and pressures so great that we wondered if we could last until retirement age. There were discipline problems among children far beyond any we had ever met before, because of existing racial prejudices among children, parents, and teachers.

When we went to the lunchroom, we did not know whether to walk at the head, in the middle, or at the back of the children in order to prevent fights. One white boy went through four years of high school without going to the school bathroom for fear of attack. "Gang" violence, which had always existed, now became more vicious and terrifying. Some parents told their children not to sit by a "nigger" or a "whitey." Others gave their children knives and like weapons. Still others told their children to just give up and "get along" at all cost. Yard, bus, hall, and lunchroom duties (never popular because they denied us even brief moments of relaxation) now became imperative but most difficult for us.

Even harder for us to deal with was the problem of instruction. We found a difference in the average achievement of our black and white children of two or more grade levels. We found a few blacks whose home environment had made it possible for them to meet the expectations we had been accustomed to. The sheer numbers and the depth of deprivation of the majority of our black children, though, was a traumatic shock to us.

We know that at the end of the year in the thirties and forties we had collected our broken crayons and scissors, and our worn textbooks "for the colored schools," but we never knew how unequal the educational opportunities had been in black and white schools. On the other hand, we had seen, during the fifties, the beautiful new school buildings erected for the blacks while we continued to teach in schoolhouses built before the depression. We did not know that we had seen only parts of the picture. We did not know of the difficulties faced by the black teachers. Most of us did not know that salaries for black and white teachers were not equalized until 1948. With our present knowledge, we are now convinced that the deficit of academic achievement could never have been overcome in all-black schools.

Our problem now as white teachers was how to teach children who came from differing environments, who spoke different dialects, and whose value systems were different from our own. Especially was this true in schools like mine where a great proportion of our students were black, a number which became increasingly larger as many of our white students left for private schools or moved to geographic areas where fewer blacks lived.

We were faced with several alternatives; among them, the following: lower our standards, have double standards, or provide individualized instruction which required different methods and materials, both of which would require a great deal more money than we had.

In my school we decided that we really believed those laws of learning to which we had given lip service all those years, such as "All children can learn," "Children grow at different rates," and "Begin where the child is." I am proud that I had the opportunity to help make this decision and to work with our children before I retired.

The first thing we decided to do was to put priority on our young children so as to help them acquire a good feeling about themselves as persons and to become proficient in reading and mathematics. We studied our test results, both as a whole and separately by race. We openly shared these results with our board of education and state and federal agencies. Because we revealed our needs, we were able to secure many additional funds which helped us give our children in the elementary grades practically everything that was needed. As a result, our average achievement is now higher than it was before integration, and in some grades it is on grade level according to national norms. We believe we have found the best way to teach elementary children. We pray that our schools will continue to have the money to do the job so that all our children can learn, whether they be "black, white, yellow, or red."

Today many of us who have retired go regularly to the schools to give volunteer help to teachers and students. We are glad to give a small part of our time to a great cause. Should funds be cut, there will be even greater need for our services.

SCHOOL MERGER IN ONE COUNTY

There were little one-room schools in every nook and cranny of our county. In the year 1924, through the Rosenwald Foundation, the black patrons had been able to raise enough matching funds to build a *new* school. This school offered a good program.

In the year 1937–38, with the phasing out of the one-room schools, the thinking was that consolidation was the panacea for all school problems.

All the white children were assigned to regional schools in the nearest vicinity, grades 1–12. The black children were to attend the one and only school designed for the blacks throughout the county with a radius of 16–20 miles. The *new* school had grades 1–12. The theory, separate but equal, was intended but not applied. Through the efforts of dedicated teachers and cooperative parents, the *new* school did produce a number of students who entered the fields of professions of athletics, teaching, medicine, nursing, ministry, modeling, civic leadership, and social workers. The children had a pride in their culture, owned a self image and were able to identify with offerings of their school, church, and community. Other counties learned of the success of our *new* school and contracts from three neighboring counties brought students not provided for in their white high schools. In the years 1955–58, as the population grew, the need for more schools became necessary. Another *new* high school was built for the blacks. There were three high schools for the whites. The buses passed through many white communities and by white schools and continued on the long route to this *new* school. They did not mind the long trip because they had something to look forward to. Each child could be a member of the band, glee club, dramatic club, football and basketball teams, and any program the school offered. One advantage of a small school, you are needed and appreciated.

Then came the 1964 court order to do something about integration. The people were panicky and then militant at the thought of mixing the races in schools. The blacks had worked hard and long to meet accreditation in Southern Schools. They had fund drives to match National Defense Education Act (NDEA) funds to get needed equipment. The graduation class boasted of 50% entering college in the fall. The school certainly had much to offer.

After much prodding, the Freedom of Choice Plan was adopted

in the years of 1965–67. Some blacks went to each of the seven white schools. Many blacks chose the white schools instead of being bussed to the *new* school, but *not one* white child selected the black school. In 1969 the Board of Education, members of the NCTA and the PTA of the *new* school had many meetings. The decision was to merge the schools on the condition that the blacks would not lose positions and status. *They* called the move *merger*. *We* called it *liquidation*.

The transition took place rather peacefully among the faculty members. But the adjustment for the children was traumatic in many respects. The stigma placed on us to bear as poor, ignorant, undesirable, went to school with both whites and blacks. Hostilities flared on both sides. Lines of communication were broken and the children wanted to run away but had no place to go. The children gave teachers and principals problems which would never have been dreamed of in the black schools. Teachers were biased in granting favors and grading, causing parents to take up the issues. Seating on the buses tried the patience of drivers and extra curricular activities drove parents up the wall. Students and parents became very frustrated.

The merger of the school broke up a way of life that had held the black people together for many years . . . the home, the church, and the school. The children lost the driving force which gave them aspirations. The ratio of college entries dropped. The feeling of being black and beautiful is about all that is left. Incidents did occur, although merger came with less friction than in other counties in North Carolina based on ratio. We can't say that merger has accomplished the intended goal after eight years. They say it takes decades for signs of improvement. Let's hope the decades are not too far in the future.

A LESSON IN PUBLIC RELATIONS

The schools designated as "Negro Schools" in the state of North Carolina varied in many respects. This variation was influenced by the attitude of the School Board, the attitude of the school superintendent, the sensitivity of the Negro parents, and the knowledge and integrity of the school principal and staff.

In one school in Western North Carolina a young man was assigned as principal. In this school there were eight teachers and twelve grades. This was termed a union school. The facilities were at the lowest ebb. The classrooms contained poor seating, poor lighting, and inferior heaters in each room where coal dust was used for fuel.

There were many more unpleasant conditions not mentioned. In the community, there seemed to have been a spirit of acceptance of these conditions among the Negro citizens. The principal of the school was asked by some of the parents not to disturb the peace and good will that existed in the community between the races by asking for too much for the school. This was the case of "Don't Rock The Boat" theory which did not prevail in this case.

To avoid a pressure drive to attain suitable facilities and a better environment for teaching and learning, the principal and school staff invited the School Board to the school for a steak dinner. All Board members were present for the annual meeting. The Board members expressed delight in the tasty food, but were disappointed in the condition of the school facilities. At that meeting the superintendent was asked why these conditions existed. The superintendent responded by informing the Board that he did not have the money nor the authority to do a project of that magnitude without an order from the Board. At that point the Board members said that was the first time they had ever seen the inside of the Negro school and did not know the conditions existed as they were.

From that point on things began to happen for the school in a peaceful transition from a low ebb facility to a bright environment with new buildings and activities conducive to good learning and living.

INTEGRATION FOR ALL

Our city hired three black policemen in 1947 when only a very few towns and cities in the South dared to do this. The experiment worked. The public library was opened to all readers, regardless of race, when some towns were removing seats from their libraries in an effort to prevent their use by blacks. The golf course was desegregated when others to the West and East of us were having their club houses burned down rather than integrate. Our city became the first town to elect a black treasurer, and a pioneer in electing a black to its City Council. Very early in the process of integration, both city and county-wide committees were integrated. Many policy-making boards were conscious of the minority and included them in the membership: such as Museum, United Way and Welfare.

Department store employees, lunchrooms, motels, and other public places were integrated before the 1964 Civil Rights Law was passed. One exception was the uptown theaters which refused to integrate and caused the only prolonged demonstration in the history of the county. The theaters did not yield until the passage of the Civil Rights Act, the next year.

Total school integration was accomplished in 1965–66 in two of our school districts without incident. Our county school system became totally integrated with the closing of one black school and the total integration of the Junior High School.

During the 1970–71 school year, school walk-outs occurred at two of our schools but were somewhat insignificant, for they were successfully concluded without violence, and required no interruption of regular classes in these schools.

A plus in the integration process can be noted with the election on a merit basis of black student body presidents at three high schools. Another plus has been the enthusiastic acceptance of the black classroom teacher as a part of the total staff, and their appreciation as excellent teachers by most of the parents in the county. The three black principals have also been accepted on their own abilities and have been a welcome addition to the professional staff of the school system.

First Encounter with Integration

On a spacious plot of land located in a rich suburban area was a beautiful school. It was modern in every way. The furniture was the last word and supplies were in abundance. The black children were speechless with amazement and to the black teacher it looked like fairyland. The only difference—the people were real.

I was qualified with both bachelor and masters degrees and over thirty-five years of teaching experience. As I looked back over those years, I remembered how I overcame obstacles that now seemed insurmountable.

Preparing to meet twenty-nine first graders, twenty-three of whom were white, appeared before me as another barrier in my teaching career. I prepared to meet this one by accepting children as children, regardless of color, wealth or culture.

When the school gong rang on opening day, I met my children at the door with a big welcoming smile. They greeted me the same way and in a few minutes we were one big happy family. The fact that the white children had been indoctrinated with the knowledge that they would have a black teacher and the black children's delight with a warm smile from anyone, especially from their teacher, contributed much to my pleasant acceptance by all children.

To get acquainted I had them tell about their experiences. They ranged from the Florida Everglades with its alligators to the Red Woods of California, including all sights in between. This report was made by the white children. They also included their trips abroad—Big Ben in England and the Leaning Tower of Pisa, just to mention a few.

The black children sat quietly and listened with an air of wonderment. They did not join the discussion until I asked them to tell about some of their experiences. The playground, supermarket and a visit to grandmother who lived in the next block were some of their adventures. Quite a difference in the comparison of the two cultures, but it gave the black children a feeling of belongingness.

Because of kindergarten training the white children were reading the first level of books within six weeks. Black children, without the benefit of any preschool training, read only after an enriched Reading Readiness Program.

People at last had begun to realize that things separate could not be equal.

I shall never forget the way the high school students reacted to the fact that the government of our county was committed to the ideals of complete integration. They were told by their leaders that complete integration was a goal toward which all people must now work. To that end all forms of segregation, whether they served a good purpose or not, must be sacrificed. All the things that the students cherished most had to be sacrificed; familiar surroundings, school trophies, clubs and organizations, certificates, including basketball, baseball, football, typing, drama, and library. The students were too young to realize fully why all of this was really happening to them and their school.

When they were told by their leaders that they would be going to another school, and about goals that had been set for them in an integrated society, they did what might have been expected of young people who had set goals for themselves in surroundings which were familiar to them. Some cried; others became sullen where before they had been lively; some threw rocks at the new school sign that replaced the old one. The students were not prepared for the challenge that faced them, for they knew they would now have to compete with students of the opposite race who had been offered better opportunities.

In the students' attempt to meet this challenge of what was termed first-class citizenship, all did not react in a responsible, thoughtful way. Some entered the new experience by using profanity in and out of the classroom; some fought for little or no reason; others carried knives and other instruments to protect themselves from people they felt were their enemies. They were truly frustrated, and fought in the only way they knew to relieve their frustration. They did not have the abilities to cope with new pressures and new responsibilities. They called their action exerting their rights in the so-called new freedom.

Second-Hand School

In 1947 the state operated a dual system of education. The black schools were often given second-hand equipment, furniture, buses, and even buildings, on the assumption that it would soon be abused and torn up anyway, new or used.

The last of January an epidemic of influenza struck the white schools and forced them to be closed for about two weeks. I was in the office of the county schools superintendent one afternoon a few days after schools were re-opened when the principal of one of the largest colored schools in the county came in.

"Mr. C," he said to the superintendent, "we are in bad shape at my school. About forty per cent of my pupils and several teachers are out with influenza."

The superintendent looked at the colored principal for several seconds and said in somewhat of a scolding manner, "Can't you colored people do anything right? Why didn't you have the flu when we were having it? You colored folk just mess around and get our schedule out of line."

After a few seconds the colored principal smiled broadly and answered, "Well, Mr. C, you know how it is, you white folk never give us colored people anything until you have finished with it."

What changes have taken place in 28 years!

Separate but Equal?

In one remote section of North Carolina where Negro families were scattered over a large area, no buses were available for use by Negro children. Because many of them had long distances to walk, attendance was sporadic. Some came one day a week while two or three came the entire week. Drop-outs were commonplace. Although this was a 1–7 grade school in one room, there were seldom any students above the fifth grade. Keeping older students motivated while explaining the intricacies of learning to youngsters just beginning to explore the joys of words and numbers is no mean feat, and *vice versa*. So it was almost inevitable that the older ones would drop out.

Anger and resentment welled up in me many days during this period because, although I never had the opportunity to enter a large brick white school, I could not imagine their conditions being as crude and as inconvenient as the one-room building a short distance around the curve where I taught. In addition, the administration seemed insensitive and uncaring about these conditions.

Effects of Love and Respect

Since I had been reared on a tobacco farm, I knew the black race better than the average white teacher did. In retirement it meant much to me when some of the blacks said, "What will we do when you retire? You understand us and are kind to us; therefore, we hate to see you retire."

One incident must be related. I am thankful to say that this was the only time I was treated rudely by a black student. During fifth period, just before lunch time, one black girl was talking as I was finishing my assignments for the next day. I corrected her twice; she continued to talk. At last I said, "I shall be forced to give you an eighth period because you continue to talk!"

She stood immediately and yelled, "I am not going to serve an eighth period for you. I haven't done nothing to have to serve an eighth period for. You are picking on me because I am black. Everyone knows that you are partial to the whites. You won't make them serve eighth periods. I hate you! Everyone hates you!"

The Lord helped me control my tongue and my temper. When she stopped making her accusations, I asked, "Are you through now? You have really accused me; I know what I am guilty of. Just serve your eighth period tomorrow."

The bell rang for lunch and the class left my room. As usual, I ate my lunch in my classroom. During that time I looked up and saw four big black boys (for all my English pupils were seniors that year) entering my room. They had come to apologize for the conduct of the black girl. They said, "Don't pay that girl any attention; she does not have respect for anyone. We know that you are kind to us, and we appreciate you. She won't ever be disrespectful to you any more. Don't you worry; we'll take care of her."

In the meantime news had reached the office that four big black boys had come to my classroom to protest my actions and my words. The office asked if I needed help. I signed the note from the office and wrote that the boys had come to apologize for the accusations which the black girl had made. Before the school day was over, three other groups of black boys had come to me with apologies for the accusations the black girl had made.

The First Driver Training Course

My school was a two-room building, nine miles from town. The biggest problem for four years was getting to and from school. Out of a salary of $57.50 we had to pay someone $10.00 a month to transport us the nine miles to the school building and back home each day. Winter was worst of all. The clay roads were nearly impassable in spots. To solve the problem, our driver made arrangements with a parent to meet us at the worst place with his mule and wagon to carry and bring us back daily until the roads cleared up.

When I finally got a car, one farmer had me equip it with blocks, chain, and shovel. He showed me how to place my blocks and dig my way across bad spots. Often, the driver of the bus for white children waited for me and pulled me across.

These experiences made me a good driver. However, I was not the only one having trouble getting to school. There was no bus for blacks, so my pupils walked to school—some six to eight miles a day.

But eventually, I found myself in a most satisfying school situation. Here, in my home town I taught 14 years in a segregated school and six years in an integrated one.

Just before integration, Federal NDEA and later Elementary and Secondary Educational Art funds were used to pour in supplies, in order to equalize. Facilities, equipment, and materials came in faster than we could use them. This assistance proved very beneficial; after integration there were smaller classes and more innovation in teaching.

An Enjoyable Year Under Integration

The experience I had in 1969 and 1970 was unique. It was my first year working as principal of an integrated school. I must hasten to say it was the most interesting year I had had in my whole career. Working with a mixed faculty and students—all seventh and eighth graders—was marvelous. At this age, though, all of them, especially the girls, wanted to get married. I was constantly counseling them to prepare themselves for good jobs first. It is provocative now to meet these girls working in the supermarkets and other stores, striving to make a living, with home responsibilities—husband and children—and trying to go to technical school. They say, "You tried to tell us; we know *now* what you meant."

My last year was my most enjoyable year. I decided to retire earlier on that very pleasant note; so I could say that everything was beautiful for 45 years.

Spirit of Hope

Working without the necessary educational tools, relying mainly on dedication, patience, and hope and seeing sparks of brightness on the faces of my none-too privileged students—these were some of the dynamics which stand out in my mind. Those were years of hope for us, because we felt that there would be better days ahead. This was a period in which we instilled *black* pride, even though the concept had not gained the notoriety it has today.

It was an era when cooperative planning between school and

community was evident. From this experience I was caught up in life's inevitability—change. I moved from this setting to consolidation. All very good. But I left a part of my soul at the two-teacher school.

Our eagerness to overcome obstacles, our spirit of hope, and our determination to move onward—I remember most and cherish most deeply.

More Ways Than One

I used the lunchroom to teach human relations. Each Friday I invited one black parent and one white person, a black minister and a white minister, to have lunch with the children. Sometimes I invited two or three black pre-school children, and some pre-school white children along with their parents to have dinner. These get-togethers went a long way in helping to integrate our schools when the time came.

Never a Dull Moment

On duty one day a small cherub came up and said, "John called me Blackie," and I patted his head and said, "Go back and call him Whitey." He started off and came back and said, "But John ain't white."

Communication Among All

One of the greatest changes that took place during my teaching career came with the desegregation and integration of schools. However, it took place smoothly and orderly in our county, because of our understanding principals, teachers, counselors and parents.

Problems? Of course, there were some problems, but I am happy to say that we held many meetings with principals and student council representatives to prepare for such problems before they arose.

The Big Move

In 1968 HEW ordered full compliance for integration. The logistics involved almost superhuman efforts in arrangement, preparation and distribution. The burdensome task of moving furniture, equipment, library books, textbooks, and remodeling to satisfy the new order was accomplished in time. Teachers who had held forth in the same room for years were uprooted and some felt it very keenly. It was long hours and hard work for all concerned.

An Experience in Integration

Flora was a frightened little black girl when she was sent to a formerly white school as a third grader. She behaved well but she was really too timid to let me find out what she was capable of doing. Finally, I saw she was talented in art; then I noticed how well she formed her letters, and before the year was out she was making charts and helping with bulletin boards. Her mother clerked at a nearby King's Store and couldn't attend the first PTA—so she sent her husband. He told me if Flora didn't behave just to whip her. She was one of the most cooperative.

My reward came at report time when her mother wrote by "comments"—"I thank God for all you have done to help Flora adjust to a different school."

"The Obscure Pioneer"

As the music teacher I was summoned to meet an affable white minister who stood smiling with outstretched hand to greet me. He said later that I was his last hope, for all other persons had refused to listen to what he had to say.

His proposal seemed simple enough at first glance. He said candidly that he wanted to do something tangible to improve race relations and that he wanted to invite our totally black school chorus to come to his church for a "Fellowship Day"—to sing, to join in the feast, and to learn to know each other better.

It took real courage for this man to make this proposal, because for many years his town had been noted for its active stand against mixing of the races.

With a degree of apprehension, all of those concerned agreed to accept the invitation. Our preparation became a challenging, stimulating, and enjoyable experience. The group felt rewarded however, for the project was a positive effort to build a better understanding between people of all races, colors, and creeds.

PRIVATE FUNDS FOR BLACK CHILDREN

Our Jeannes teacher was paid by a rich Jewish man, Mr. Julius Rosenwald, who also built many schools in the South for black children. All of the schools he built had kitchens.

After completing the eighth grade, we had no high school for blacks. My parents sent me to a Normal and Industrial Boarding School supported for blacks by some wealthy New York Quakers. It no longer exists.

GETTING A STEP AHEAD

In the words of the poet, "Life for me ain't been no crystal stair." Born the youngest child of a family of five to a couple of ex-slaves, I can truly say that my life has been quite eventful.

My father died when I was six years old but my mother had a burning desire for me to get a step ahead, so I attended the two-months-long local schools, completing what was offered.

After this time I became a house servant to a Northern doctor during the summer and went away to school during the winter.

My schooling was interrupted when my mother became an invalid, but she lived to see me become a teacher, while in my teens, by passing an examination and receiving a grade "B" certificate which paid $14 per month.

With this meager beginning I continued my education through

summer school and extension classes, and when I retired I had a class "A" certificate and a college education.

My experiences have truly been unforgettable. I have taught as many as 60 pupils—some even older than I—in a one room log building, heated by an open fireplace, in which there were no kinds of health facilities provided inside or out.

We brought our water and food from home. I served as custodian, mother, and teacher. . . .

FREEDOM OF CHOICE

In 1965 a Freedom of Choice Plan was submitted to HEW. A few teachers and students transferred. They were truly in the foxholes of education. To them, the county school system is deeply indebted. Their tolerance, patience, humanity, and integrity paved the way for the upheaval ahead.

EARLY AND HAPPY RETIREMENT

My position was to serve as assistant to persons whose training and experiences were limited. After working under such conditions for three or four years, I realized I did not have the drive and dedication that I think a teacher should have if he is to motivate students. The above and similar experiences resulted in my early and happy retirement in 1972.

MAKE BELIEVE

One day we were using flour and some fell on the counter. Since there were no white pupils in the class, some of the girls rushed to the flour and covered their faces with it. They giggled and giggled and had a good time pretending.

A BI-CENTENNIAL GOAL

Integration has come to our county without the violence and disruption experienced by many other communities. It has been marked by a great degree of tolerance and understanding. Both races have entered into it with determination. Lines of communication have been kept open and many options have been available. This statement does not mean, though, that there have not been some problems. The way to integration has not been completely free from pressures.

Now as we approach our Bi-Centennial in our state and the rest of the country, we can look with pride on what has happened in North Carolina and with hope that the last quarter of the 20th century will see the complete realization of our dream of a colorless society.

SHOW AND TELL

In an oral composition class, Johnny brought a lot of toy dogs of different kinds and described them to the students. Another object which he placed on the desk elicited the question from a student: "Johnny, What is that?"
Johnny replied, "Oh, that's a fire hydrant!"

THE SYMPHONY OF LIFE

I do not fret if my students remember little or nothing of the subject matter in my classes. My fervent hope is that I offered them the ideals to develop a true sense of high moral values that have contributed to an appreciation of beauty, an understanding of freedom in contrast to undisciplined liberty, a faith in a Supreme Being, and a desire not only "to read poetry and to recite poetry, but to live poetry, which is the symphony of life."

LIVES ON

After all, what is a teacher? In the beginning she is a complicated human mechanism. If she is dedicated, she develops and grows in skill and understanding and the beauty of her existence lives forever.

IX Showing the Way

Schools That Left Their Mark

In the years before the advent of public education, and for some years afterward, there were scattered throughout North Carolina many educational institutions which made distinctive contributions to the cultural life of the state. A few were founded by individuals, some by church organizations, and others by the communities themselves. There are teachers living today who attended some of these schools or taught in them, while there are others who grew up in communities where their influence is still felt and discussed. Ranging from a one-room school enrolling students of all ages to the more sophisticated "Academy" and "College," these pioneer institutions were operated by men and women of culture and superior education.

On the anvil of almost unbelievable hardship, these teachers hammered on both academic "metal" and personality mettle; heated, beaten, tempered into capable, dependable, and durable character. There was always wholesome fun, a deep religious interest, and a surprisingly-high quality of academic advantages. Their equipment and quality of formally-trained leadership have been well replaced with what money can do, but nothing, really, can replace the charisma and personal dedication of their teachers.

Early private schools had a decided impact on the development of education in North Carolina. In the following pages we describe many of them. No effort has been made to include all that existed; rather we attempt to record memories and impressions revealed by retired teachers throughout the state. For simplification, the schools are grouped in the following order: oldest schools, church related schools, non-church related schools, and an assortment of private and public schools, including elementary.

OLDEST SCHOOLS

Old Queen's College

Undoubtedly, old Queen's College, in Charlottetown (Charlotte), was the first school of higher education in North Carolina. Some Mecklenburg citizens petitioned the General Assembly to establish a school for the education of youth, hoping that a local college would "keep their sons and their money away from distant Nassau Hall." (Princeton University was then called Nassau Hall.) The charter was granted in 1771, empowering the college to confer BA and MA degrees. It also specified that "the rules and ordinances correspond . . . to the Laws and Customs of Oxford and Cambridge Universities or the Colleges in America." The school was open to males only. It was not the ancestor of the present Queen's College. To support it, a six-pence tax was levied "on each gallon of rum or spirituous liquors brought into Mecklenburg."

In addition to offering classical studies, Queens sponsored literary societies and encouraged political debating. The latter activity probably prompted George III to revoke the charter. The trustees then simply changed the name to Queen's Museum and continued operating. In 1777, when the state's first legislature met, the school was re-chartered and named Liberty Hall Academy. During the Revolution the Academy was converted into a hospital, first for American wounded, then for British. After the War the trustees moved the school to Salisbury where it became Salisbury Academy.

The college claimed many distinguished alumni, including a future president, Andrew Jackson.

Salem Academy (and College)

"Salem Female Academy was begun in 1802 by the governing board of the Moravian Congregation at Salem, North Carolina." The Moravians' interest in education was indigenous, for they always coupled intelligence with labor, with both based in their love of God and service to their fellows. Although a religious spirit was fostered in the school, no attempt was ever made to proselytize students of other faiths; and to this day the Academy and College are completely unsectarian.

As travel was difficult in those early days, the students arrived on horseback or were brought in chaises with a servant in attendance. They remained during most of the year, and "a few weeks' rest in midsummer with a picnic or two" kept them content.

By the time of the Civil War the Academy was widely known, and parents in all parts of the South were enrolling their daughters, "believing that they would be safe in Old Salem." Because of the resulting crowded conditions, parents were informed that if they would bring beds, room would be made for all the girls.

When Stoneman's Cavalry Brigade moved on Salem, valuables were quickly concealed under the stone flooring, and the Academy's two fine horses were hidden in the basement under Main Hall. Tradition says that when the soldiers marched by, one student gave the Rebel yell and waved a Confederate flag from a third-story window. The only thing that saved the Academy from being burned in retaliation was that the principal and the Union Commander had been schoolmates at the Moravian School for Boys in Pennsylvania, and the Union officer "gave reassurance that the school would be protected in spite of the demonstration."

Caring for the students in the latter years of the war was a tremendous task. There was a scarcity of everything, but Salem "kept the faith in the dark days of the war" and managed to provide the necessities. However, the large bundles of Confederate money still kept in the old iron safe in the College office are mute evidence of the loss sustained by the institution.

High standards in scholarship and character were maintained

in an expanding curriculum, and, in 1866, "the incorporation of the school as a college provided legal recognition that college standards had been achieved."

With the passing years many changes took place. The physical plant became more up-to-date: water coolers replaced wooden pails in the halls, chairs replaced stools in the dining-room, and candles yielded to gas and then electricity. A bowling alley was installed; small dressing rooms were converted into piano practice rooms; beds were separated by curtains, affording privacy; and finally, hot air heat and inside toilets were provided. Eventually, an infirmary, a library, and a large hall for concerts, gatherings, and commencement exercises were built.

Strong emphasis on the liberal arts was always paramount at Salem, although, for a while, a business course and an industrial department were included in the curriculum. Art and music were introduced, with a regular course in music leading to a diploma.

Without doubt it has been the deep concern, the personal interest and affection shown by Salem Academy and College for its students, which explains the deep sense of loyalty and dedication noted in its alumnae.

New Bern Academy

The "Academy" building built in 1806 still stands on the school green in New Bern. The 1975 North Carolina General Assembly passed an enabling act whereby this building will be turned over to a commission to be appointed by the Craven County Commissioners. As the New Bern City School Board has voted to give land to the commission, this beautiful old building can be restored on the site where it has stood for one hundred sixty-nine years.

The school's history goes back for another forty-four years when Thomas Tomlinson opened the school on January 7, 1764. A building completed in 1766 burned in 1795 and school continued in either Tryon Palace or the Episcopal Church until the new academy was completed.

Ebenezer Academy

Among the historical landmarks in Iredell County, none is more outstanding than Ebenezer Academy. In the *Western Carolinian*, under the date of December 9, 1823, this advertisement appeared:

> Ebenezer Academy was incorporated during the session of the General Assembly in 1822. It is now open to all who wish to pursue a course in liberal education or study English Grammar and Geography. All branches of Education required for college admission will be taught. We are happy in stating to the public that a new and commodious academy will be completed in a few days. This academy is in a rural situation, six miles from the city of Statesville, so that students will be measurably free from temptations to vice. It is convenient to church, where there is preaching statedly.

The academy's code called for "full respect for teachers, the institution, the state, and divine law." Ebenezer functioned as a private academy until 1856 and as a public school until 1903.

Many men who later became prominent in local, state, and national life in the fields of religion, medicine, law, politics, and education, as writers and historians, were well prepared at Ebenezer Academy for college entrance. A large percentage of the students, having been cradled in the Presbyterian faith, chose to pursue further education at Davidson College.

CHURCH RELATED SCHOOLS

Davenport College

In 1857 a group of prominent Caldwell County citizens met and drew up plans for a college for girls. It opened the next year with fifty-six students and was given the name Davenport College to honor a prime promoter and large contributor. It was chartered in 1859 by the Methodist Episcopal Church South, and, except for the Civil War years, operated continually until 1933.

An imposing colonial building was erected on a prominent hill in the town of Lenoir. This large three-story building was all-inclusive, with a dormitory area, an auditorium, classrooms, spacious parlors, dining-room, music rooms, and administrative offices. In later years a large dormitory and a dining hall were erected, with space in the latter for the Music Department. These, along with the original building, took care of the growing number of students who came from many places in North and South Carolina and a few other states.

Originally a two-year college with a preparatory department, Davenport added a third year of college work in the early 1900's. In 1924–25 a fourth year was added and three women were granted degrees. The next year the three-year status was resumed. Dynamic teachers and able administrators demanded excellence in fundamental subjects, and a superior Art Department and an outstanding Music Department gave opportunity to talented students. A glee club and a dramatics club afforded participation in the performing arts, and two rival debating societies gave practice in forensic development. Calisthenics and tennis kept the girls fit.

In the depression of the 1930's the Methodists found it advisable to combine some of their small colleges, so Davenport was closed in 1933, and records and assets were transferred to Greensboro College, the first woman's college chartered by the Methodist Church. (Greensboro College was the first woman's college chartered in North Carolina and was the second woman's college chartered south of the Potomac river.) The city of Lenoir bought the real estate and operates Davenport Elementary School on the site.

A former student says, "I did love Davenport, and from my experience as a teacher and with other colleges, I am convinced that the education we received there was of real quality."

Boiling Springs High School

Boiling Springs High School, a private boarding school owned by the Baptists, was unique in many respects. The student body was made up mainly of students older than found in high school. Although there were quite a few of average high school age, some of the students were older than many of their teachers. They were, for the most part, boys and some girls who had dropped out of school for one reason or another. They had finally realized their mistake and wanted to finish their education. They were there to learn and wanted to learn; therefore, there were few disciplinary problems.

Classes were held from Tuesday through noon Saturday. Monday was a holiday so that the students and teachers who went away for weekends would not have to travel on Sunday. It was also a help to the ministerial students who were preaching or teaching on weekends in the churches of the three Associations near the school. Since the office personnel took care of all the record keeping, the teachers had more time to plan for and to teach the students.

This school was the parent of Gardner-Webb College.

Traphill Seminary or Academy

In the midst of Reconstruction following the Civil War the progressive citizens of the pioneer community of Traphill in Wilkes County realized the need for educational advantages beyond the common school. The time was ripe for Traphill's golden age of Christian education.

In 1871, under the sponsorship of the Methodist church, Methodists and Baptists joined forces to open an interdenominational school, Traphill Seminary (later called Traphill Academy). A two-story frame building was erected on a prominent elevation above the village. There was no charter. No record of students can be found, except a statement for tuition ($2.95 a year) in 1885. A number of homes in the village were open to students at the rate of $5.00 to $6.00 a month. Wholesome co-operation existed among patrons until 1886, when the trustees were promised aid if they would convey the school property to the Methodist church. Rivalry between the Methodists and the Baptists resulted in a division. In the 1887 Official Journal of the Blue Ridge Conference, we find this entry: "In pursuance of the action of the Conference . . . arrangements have been made and the property at Traphill . . . valued at something like two thousand dollars, has been secured and deeded to the M. E. church."

Traphill Institute

The Baptists withdrew and organized a Missionary Baptist church in 1887, and in the next year established a new school to promote growth in their denomination, as well as to prepare students for college entrance and "for life and its duties." Traphill Institute opened February 3, 1889. The first year, classes were held in the Baptist church while a building was being constructed.

In 1893 Traphill Institute was chartered "for the purpose of maintaining a school of high grade at Traphill . . . for the mental and moral training of children of the white race of both sexes. . . . The faculty . . . by the advice and with the consent of the directors . . . shall have power to grant certificates of merit. . . ."

In catalogues from 1894–95 and 1895–96 there are references to discipline: "The government is lenient and parental, yet firm. The moral interest of the student receives special attention. . . . Each student is required to render cheerful obedience to the few rules that are necessary." "The cooperation of parents is invited by reports and correspondence." "The habitual indulgence of profane language, the reading of pernicious literature, the use of intoxicating drinks or tobacco, and the carrying of pistols or other dangerous weapons would be considered grave and treated accordingly."

In the early 1900's the school declined and in 1912 it closed.

Fair View College

For four years after the Baptists withdrew and the Methodists took control Traphill Academy was still called by that name and by Fair View Academy. In 1891 it was chartered as Fair View Male and Female College, then was shortened to Fair View College. Power was given "to grant diplomas conferring such degrees as are usually conferred in colleges and universities." In 1895–96 the Normal Course was expanded to include pedagogy and psychology "necessary to convert the scholar into the teacher." The college was closed from 1904 to 1909 but reopened in 1910 with dormitory space provided.

Directions on admission are found in the 1911–1912 catalogue: "Candidates must present certificates . . . or take . . . examination on entrance. The school is open to both sexes of the white race. . . . None but worthy persons will be tolerated. When it becomes evident that any student has no settled purpose to study, parents will be requested to take their child home."

The college closed in 1918 when Traphill High School opened, marking the end of Traphill's golden age of Christian education, but the influence of the three schools has lasted and spread, having sent out from their walls local, state, and national leaders. Among alumni were six Representatives to the General Assembly, a U.S. Congressman, a North Carolina lieutenant governor, the mayor of a large northern city, several doctors and lawyers, successful business men, and a large number of teachers.

Linwood College

In 1883 a maiden lady from the North came to All Healing Springs and built a rather large structure on the mountain slope above the springs to serve as a school for girls. In those early days neither the boys nor the girls of this section had much opportunity to get an education. The school was supported by the Northern Presbyterian Church and was projected on the self-help plan, the students doing most of the work in preparing the meals and keeping house. Many fine and capable young women desiring college training took advantage of the school and received a valuable education at a minimum cost. The neighboring people soon began to see the worth of the school at their very door, and many young women in this section received college training, who, without the school, would have been denied the privileges of college culture and education.

The school was first called Pruden Hall, named after Miss Emily Pruden, the founder. Having established the school, she turned it over to Judge Jones, of Minneapolis, Minnesota, and went on her way to establish other schools of like character. It then was renamed Jones Seminary. In 1898 Judge Jones offered the use of the school property to the First Presbytery of the Associated Reformed Presbyterian Church. The offer was accepted, and under the new auspices it had the support of the many churches of the supporting denomination. The name was changed to Linwood College when the property was bought by the pastor of the Pisgah A. R. P. Church in 1903. In a few years boys of the community were admitted, and many educated men, as well as women, went out into places of honor and service.

Penelope Academy

Penelope Academy of eastern Burke County was established in 1887 by a young educational enthusiast, Claudius M. Murchison and his wife, Penelope. There was a modest dwelling for the principal's family and two buildings used for dormitories, one for girls and one for boys. The *Penelope Baptist Church History* relates the following:

> In 1887, at the annual meeting of the South Fork Association, Penelope Academy was acclaimed worthy of the patronage of all persons as a primary and preparatory school.
>
> In 1897 Penelope Academy was reported in good condition and doing excellent work; the teaching able and efficient; the discipline strict, but mild and religious; and the charges reasonably low. A splendid building was erected for the accommodation of the students who wished to stay in the Academy. The enrollment was 80 students from six North Carolina counties.
>
> The Academy ceased to operate with the establishment of high schools by the state, but the effect of its existence is still felt and seen and will echo and reverberate through the years.

Pee Dee Institute

The First Baptist Church of Wadesboro was under the supervision of the Pee Dee Association in the 1880's and 1890's when its members decided to build a school to help "deserving boys and girls," as well as local students. There were no public schools, and private schools were both scarce and expensive.

The Institute was financed by the Association and some students were given scholarships. The school opened in Wadesboro in 1897 and became known as Pee Dee Baptist Institute. The main building had a large auditorium and classrooms. There was a dormitory for girls and one for boys. Some pupils lived in private homes. The school was run by a fifteen member board of the Pee Dee Baptist Association. Fees ranged from $1.00 to $3.00 per month, and board was $7.00 per month. Preachers' children received favors. The 1903 catalog listed 257 students.

Pee Dee Institute was a citadel of influence and helpfulness until it was closed in 1907 to make way for a public school.

South Fork Institute

South Fork Institute was established in 1903 in Maiden by the South Fork Baptist Association, the site being chosen because of the good water and the high elevation. It was attended by people of any or no denomination. There was a dormitory for boys and one for girls. It was a high school with preparatory work in the grades. The school was noted for its very good music department. The spread of tax-supported schools, however, made denominational academies unnecessary, and in 1917 the property was sold. The building was then used for Maiden High School for approximately five or five and a half years.

Lincoln Academy

In the late 19th century Miss Emily Pruden, a New Englander with a vision and a true pioneer spirit, chose the foot of the beautiful Crowder's Mountain near All Healing Springs near King's Mountain as the ideal spot for an educational center. Thus began Lincoln Academy, which functioned under the auspices of the American Missionary Society.

From Lincoln Academy have gone out thousands whose lives have been indelibly etched by the cultural and Christian way of life on the campus of this boarding school.

Having outgrown the facilities of the Lincoln Academy plant, and through the intercession of the county superintendent, the high school department was moved in 1955 to a new and larger modern plant in Bessemer City and became Lincoln High School. With the improved facilities and expanded curriculum and activities program, the students continued to feel pride in the school and its great heritage. The high school was absorbed by consolidation and the plant is now used for a junior high school, retaining its traditional name, Lincoln Junior High School.

Mountain View Institute

Mountain View Institute was established in 1912 by the Stone Mountain, Brushy Mountain, and Elkin Baptist Associations. The citizens of Wilkes and adjoining counties supported it liberally and the Southern Baptist convention made appropriations for its operation. It was located at Hays, in the valley between the Blue Ridge and Brushy Mountains, with a splendid view of the mountains. A stump puller was bought and the boys cleared the thirty-five acre campus.

The first session of the Institute began in 1913 in an existing wooden building which was later remodeled for a dormitory for boys. The first new building was the Pearl Kilby Home built in 1918 for the girls. To foster a spirit of helpfulness and industry, each resident girl was expected to help in the kitchen and dining room. The first floor was used for classrooms. The next building was the Administrative Building, housing offices, seven classrooms, the auditorium, two Society Halls, and the library, where each student was required to spend a short while each day.

Five periods each week were devoted to Bible study, and all boarding students were required to attend Sunday School and church.

In 1923 the school was chartered as a junior college and operated on that level for several years. By 1927 the Associations had decided to concentrate primarily on supporting their larger schools, and Mountain View began experiencing financial problems. Despite the far-reaching influence the school had enjoyed, it was found necessary to close.

Mitchell College

Mitchell College in Statesville, one of the oldest colleges in North Carolina, has undergone many changes in its 119-year history. Founded by Concord Presbytery of the synod of North Carolina as a school for girls, it opened its doors in 1856, offering both preparatory and college courses. It had high scholastic requirements and adhered to strict rules of conduct. It took morals and religion seriously. For example, under one president's tenure, on Sunday no newspaper could be read, baths could not be taken, no walking was allowed except to church, and no studying except the Bible. A "no-smoking" pledge was required of all boarding students. By order of the trustees, card playing and dancing were taboo.

In the 1932 depression days Mitchell experienced many changes. The enrollment increased as students could not afford to go away to college; the school became co-educational when five local boys were admitted. Other changes followed: the Academy was closed in 1945 as more students began attending the state-supported local high schools; after World War II, the college accepted G. I. students, and along with them came surplus war buildings, supplies, and furniture.

In 1956 the church support was discontinued and Mitchell became an independent community college. The community raised $350,000 for endowment and aided in the expanding and improving of facilities. The college, once a traditional church institution, is now owned and controlled by the State of North Carolina with emphasis placed on vocational and technical courses.

Carolina Female College

The community of Ansonville was settled about 1844 by planters from along the Pee Dee River who were seeking relief from malaria. These affluent planters wanted a school for their daughters nearby so that the girls would not have to be sent to Salem or other distant points. They collected $10,000 and employed a man from Philadelphia to build the college, plus a president's home at Ansonville. Girls came from as far away as Mississippi. One girl arrived from South Carolina in a carriage with a driver.

Its curriculum emphasized music, Latin, and classical studies. The school was later taken over by the Methodist Church. After enjoying a seventeen year existence, the institution closed its doors in 1867, a victim of typhoid fever and Reconstruction.

Rutherford College

Regarded as one of the State's most influential early schools, Rutherford College operated for about sixty-five years. In the fall of 1868 a committee of men of the community of Excelsior in Burke County appealed to a local teacher, Laban Abernathy to join them in establishing a school of better quality than they had. He had taught about ten years in Caldwell County before coming to Burke. He had also been admitted to the Methodist Conference in South Carolina and was a circuit-rider. His success as a teacher and his ministerial experience well qualified him to operate a school such as the people of Excelsior wanted. The fame of the little school began to grow and enrollment increased. It was named Rutherford Academy, in honor of a local citizen who donated 200 acres of land and his private library. In 1871 Rutherford Academy became Rutherford College and was granted the right to confer degrees. In 1881 the village was chartered and renamed Rutherford College, after the school which was by now well established.

A destructive cyclone in 1879 caused the trustees to lose heart and allow the school to be sold for the mortgage. Mr. Abernathy borrowed money and bought the school. For the next ten years the institution enjoyed a very successful period; then disaster struck again. In 1891 fire destroyed not only the building but also money, deeds, private papers, old relics, and an accumulation of valuable books. The venerable head of the school went to the people and they responded to his plea and the buildings were rebuilt. Though the buildings were incomplete, the school reopened in 1893.

In 1900 Rutherford College was bought by the Methodist Conference. In 1907 it had the distinction of being presented a Carnegie Library. The college ceased operation in the mid-30's when the Conference decided to combine its small colleges. The influence of the religious atmosphere and the moral standards upheld by the founder of the school and his successors permeated the lives of the many young men who went on to enter the ministry.

The Dell School

Another school which was first supported by private citizens and then taken over by a church was the Dell School in Sampson County. It opened in 1902 in a remodeled old frame building with ninety-five students from five counties and two states. In 1908 the Baptist church took control of it and new brick buildings were erected, "all with indoor plumbing." Board in the dormitories was $13 a month, and $190 would pay for room, board, and tuition for nine months. While the Dell School was one of the private academies which never attained pre-eminence, it filled a need for schooling beyond the seventh grade before the state and local governments assumed that responsibility. It was closed in 1923.

Flora Macdonald College

Flora Macdonald College in Red Springs, a Presbyterian liberal arts college, was established at the turn of the century by Dr. Charles Graves Vardell, Sr., who envisioned it as a place where a young woman of moderate means could receive a Christian education of quality. For over a half century, graduates enjoyed an enviable reputation for their preparation in their chosen profession and for their deep-rooted philosophy of service. Despite the efforts of its founder, the college was never a large institution, but the influence of the successful teachers, directors of religious education, missionaries, and musicians receiving its programs of preparation, was far greater than its size would indicate.

Dr. Vardell gained the support, among others, of the Scottish communities and churches of Eastern Carolina who saw in this institution a rebirth of Floral College which had been in operation during the nineteenth century. He also was able to attract benefactors from many states and nationally-respected faculty members to assist him in accomplishing his dream.

During the 1960's Flora Macdonald's accreditation was transferred to St. Andrews Presbyterian College in Laurinburg. For several years Vardell Hall, a girl's preparatory school, occupied the Red Springs site; then, in 1974 the buildings were turned over for use by the Robeson County Day School.

NON-CHURCH RELATED SCHOOLS

Pineland College

Pineland College had its beginning as Salemburg Academy when in the autumn of 1874 certain civic-minded persons in Sampson County sat down and drew up a charter for a private school. The school operated for many decades, realizing its goal of better education for young people.

In 1908 Mr. and Mrs. W. J. Jones became co-presidents and set themselves the job of expansion and financial reinforcement. Though buffeted by many fateful events, they served with notable success. The name was changed to Pineland College, and new buildings and equipment were added steadily. One gift of $70,000 came from B. N. Duke. Considered a finishing school, Pineland admitted girls only. At the urging by parents to provide a school for boys, Edwards Military Academy was opened in 1935 as a boys high school and junior college.

In 1926 Mr. and Mrs. Jones deeded the property to a Board of Trustees from all over North Carolina and Virginia. This corporation provided Christian training of the non-denominational type and a fine accredited education in a homelike atmosphere.

In 1972 the state of North Carolina took control of the buildings and campus. Today, the Justice Academy of North Carolina occupies the grounds.

Smithfield Collegiate Institute (Turlington Graded School)

In 1886 Ira T. Turlington founded Smithfield Collegiate Institute, the name of which was changed in honor of him, in 1891, to Turlington Graded School. At that time the school occupied a large wooden frame building. The enrollment was 239 and the faculty consisted of five members.

Mr. Turlington helped establish private schools to extend the teaching time from a month, to six weeks, to four months, to six months, and finally to nine months and eleven grades. Many students from surrounding counties came to Turlington Graded School—some walked many miles and some came in wagons.

It was at Turlington Graded School that Johnston County's own Albert Coates, founder of the internationally-acclaimed Institute of Government at the University of North Carolina at Chapel Hill, started to school in 1901.

Pembroke State College

For many years there existed in Robeson County a unique and unfortunate situation. Among the population were a great many Indians who did not live on a reservation but resided on farms and in towns. Because of prejudice they were not admitted to the white schools, and were too proud to attend the Negro schools. To remedy this situation the State, in 1887, attempted the establishing of a separate school system when the legislature appropriated $500 for a school for Indians, with the stipulation that the students be over fifteen years old and sign a contract to teach at least one year. Several years later $1,000 was appropriated, and in 1909 the amount was increased to $3,000. In 1924 the school was given high-school rating.

Though the legislature in 1885 had created a normal school, that level of work was not begun until 1926. In 1939 the college and high school were separated, and in 1940 four-year college diplomas were awarded. In 1952 the college was admitted to the

Southern Association of Colleges and Universities. The next year white people were admitted!

Born of necessity, the school has made long and rapid strides and now belongs to the University system with an Indian as president.

Moravian Falls Academy

For many years the villagers of Moravian Falls relied on the "subscription school" for educating their offspring and for this purpose had erected on the outskirts of the village a one-room log building, which they called Edgewood. In the summer of 1874 a young teacher, Joe F. Spainhour of Burke County, came to visit his brother, a highly esteemed local citizen. Joe had been teaching in Illinois but was persuaded to remain and teach at Edgewood. Pleased with the success of the school that year, he urged that a better school building be provided for the community. The response of the citizens was hearty. They ground their axes, whetted their saws, cut timber, sawed lumber, and hauled it to a wooded knoll in the center of the village. Volunteers came. Carpenters served without pay. Men worked two weeks at home and one week at the schoolhouse until it was completed, a large two-story frame building with several classrooms and an ample auditorium. Thus Moravian Falls Academy came into existence.

The academy gained a reputation for providing a sound education that attracted students from a wide area. The 1878–79 catalogue listed students from nine North Carolina counties and three other states. There were no dormitories, but everyone in the village who had a spare room took in student boarders at $6.00 to $7.00 per month. As the school grew, the community was unable to accommodate them all; so, small two-room buildings, called "offices," were erected and rented for 50¢ a month. In each of these, several students, usually brothers and sisters, "batched."

In the fall of 1878 Dr. George Greene, a graduate of Wake Forest College and the Southern Baptist Seminary, succeeded Professor Spainhour. Under his administration the school broadened its course of study and established a reputation for academic excellence. Early school catalogues show that Latin, Greek, higher mathematics, natural sciences, history, vocal and instrumental music, and Military Science were taught. In 1878–79 tuition fees were $1.00 per month for Primary, $2.00 for Intermediate, and $3.00 for Academy students.

Able principals, who stressed the development of manners and morals, helped to elevate the standards of life of the community as well as the character of the students. Dr. Greene departed in 1887 to teach at Wake Forest College, but the Academy continued under a succession of competent principals until it closed in 1900, when it became a public school.

Kings Mountain Military School (W. T. R. Bell Military Academy)

In 1876 Captain W. T. R. Bell opened a private school in Kings Mountain with an enrollment of eighteen, which became a military school with young men attending from the Carolinas, Virginia, and New York. The cadets wore gray military style uniforms. There was no distinction between grades, and when the boys left the military school the great majority of them went on to college. Many of the leaders in Virginia and the Carolinas were former students of Kings Mountain Military School.

There were no dormitories, so cadets boarded with families in the community. Girls were permitted to attend as day students.

In 1879 the school was changed to become the first public school in Kings Mountain, including grades one through high school.

Bethel Hill Institute

Rev. John A. Beam, a man of vision and courage, went to the Bethel Hill community in 1886 as a minister, after receiving an A.B. degree from Wake Forest College and attending the Southern Baptist Seminary. He decided to combine his ministry with teaching and started by purchasing the old Flat River Association school building, naming his school Bethel Hill Institute. The young minister-educator advertised in the newspapers of the day:

"If you want an education, come to Bethel Hill Institute. If you have no money, come anyway."

In 1888 the school opened and Miss Mollie Lucas came to teach music. They were married the next year and together operated the school and did other educational work for many years.

According to an issue of *The Roxboro Courier Times*, "The little two-room building gave way to a splendid building of good proportions and architectural beauty." It opened with a mortgage on the Beam home, five dollars in money, faith, and the good will of the community.

This boarding and rooming school became recognized over the state as one of the best. Bethel Hill Institute was duly incorporated as a school of high grade by the Legislature of 1897 and was given power to grant diplomas. It enjoyed a liberal patronage from the community and from many counties in North Carolina and adjoining states.

According to the 1897–98 catalogue: "The design of Bethel Hill Institute is to equip young men and young ladies mentally and morally for the varied vocations of life; to furnish them with the knowledge adapted to the needs of one in business life; and to lay broad solid foundations for a more extended and liberal education." During the seventeen years that the institute existed, more than 100 ministers were educated there.

Disaster struck in 1905 in a destructive fire, and the school was never re-opened.

Virginia-Carolina School

The Virginia-Carolina School at Grassy Creek occupied a unique position. Built in 1913 it was a boarding school with dormitories for boys and girls in grades one through eleven. The school, a wooden structure, was built diagonally across the Virginia-Carolina line and was run co-operatively by both states. Virginia supported and directed the elementary grades and North Carolina controlled the high school. All graduates received North Carolina diplomas. Students were required to study both North

Carolina and Virginia history. Agriculture classes were taught in North Carolina but the workshop was in Virginia. Students attended classes in North Carolina and ate lunch in Virginia.

Roads were impassable in winter; hence, dormitories were needed. Horseback was the safest and surest method of transportation. Covered wagons were used for local rural students, but they sometimes had to unload and walk.

This unique consolidation seemed to work well in providing good schooling for a sparsely populated area in adjoining states.

Sulphur Springs Academy

In 1875 Sulphur Springs Academy was established about seven miles north of North Wilkesboro. Though called an academy, it apparently included only the first seven grades; but perhaps it included at times some grades above that level. The one hundred year old building erected as a community project still stands, and the proud community hopes to have it preserved as a historic landmark. Many leading citizens of the area were educated at the school, which closed in 1934 when it became a public school.

OTHER SCHOOLS

Catawba County Farm Life School

Catawba County's first consolidated high school was Startown, later to become Catawba County Farm Life School. In July, 1904, two school districts were consolidated and a local tax was voted to supplement state funds. The first building had two classrooms and an auditorium, which was soon divided into more classrooms. In 1911 the high school was made a separate department. Soon dormitories were built and the curriculum greatly expanded. Agriculture and Home Economics were added, more land was acquired, and in 1921 it became a recognized Farm Life School, operating on a sixty-five acre campus. With still more consolidation and with a broadened curriculum, it developed into one of the best schools in western North Carolina. It functioned as a Farm Life School until 1931 when it became a regular high school.

Balls Creek High School

Another outstanding early high school in Catawba County was Balls Creek, which opened in 1927. In addition to the regular secondary school courses, Balls Creek had a Business Department in which students who had already graduated from high school could enroll to take commercial subjects.

The Commercial Department ran the school store, thus giving the students first-hand experience in record keeping and in managing a business. In 1935 the business students began publishing the school's first annual, with all of the work being done by the students. Typewriting was also offered to the high school seniors.

Men and women from all over the county attended Balls Creek. Students who enrolled intended to learn enough to go out and get jobs, and many of these same individuals are still working without having taken further training.

Penderlea

The U. S. Department of the Interior in 1934 purchased 4,500 acres of land in the woodland and savannah northwest corner of Pender County for the Subsistive Homestead Corporation. Penderlea School, which was built on the project, was considered one of the finest in the United States. The Penderlea School building, completed in 1938, was one of the Homestead Projects of the Franklin D. Roosevelt Administration and a special interest of Mrs. Roosevelt. And were the people proud of it! There were twenty-six classrooms, a library with more than 8,000 volumes, a cafeteria, a teacherage, an auditorium, a well-equipped playground, and a large agriculture building and machine shop. The lighting was exceptionally modern, and there was an outside door and a workroom for each classroom.

The efficient and comprehensive Home Economics Department was the pride and joy of students and parents. The lessons the girls learned have had a most valuable influence in their homes and communities. The athletic program was well organized and included both boys and girls. The Ruritan Club was very helpful in encouraging the boys to strive to achieve their goals in corn production and the girls in homemaking projects.

The school gained such a wide reputation for its outstanding work that educators came from all over the country to observe.

It was, indeed, a sad occasion when, because of consolidation, the last graduation exercises were held in May 1975.

Crossnore School

In the year 1911 Dr. Mary Martin Sloop and her husband, Dr. E. H. Sloop, went to Crossnore in the North Carolina mountains to practice medicine. Finding a little neglected one-room school-house at the crossroads there, Mrs. Sloop became deeply concerned and appealed to the parents to help repair and renovate the building and to send their children to school regularly. Gradually she overcame their innate reserve. She won their confidence and succeeded in developing an institution that is widely acclaimed. In need of financial help, she called upon friends to contribute used clothes to sell to the mountain families. The response was so generous that the sales amounted to thousands of dollars annually in the following years. Consequently, the school became known as "the school that old clothes built." Other contributions from individuals and organizations, especially the DAR, have been significant, too.

The little school was inadequate after awhile and was replaced. In a few years many buildings occupied a large campus: dormitories, a teacherage, a store, a church, a weaving building, and farm buildings as well as a large school. While the young residents attend public schools in the area, they live on campus where they do much of the housekeeping and farm work. Hundreds of boys and girls, orphaned or from broken homes, have gained an education and a temporary home through the Sloop's dedicated work.

Canton Schools

Until consolidation of the schools in Haywood County, the Canton area had one of the unique systems in the state. It operated under a special state charter and was the first school west of Asheville that was accredited by the Southern Association. The Beaverdam township schools were operated in such a way that five elementary schools fed into Canton High School, which initiated many modern practices. Before team teaching became current, it was used in the Canton system. Their Student Government was one of the state models. In co-operation with the Champion Paper and Fiber Company, vocational and shop classes were established. The Champion YMCA, with its gymnasium, swimming pool, ball field, and tennis courts was made available to the school.

Teachers in the schools say, "It was a great and unique system."

Ellerbe School

Ever hear of Ellerbe? This was a caption to an editorial that Gerald W. Johnson wrote for the *Baltimore Sun* in the mid 1930's. It applied to an outstanding public school in Ellerbe, in the North Carolina sandhills. Richard F. Little was principal and guided the development several years.

At Ellerbe the child-centered activities and the methods of developing them were considered revolutionary. It became known as a "progressive school." A school store, a printshop, and a horticulture department provided students with actual experience. A Student Council, thought to be the first in a North Carolina public school, governed the student body and also assumed housekeeping duties.

Visitors came from many states and a few foreign countries to observe. During one year they numbered 4,800, and in addition the school received 17,000 letters of inquiry and commendation. The State Department of Public Instruction even asked the school to operate on Saturdays to accommodate observers who could not come during the week.

How the teachers and students loved their school! At one time a little tyke came puffing into his classroom only minutes before dismissal time, panting, "I missed the bus! I've been walking all day!"

In Richmond County, at Hoffman, a quiet village in a 50,000 acre government wildlife reservation, there once nestled among the long leaf pines a rural high school which offered a real stimulant for pride in America. At school, students watched as beavers built their homes, deer roamed, quail flourished, and fish spawned both in the natural lakes and in the government hatcheries.

Then the tempo of the area changed. World War II was in the making. Camp McCall was constructed just three miles from the school and the 82nd Airborne Division began training there. Forty thousand soldiers came and with them came many of their families. Where once only children from the wide reservation area were bussed in, now children of the military personnel began to enroll. From all across the nation they came—from city schools, progressive schools, large schools, small schools, poor schools, and just average ones.

Now, students were provided many rare learning situations. They watched perhaps the very last cavalry unit as the hundreds of horses and their riders and the huge tank division rolled by enroute from Fort Bragg to another camp near the school. Paratroopers were constantly jumping within view of the school, and the students learned a lot about the meanings of some of their routines. They also learned what the inside of a tank looks like, how K-rations taste, how the Red Cross performs, and how gliders soar. Meantime, they learned great lessons in courage and patriotism.

Frequently military engineers, artists, scientists, musicians, and athletes supplemented regular class schedules; chaplains at times conducted worship services (before the outlawing of school prayers); German prisoners of war helped in the school's large cannery and taught a few students a little German. The Home Economics Department and the Air Base co-operated in securing Federal aid for a lunchroom; and some commercial students found part-time employment at the Base.

Despite the unusual school situation, dedicated and cooperative teachers managed to adhere to the basics and prepared the students well for college entrance and for life.

Newton Preparatory School

One-room schools played such a significant role in early North Carolina education that a full chapter could be devoted to them, but we shall discuss only a few about which specific information has been given.

About 1899 Miss Matt Cochran ran a private school on family property in Newton. The school day began when Miss Matt appeared at the doorway ringing an old dinner bell. Students ranging from six to twenty-one years of age entered and were seated at wooden, unpainted double desks. Light came from windows on each side and heat from a wood-burning stove in the middle of the room. Everything was very primitive.

The day began with devotionals, songs, and memory passages from poetry. Assignments and programs throughout the day were stimulating and inspiring. Instruction ranged from primary level to preparation for college. Each pupil progressed according to his ability. During the hour-long lunch period, most pupils and the teacher went home, but some brought their simple lunches and ate at school. Often it was late afternoon when the day's work was finished. The building was then swept and dusted by some pupils to pay for their tuition.

This school closed in 1913 when Miss Matt joined the public school faculty in Newton.

Some Early Burke County Schools

Old Zoar, the first school in the George Hildebrand area, was started in the late 1700's in the old Zoar Lutheran church, a large log building. The early teachers were usually the ministers.

Before 1850 a subscription school, called the *Old School,* was built between new Highway 18 and Sugar Loaf roads. It was a thirty-foot long building with a fireplace at each end, a door on one side, and two windows on the other.

The Meadows was a one-room log house built before 1850.

It had a fireplace, one shuttered window, and one door. The children sat on puncheons, wrote on slates, and got their water from a spring.

The Little School was built about 1890. In this primitive school the children had split oak baskets in which they carried their lunches: meat and biscuits, molasses, fried pies, gingerbread, baked sweet potatoes, and often a jar of buttermilk. The pupils were classified according to the Reader they were in. School was in session only forty days a year, and one teacher taught 20 to 70 pupils from age six to eighteen.

THESE PEOPLE DIDN'T WAIT FOR WASHINGTON

During the 1940's and 1960's schools in many areas were centers of community activity and interest. In some communities, once a year, in the fall several pigs were barbecued, bushels of potatoes were made into potato salad, bags of cabbage were made into slaw, and two or three hundred pies and cakes were baked. Everyone worked steadily for weeks tabulating donations, making lists of needs, preparing and serving. Men of the community stayed up all night cooking prior to the meal, which was usually served to more than a thousand people. Then the PTA, the sponsoring agent, paid the salary of a much needed teacher.

DEGREES

The Sophomore Class was studying the degrees of comparison. The teacher asked if any one could compare "much." One of the students very enthusiastically answered, "Much, Muchier, Muchiest."

X ᔐ Helping Children

"To me the experience of seeing a human being grow and develop is a sacred responsibility and a joy." This statement by one teacher expresses the dedication common to teachers as a whole—a dedication that prepared them to act creatively and helpfully in many situations not necessarily in the academic field.

In the early working years of now retired teachers "there were no health nurses, no lunch programs, nor any of the agencies that exist today for the welfare and safety of the child. The teacher had to be all things to everybody, or at least to her children and their parents." This chapter is concerned with certain auxiliary services, such as nutritional supplements, clothing, textbooks, health services, guidance and psychological services.

Meeting Nutritional Needs

Of all the "non-bookish" problems teachers faced perhaps the one that concerned them most, especially in the 30's and 40's, was that many of their children were too poor to have nutritious diets, and all of them had cold lunches.

Signs of deprivation were everywhere. Lunch boxes with one sweet potato, a paper bag with two cold biscuits, sometimes even a solitary cooked Irish potato or a turnip—these were representative lunches for many children. One teacher recalls that one day four children who had been bringing a pail of chicken stew to school each day announced they could not come to school anymore. The reason? The children's father cooked for them, and "we don't have but one more rooster, and that's all Daddy knows how to cook."

Resourceful teachers, however, found ways to supplement the diets of their students. In general, hot soup was the answer.

During the Depression a teacher was serving hot soup in her one-room school long before the Federal Government began to give food to the schools. She had "bowls and spoons given . . . by a fine merchant in the county." There were also "other merchant friends who gladly donated soup bones" and "farmers gave potatoes and other vegetables."

In another school the "children carried their lunches in one-gallon pails." Then a plan was devised to serve, under the supervision of the teacher, hot vegetables to go with their lunches. Each child brought a small glass jar of vegetables to heat on the iron wood-burning heater. "At 11:00 A.M. each day these jars were submerged in a ten-gallon lard can which had been partially filled with water." By 12:00 noon the vegetables in the jars were ready to be eaten with lunch.

A woman in one county "started a small lunchroom in the one-room school building with one teacher cooking on a pot-bellied stove." The parents canned food in the summer and "a local butcher supplied the meat to add to it for no price at all."

An early portable lunch was described as a "soup kitchen staffed by one cook. . . . Soup was sent to the classroom in pitchers and served there. If there was a good quantity of meat on the soup bone, the meat was ground to make sandwiches."

Sometimes the teachers met nutritional needs by stimulating students to act for themselves. Recognizing her students' needs for milk, one teacher in the eastern part of the state took a survey of cows in the farming community. "It was found that only 35% of the students had access to milk. . . . We talked to the children about the importance of milk in the diet." A survey made the next year showed that the number of cows had increased to 70%.

The teachers were not alone in their efforts to provide adequate food for their children. Everywhere they enjoyed broad community support. In one community it was the mothers of the affluent well-fed children who spearheaded a drive for better lunches.

Most of the women belonged to a Home Demonstration Club. One group had a club house in which they could work. Another group . . . used a room in the school house basement for their meetings. The husbands of the latter group got hold of scrap lumber and built a work shed near the basement and counters in the club room. The women bought a secondhand oil stove to be used for cooking soup.

During the summer, with the help of the Home Demonstration Agent, regardless of the heat, the women met from time to time whenever vegetables ripened and canned tomatoes, okra, corn and beans.

When school opened, each child was asked to bring a mug and spoon. Mugs were bought for those who could not bring their own. Later the club bought bowls for all the children.

Different mothers furnished the soup bones at different times . . . One kind father who had a country store furnished soda crackers at cost. All children were asked to bring a turnip or potato, or whatever they could for the soup. Since no child was expected to bring something everyday, no child was arrogant about what he had furnished, and no child was embarrassed if he never brought anything

This account comes from a two-teacher school:

My father converted a stove-wood closet into a lunchroom, installing a window, shelves, and a built-in table. Parents and teachers donated pots and pans and children brought bowls, spoons, and jars. The Federal Government issued free food, such as peas, beans, cabbage, butter, cereal, and meat. In winter we cooked on the heater, but in the spring we used a two-burner stove (purchased with money earned by picking cotton—teachers and pupils alike.) The kitchen and food would never have received an A-1 cafe rating, but it certainly filled the needs of the pupils.

Ways were found to use food to assist with other projects. For example:

There was no place in the school where a hot lunch was served. The boys and girls in our classroom brought milk and sugar to school.

The teacher took chocolate and a small oil heater. Early in the morning hot chocolate was made and placed on the heater until serving time. The hot drink was purchased by many students in all grades to enjoy with their school lunches. The money was used to purchase library books in our classroom.

When the government began to give food with a value of nine cents per lunch if the school would supplement the food in order to have a balanced meal, a black teacher appealed to the community for help. Both races responded.

The Woman's Club gave the dishes and the silver.
The lumber men gave lumber for tables. One man gave a stove. Many interested persons gave pots, pans, dish cloths and bowls. I picked up the milk each morning and carried it to school. I taught the children to make menus and help in preparing the lunches.

We had a school garden. Everyone in the community helped. During canning season, I went out to the school and taught the children how to can for the school.

In one school the lunchroom program began with five-cent lunches which could be paid for by bringing in canned goods and farm products. The teacher remembers they "ate an awful lot of blackberries."

It was common practice for the teachers to help with the lunches, both in securing food and preparing it; and there is testimony that in some cases "the teachers ended their first year spending most of their small salaries financing the lunch programs."

In schools which had no lunchrooms, the teachers, like the students, usually brought sandwiches for lunch; and some of them discovered that their own eating habits influenced their students in surprising ways. After observing that the teacher always had lettuce in her sandwiches, one child brought a sandwich with a collard leaf in it.

Another teacher used the children's tendency to imitate the teacher to befriend an embarrassed child.

Lunch was eaten daily in the classroom. One day during the lunch period, it was noticed that a child was hiding behind a newspaper eating a sweet potato. The following day the teacher took a sweet potato for lunch and openly enjoyed it during lunchtime with the class closely observing. The next day practically every child in the class brought a sweet potato for lunch.

Teachers approved the Federal lunch programs, but they also faced problems with their administration. A teacher often remembered with longing the "warm hearts and ready hands" of the community in which she taught when the government lunch program began. However, she also remembered that

> in those early years of Federal lunches, Monday mornings became nightmares, extending their demands into the best hours of the day in which bright minds most readily grasp fundamentals and ideals. In those precious hours teacher sat collecting lunch money and making out tickets for those who could pay, and checking the list of those present who were to receive free lunches.

As they surveyed changes in schools over the years, teacher after teacher rejoiced in the clean lunchrooms of today and the nutritious meals they serve; but a few teachers saw present-day lunches in a different light. One teacher even suggested that elaborate lunches of today are "almost as dead as a Dodo Bird" and recommended simpler fare more in keeping with children's tastes. A fellow teacher remarked "All my life I have heard of the 'poor child's meal' of a sweet potato and a biscuit. Now we know that the sweet potato did have a lot of nourishment . . . better than the coke and potato chip snacks some of our affluent eat today."

Transportation was an area guaranteed to generate emergencies for teachers; and dealing with these emergencies called for patience, imagination, administrative ability and a highly-developed sense of humor. Helpfulness with transportation took many forms. Here is the testimony of a teacher from the walking-to-school period:

Transportation

> To get to _____ School, most of the children had to cross the river on a log. Most of them could nimbly walk any kind of log, but, sometimes the river would get up over the log, or freshet

waters would wash one end around. Then I would wade across with the children, each carrying his own stockings and shoes to keep them dry. One year I paid a man a dollar a month to keep up the log.

An elementary school principal began his teaching career at eighteen in a school five miles from his home. He paid a man a dollar to let him ride his horse to school and fifty cents to bring the horse back home.

His next school wasn't so isolated. He got to it by walking to the train tracks and by flagging the train and riding it to his destination. As the pupils got older, their parents often took them to a larger community where they boarded and attended the village school . . . . By 1924 two state school buses arrived in his county. Now the pupils could once more attend a school twelve miles away.

An Oldsmobile truck and a Ford truck provided transportation in one community.

The following illustrations preserve the story of bygone days in one county school system:

During the years 1900 to 1924 in a rural area a school was organized. This school is known to have developed, not only the *first form of school transportation* in this county, but also the first in the state. During this same period this school became not only the first *consolidated* school in the county, but also the first in the state.

It is said that three of the outstanding leaders in the community, who were also members of the school board, visited another state to investigate a type of transportation being used there. Following their visit, their own school developed a horse-or-mule-drawn wagon type of vehicle, which was used until the beginning of the present mode of school bus transportation.

The coming of the buses brought new duties and exasperating experiences for the teachers, especially for the men. This story is from a retired principal:

One day during my first year of teaching the principal became ill. . . . Said the principal to me, "Chum, serve as principal today. Stick around the office when you are not teaching, and look after the school buses." So the day began.

After learning that a bus was mired deep in mud and after having received instructions by way of a visit to the ailing principal's bedside, the substitute principal was met by a mud-spattered runner who had a report. A bus, loaded to the hilt with school children, was in a ditch with the youngsters screaming their heads off with fear.

Returning from a trip to the sick principal, the principal-for-the-day found a "rather bewildered youth mumbling that their bus had exploded a mile away "and was belching like a volcano." Another quick conference with the sick principal yielded this advice, "Tell the driver to let the motor cool for thirty minutes; then pour water into the radiator and drive to school. Tell the children to walk the mile." The children walked.

Still another bus had flat tires, and the at-home principal had still another conference. Finally, the bewildered teacher received this advice from the harassed principal: "I am sick, never been sicker. But if I am going to be compelled to run the school anyway, I'll get up and do my work while miserating. Get back to your classroom duties. I hope you understand teaching, much better than you do dealing with school buses."

Later, as a principal himself, the above teacher secured the help of the school board in dividing his district into "spheres of influence" in order to insure proficiency in bus service. All went well until one day a blizzard struck. . . . Trees were hanging low; telephone wires had snapped; and the ground was covered with a thick glaze of mist. The teacher, now principal, went to school but entertained no thought of school that day. That was entirely out of the question.

But the buses came to school. The first bus put on chains and delivered the children at the school door. The second bus arrived empty with a driver who inquired whether or not they would have school. Then the coordinator for the five "spheres of influence" appeared in a pick-up truck with this triumphant report: "I have been personally to every driver's home. We are to have school. Buses not here will arrive." The buses came—just after 12:00 noon. What a day for the principal!

A high school teacher recalls that "One cold, rainy, and sleety day one of the buses turned over. No one was seriously hurt," but "there was very little school that day because we teachers were acting as nurses and helping the students get over shock."

One teacher relates that

> in 1926, there were no buses nor any type of transportation for blacks. A man and woman were hired at the price of fifteen cents per child to transport pupils who lived over a mile from the school each way. . . . After talking to the superintendent of county schools and committee members, they decided to remedy the situation. Blacks were bussed, too.

From a principal of a school came this account of a chilling experience with transportation: A teacher had left five Head Start children alone in a car for a few minutes, two in the front seat and three in the back.

> Soon after she left the car, someone yelled, "Look-a-yonder!"
>
> One of the children in the front seat (it was assumed) pulled the gear shift lever of the car into reverse. Immediately the car began to go around and around backward in a circle of about a hundred feet in circumference. . . . I, of course, was called to the scene immediately.
>
> The chief of police was called, and he suggested we call one of the larger wreckers in town, asking them to pull in behind the car and meet it bumper to bumper. This seemed a good scheme to stop the car, but what about the five children in the car?
>
> I placed myself just as close to the path where the car was rotating as possible. I then proceeded to tell the children, (who were frightened but not frantic), our plan and asked those in the front seat to climb over the seat into the back, which they did. Then I asked all five children to lie down flat on the floor between the seats, which they did.
>
> The wrecker then pulled into the backward path of the Ford; and when the impact was made, the car stopped still. . . . The children were not hurt.
>
> We did not count the trips which the car made, but it was estimated at between 150 and 175 trips around the circle.

A county librarian called herself a "peddler of books" whose "book truck was a Model A Ford with a small box for books on each running board and a big box on the back." Her bi-weekly route included Knott's Island and Corolla Beach.

Like the proverbial postman, no matter what the weather or the circumstances, teachers and students kept their appointed schedules and went to school.

Meeting Individual Needs

Children always had many individual needs, needs that were peculiar to their own personalities and circumstances; and individual teachers devised individual solutions for individual needs.

A former first-grade teacher remembers that her most rewarding experience was in knowing that she taught children to read "who had never seen a book before they entered school."

And imagine the plight of the teacher who discovered she had a student who could speak no English. Here is how she managed:

When Mario entered my room, he knew one English word, "come." He was a very observant child, very eager to learn to communicate with his classmates. When others were speaking, he tried to read their lips and make the sounds they made even though he did not understand what they meant.

We began working with pictures he was familiar with, associating English words with them. We continued this process until he had a speakable vocabulary. The children . . . helped in the classroom and on the playground. His father was a marine, and he was transferred to the marine base in five months with Mario having "an unbelievable English vocabulary."

Holidays have always provided teachers with challenges to overcome handicaps and still give the students the excitement and pleasure they anticipated and deserved.

A teacher during Depression days recounts that one year when it snowed at Christmas the children "persuaded their parents to take mules and clear the snow off the roads (or paths) from their homes to the school" so they could have their Christmas "goodies" and their Christmas tree. The "goodies" were "a small colored bag with an orange, apple, hard candy and nuts." After the party the teacher mounted her horse and rode home alone, a distance of three or four miles, partially cleared of snow.

A high school guidance counselor faced a delicate personal problem. A mother in an affluent family had decided that her daughter, a high school senior of average ability and well-developed social attitudes, must go to a university, noted for its academic quality. The girl found excuses to keep from taking college board tests. The counselor understood the girl's fear of a highly academic university, and suggested to the perplexed mother that she "select a small group of less prestigious colleges of which you approve, where the numbers are not so great, where the pressures are not so heavy as at some of the institutions which have such demanding requirements."

The mother followed the advice and then "on Thursday morning, before the opening of school, she met me in the hall with this question:

Do you have a catalogue of College _____?
Yes, would you like to see it?

On the way to the guidance office the girl confided,

My mother and I were talking this morning at breakfast about colleges, and I got interested in _____. The girl decided to go to _____, and mother, father, counselor, and the young woman were all happy with the results.

Cleanliness was often a problem for which teachers had to find solutions. Sometimes the solutions did not work.

Noticing that a child needed "special cleanliness emphasis," a teacher ordered free materials to implement cleanliness teaching, including the whole class in the project. "After an enthusiastic presentation each child was given a chart and a small bar of Lifebouy soap to take home."

The next morning during health inspection the teacher observed that the boy still had very dirty hands and nails. She inquired about the soap she had given him, and he replied: "Pa said it smelt like a horsepital, and he would give me a nickel if I would throw it as far in the field as I could send it."

During routine health screening a teacher discovered that a child's tonsils were greatly enlarged. When she questioned him, the child told her his tonsils had been removed by Dr. B———. The teacher recognized the name of the doctor as that of a veterinarian.

During the Depression many children came to school from homes where no member of the family was employed. An annoyed teacher complained to the principal about some children who "came to school poorly dressed and not very clean," and whose faces and hands were very dirty. The principal answered, "Would you wash your face each morning if you had to break ice in the pan of water before you washed?"

"After that," said the teacher, "I kept soap and cloths for children to use after they came to school. I realized that school was the warmest, cleanest, and, probably, the happiest part of their lives."

Teachers recognized the many-sided needs of children, and stretched their imaginations and, often, their pocketbooks to try to meet those needs.

> During all my years of teaching, I tried to teach the whole child. In my one-room schools I was able to teach sewing, art, and other needed experiences. The boys were taught to build bird houses, doll houses, and make some small furniture for each room. The girls made their own clothes, panties, slips, dresses, hats and gloves. They also made small curtains for the doll houses. They made their own cookbooks. . . . They made herb medical books that told them how to use them.

A warm-hearted generous teacher used an unusual method to inspire black boys to finish high school:

> During my teaching in this small school, we did not have a high school for blacks. I promised every boy who would finish high school, I would give him his shoes to march in. To my happy surprise, several of them went into other counties and finished high school. I gladly gave them their shoes.

> Later, we had a makeshift high school. I challenged one class that, if the boys would finish high school, they would get shoes, and if they finished college, they would get a suit to march in. I gave away

many pairs of shoes. To my surprise, one young man notified me to buy the suit. I was happy to do it.

In some cases the teacher discovered many years after he or she had performed a kindness that the act had made a real difference in the lives of their one-time students.

Such was the case of one teacher who recalled a visit from a former under-achiever 6th-grade-student who came by to show her his high school diploma from a technical school. He reviewed his many problems over the years. He had been expelled from high school and had spent some time in prison for burglary.

> He reminisced and told me how I had encouraged him to paint a picture of a ship which won for him a blue ribbon; and I found "tall stories" in the library for him to read and later tell the class; how I went to church revivals with him at night so he could be recognized for bringing the largest number of visitors.

> Because you believed in me, I have earned this diploma by studying bit by bit at night for years. I came by to thank you for your lasting influence that caused me to reach for high goals.

Then there was the high school football coach who remembered an afternoon when an unruly gang of boys, mostly dropouts, came to watch his boys practice football. The antics of the gang were very disturbing to his team; so he went to the crowd and ordered them to "Scram." All except one big brawny fellow immediately turned to leave. The husky lad, with a dazed expression said, "I'd like to play that."

After a little questioning, the coach assured the stranger that he could be reinstated in school and play football. But the boy blurted out, "I can't do that—just look at me! I'd be the goat of the school with these rags on, and this is all I've got. No!! I just couldn't do that."

The coach asked him to wait around after practice. The boy waited, and the coach who was the same size as the boy took him home and fitted him with clothes from his own closet.

The boy came to school the next day immaculately dressed. He played football and he was a success! He had stamina, school spirit, old football guts, and a compelling desire to win.

The boy became a grammar school teacher, loved young people and championed their causes. Asked how he became so involved with youth, he replied, "When I was a wayward boy, an unknown friend snatched me from the dark alleys, gave me his own clothes to wear, and planted my feet on higher ground. I can do no less."

A former superintendent of schools in an Eastern North Carolina city went into court to help a boy.

> One day while a boarding school principal, I was called to the telephone. A court solicitor . . . said "Mr. W_____, we need you in court today. One of your students is involved in the case just starting. He is B_____ W_____. Do you know him?"
>
> "Why, yes, a fine boy."
>
> The principal went to the courtroom, and saw the boy in the witness chair. The boy was being questioned about having a gun near a still, and had said he "was a-squirrell huntin'!"
>
> After undisguised merriment over the answer, the judge called the principal to the stand.
>
> "Now, then," said the judge, "what kind of boy have we here?"
>
> The principal replied, "A fine, hard-working boy, who wants to amount to something."
>
> "Well," said the judge, "what possessed this fellow to leave school and go slinking out to a filthy still?"
>
> The principal replied, "Forced into it by his father. Sir, when you and I were 17, we'd have obeyed *our* fathers, no matter what they required us to do."

Before the coming of compulsory immunizations, there was always the problem of epidemics. "Often schools had to be closed because of epidemics of such diseases as measles, mumps, scarlet fever, whooping cough, and diphtheria. Often students would fail to pass their grades because of these diseases." Every teacher automatically accepted the duties of part-time nurse.

Teachers were well aware of the relationship between the emotional lives of their students and their academic achievement. Many teachers remembered non-academic experiences which developed emotional sensitivities and provided the means for some excellent teaching opportunities.

A poignant story of the death of a bird which collided with the schoolroom window pane illustrates how a meaningful experience to children can be used to teach skills and facts, as well as to inspire interest in new fields. The class provided a casket, dug a grave, and buried the bird in a funeral ceremony which featured music and poetry which they themselves had selected.

For the remainder of the year, the children were most interested in birds. In the spring a girl brought in a red-winged blackbird with a broken wing. An interested parent donated a cage; a local veterinarian prescribed treatment; but most help came from the editor-in-chief of an encyclopedia. For ten weeks the children followed the editor's instructions; and when the bird, "Crip," was well enough, he was released to the free world of nature.

Academically, the teacher observed that vocabularies improved; geography was learned through maps of flyways; the speech choir learned bird poems; children became interested in recordings of bird songs, and piano students learned to play bird songs; bird portraits were painted; and bird houses were made. A bird Christmas tree was decorated with cranberries, popcorn and doughuts. Most important of all, the children developed a permanent interest in conservation and the natural world.

A first-grade teacher used an experience with nature as a springboard for an ancedote to inspire creativity and self-confidence in a child. She recalls a boy who had a hostility for books until, one day, she took her class for a walk in the park. There the boy was enthralled with catching minnows from a brook. Back in the classroom the teacher used the story of "Tim Tadpole and the Great Bullfrog" to inspire the child to believe that reading was fun and he could read.

A high school teacher, confronted with a boy whose mother had always helped him too much, found a simple remedy when his mother could no longer help him with his algebra. The teacher suggested that the mother provide "a suitable time and place for him to study, and to see that he did so daily." It worked.

In one school system a resourceful superintendent solved the need for books for the libraries. The project began with a symposium to choose books. An exhibit was prepared with the help of the book center of a university, the state Library Association, an interested publishing company, and the administration of the county schools.

Children, teachers, and parents came to examine the books. A night session was known as "Book Night for Parents and School Patrons." Books were chosen in cooperation with teachers. When the books came, they were processed in "assembly-line" fashion with inexperienced people processing over 40 books an hour. Over 1700 books were processed by this method, and because of enlarged libraries six elementary schools were accredited in five years. This school system was one of five school systems selected to help film the movie "Let's Visit School Libraries."

Community resources were tapped for many needs of the schools. A teacher says he used all the community to help—"the postmaster, the policemen, lawyers, doctors, business men, bankers, building and loan men, beauticians, ministers, nurses. All these people came on different occasions to lecture to my students."

Banking personnel worked with teachers to teach children habits of thrift by having banking days in their classrooms. One teacher recalled that

> saving was always taught in my schools, and Monday was banking day. The children brought what money they earned doing different chores for their parents or neighbors over the weekend to school. It was put in the bank. At the end of the spring school term each child was given a check for the money he had saved. Prizes for 1st, 2nd, 3rd were awarded to those who had saved the most. The parents let their children open savings accounts by adding to these accounts, and when they were ready for high school, they were allowed to use their savings or continue to add to the amount.

One attendance worker echoes praise for community help. In connection with her work she "kept one civic club informed about the community children's needs. This club allocated fifteen hundred dollars yearly to be used for the benefit of the school children—most of which money was used to buy shoes and clothes."

The same attendance worker recalled with great satisfaction how

the climate of the community made for strong, high quality schools. There was constant cooperation on the part of neighborhood families, the neighborhood stores, the neighborhood churches, the community clubs, the city officials, and the school administration.

Inspiring Citizenship

As citizens with rights and great potential, children were taught to respect their history, love their country, and be loyal to their institutions.

As one teacher expressed it:

I found early in my teaching career that I could combine my language arts, crafts, and music and history in such a way that students did not realize how much of the history of our country they were learning. . . . I think I began the first excursion to mills. These children really did research on whatever we were going to see, whether it was an annual picnic to Kings Mountain Battleground or a trip to Old Salem. The next day was given over to quiet reading, study, art, poetry, prose, diaries, stories; and many learning experiences of value came from these field trips.

Another patriotic teacher reported how one 7th grade got so interested in American history that they prepared a tape and display and sent it to the Freedom Foundation at Valley Forge, where they won an award. A citizen gave $600.00 to charter a bus to take students to Valley Forge.

About this time the doctor made me give up that work, and I was given a class of highly gifted 7th graders in another school. I led this class and school in another intensive history study which also won a Valley Forge award.

Among black teachers in particular there were those who strove mightily to give their students an exalted vision of the true greatness of their country. They found ways to do it.

A history teacher at a state university describes her efforts:

I wanted to have a flag raising and an outdoor patriotic program. I wrote the script. The veterans gave a flag, and a citizen in the community gave the pole. . . . The program was held outside. A college band furnished the music, and there was a guest speaker. Over three hundred people of all races witnessed the program . . .

Also, annually, a brotherhood supper was held on February 22. People invited were religious educators. Deans of men and women, black and white, came from the colleges nearby, bringing some of the international students dressed in their national costumes. All this gave me an opportunity to teach love and interest to our international students, letting them understand that all races could meet together in America in brotherhood.

Teachers recognized the importance of the flag as a symbol of this nation, and acted to enhance reverence for it. One teacher declares that

My classroom flag was on display each day . . . Before the work began each day, we learned to stand properly and pledge allegiance to the flag and follow this by singing, with the recorder, the stirring arrangement by the Chicago Symphony orchestra of the "Star Spangled Banner." All during the years each class studied the story of the flag—how to display it and respect it . . .

Especially in the troublous '60's teachers were concerned about the disrespect being shown the flag. A veteran teacher describes his joy when, in Britain, he met "officers of some of America's mightiest naval vessels anchored in the mouth of the Clyde River (1957) all flying the American Flag." This veteran teacher saw the need "to learn the difference in flag protocol and flag anti-discrimination laws . . . and decide what attitude to take about flag gimmicks that are all about us." He observed that others, sometimes even campaigning politicians, violated the rules for the display of the flag.

"My foremost thought in everything I taught or did was to build good human relations and love for our country, to teach each community that togetherness is the only way we can build good citizenship and keep America a great country" is how one teacher summed up his concept of the teacher's role in teaching today's young citizens.

Thus, in many ways and in many circumstances—some simple, some baffling—teachers found ways to contribute to the development of human personalities above and beyond the prescribed learning in the classroom.

MY FIRST ENCOUNTER WITH PANTYHOSE

As principal of a large combined high school and elementary school, it was not unusual for students to come to my office for first aid treatment.

One day a little girl in about the 6th grade came in with a skinned knee. It was bleeding and covered with dirt from the fall on the ground. When I told her that I could clean it much better if she would take the torn hose off—as I had done over the years—, she became excited and seemed to be actually frightened. This was very strange because children responded to such a request with no reaction at all. I completed the first aid as well as I could over and through the torn hose.

It was not until I told my wife about the incident that I learned about the "newfangled" pantyhose the girls were wearing.

VOICES

The Junior English class was in progress when the teacher asked, "How many voices do we have in English, Tom?"

"Mrs. J., we have four voices in English."

"Name them, please," requested Mrs. J.

"Alto, soprano, bass and tenor," replied Tom.

XI ☙ Serving All Children

Curriculum for Education for All Exceptionalities

Teachers, as well as parents, have always had a special concern for children who were mentally or physically incapable of relating to school requirements and activities on an equal basis with the average child. In recent years educators have realized that gifted youngsters also have special needs, and most recently have begun to make provisions for the emotionally disturbed.

A retired state supervisor for education for the exceptional child furnished this information:

> Although residential education of the blind and deaf had been provided from state funds as early as 1845, exceptional children did not begin receiving special education in the public schools from state funds specifically allocated for this purpose until the beginning of the 1949–50 school year. Prior to that year a few local school units had employed some special teachers for mentally or physically-handicapped children.
>
> In 1947 the General Assembly enacted Chapter 818 of the Public School Laws which laid the foundation for the establishment of a state-wide program except the salary for the director of the state program and one secretary. In 1948 a division director was appointed.
>
> For the 1949–50 school year the State Board of Education allotted 25 teaching positions to be used in serving handicapped children. These positions, along with 30 additional positions funded locally, served crippled, educable retarded, visually-impaired, speech-impaired, and hearing-impaired children.
>
> The 1954 General Assembly enacted legislation to enable local boards of education to operate programs for trainable mentally-

handicapped children and approved funds of $300 per child per year. In 1961 the legislature provided special state funds for the education of exceptionally gifted and talented children, and the remaining years of the decade saw state-funded special education services grow to embrace programs for emotionally-disturbed, learning-disabled, homebound, and hospitalized children as well.

An act of 1974 established the right of children with special needs to equal educational opportunities in the public schools.

Years before the State funded such a program, in one city an admirable combination of teacher initiative, community resourcefulness, and business-world cooperation provided for the mentally retarded. This city set up a Special School for mentally retarded children in 1954 as a private institution co-sponsored by the local Association of Parents and Friends of Retarded Children and the local Woman's Club.

Concentrating upon helping the trainable retarded, this Special School was housed in a space at the local college, and was under the direction of a board composed of a psychologist, a psychiatrist, public officials and business men. The board provided scholarships of $300 per pupil per year.

A teacher, assisted by a 16 year-old retarded girl, taught the six retarded children.

> The program included habit training, music, field trips and social events. Areas included in the curriculum were: control of emotions, proper ways to work and play, good manners, social adeptness, academic readiness and progress, good health and hygiene, harmonious group relationship and happiness.

Because of increasing enrollment in 1955 a second and third classroom were added through the cooperation of the college. To fill the need for trained teachers this college began a training program for Special Education. Two businessmen raised the needed money. This course was the only complete undergraduate course in North Carolina leading to an A certificate in the teaching of speech-handicapped and mentally-retarded children.

The community at large responded. Parents and teachers appeared on TV stations, telling of the school and its needs. In

1956–57 the Special School received $9,460.00 from the United Fund. In March, 1957, the United Fund authorized this Special School, and the community began a campaign for $50,000. A member of the Woman's Club designed a special Christmas card and sponsored sale of cards. Three printings of the card sent Season's Greetings to 40,500 people. Bridge benefits, a puppy sale, and projects by the Junior Chamber of Commerce, a civic club and others assured raising of funds.

By October, 1956, a near-by city joined efforts with the original Parents and Friends of Retarded Children and began a drive for a part of the state school funds. Working with the State Superintendent, an appeal was made to the General Assembly. In 1957 the legislature appropriated $330,000 for the establishment of schools for the trainable retarded.

When the fire department condemned the facilities at the college, four churches in the community offered the use of their facilities. In 1957 the Special School opened at one of the churches where classrooms, auditorium, kitchen and recreational facilities were all available. A city park nearby was also used.

In 1959 the Special School moved to an elementary school. The students used all facilities at the school but on a different schedule. They took part in school clean-up programs, safety patrol, fire drills, and other activities. The older children at the school planted a garden. They took field trips, built bird houses, and planned special celebrations such as birthday parties.

In the history of this Special School a local teacher names more than 80 organizations which helped and continue to help. What a tribute to community concern and cooperation!

This city was not alone in having a special school. Such schools existed in other communities. One of these cities started its first class in 1954. There the class was housed in an elementary school. A teacher with broad experience in elementary education journeyed to Raleigh and helped to set up a curriculum for the North Carolina Trainable Classes. This school system provided in-service training for the teacher, and also cooperated with special training when this became available at a North Carolina college.

In retrospect the pioneering teacher observed that "The majority of trainable adults, who have graduated from the public school program," are "neatly self-groomed and dressed and partially self-supporting members to home and community."

In 1970 a project in another school system was one of 34 projects in North Carolina "to determine the effectiveness of the Resource Program in teaching the educable retarded students." This beginning of diagnostic and prescriptive teaching for Educable Mental Retarded (EMR) children spread throughout the county, and this school was used as a model for other schools having similar programs.

A worker for two years with the resource center program in this school described the experience as the "icing on the cake" of her teaching career. Another teacher of the EMR in another community thanked "God for letting me live to be a part of this work," and said the best Christmas present she ever had was a Christmas card made by one of her students.

While the state was gradually awakening to its responsibilities to the exceptional child, teachers in the community-sponsored special classes for the mentally and physically handicapped were transforming the once-forgotten children into contributing members of their schools and communities. Warmhearted, alert teachers devised programs, responded to individual needs, and solicited help and materials from sympathetic communities.

In the 1930's little provision was made for under-achievers in the school systems. One class in a high school was called 8BX and was made up of students whose IQ's ranged from 60 to 70 and who were too old to stay in normal classes. Enrollment was limited to 15.

Among the students assigned to her 8BX class one year, the teacher recognized a boy who appeared to have average intelligence and had scored 85 on an IQ test, but who could work only on 4th grade level or below. The boy had a father who was a serviceman and an uninterested mother. He had always been a failure, and no one cared.

The teacher arranged for him to go to "woodwork an hour each day, and there he was expected to do his best. He was also thrown with a class of normal children." After three years in her class, the boy went to a normal 8th-grade class. Four years later the teacher attended his high school graduation, and eight years later, he graduated from a university in North Carolina.

A bewildered high school teacher in one of the large school systems of the state learned when she reported for work in September that she was to have a special class of students, age 14 to 19, and with IQ's of 70 and below. One student was a bright Greek boy who knew no English.

At the first break in her school day the principal came and told the teacher she was to teach half a day and do crafts in the afternoon. He gave her $5.00 to buy "hammers, saws, crochet needles," and she "could do only one crochet stitch, could not hammer, could not saw" and at that moment "could not speak one word."

But the teacher's resourcefulness and help from the community solved problems that looked insurmountable. A furniture industry furnished veneer scraps for plaques; a lumber company gave discarded planks; paint stores gave paint and varnish; a factory supplied T-shirt strips to crochet rugs; and supply houses gave metal barrel tops.

> A young man from the city traffic department came to school and helped construct the model of a highway on a large table, complete with small cars and traffic signs—the works. A young electrician brought all materials and spent a few hours each day until every boy had made his own little motor.

At the end of the school year the teacher was disappointed that the community did not seem interested in providing jobs for her students. Today she is grateful for more community concern, special schools for special children, highly trained teachers to work with them, materials furnished to serve the special needs of special children. Above all she is happy that now the social needs of these once-ignored children are recognized—happy also that school systems, churches, social agencies, and civic organizations provide special services for special needs, such as sheltered workshops, classes for pregnant girls, and home-bound teaching for bed-ridden children.

The teacher hoped that others had learned what she had learned: "to practice compassion without pity," to "listen and hear," to "emphasize with humility and gratitude," to "appreciate students in perspective relative to their backgrounds and ambitions."

The teacher found her students fiercely loyal to each other and to her. The greatest personal satisfaction, however, came every day when they said they loved her.

In 1965 a teacher took over the first class of trainable children in her county. Many of the children, who ranged in age from 6 to 21 years, were physically handicapped in some way. One was subject to convulsions, and some had compulsions to destructiveness.

Some were in wheel chairs; many had speaking and hearing problems; several were on tranquilizers; one boy weighed 325 pounds; a ten-year-old weighed 46. The children were happy and loved coming to school where they could learn to take care of their personal needs.

The teacher of this challenging class for ten years described those years as the "most wonderful and rewarding years of my life." The reason? The teacher's explanation was simple: "We all spoke the language of love," and "it is unbelievable how much love has been given and taken in working with them."

From a small eastern town came the story of how a teacher taught the unteachable child. A boy was considered retarded because of a speech defect. When he came to her room in the first grade, the child had already been refused by Head Start, kindergarten, and another first-grade teacher in the same school. A righteously-angered father brought his child back to school and demanded that he be taught. The teacher taught him as a class of one; and to the amazement of everyone, he learned to read and write. At last report the unteachable child was still moving along slowly but surely.

As in other communities before the state began providing funds for special education classes, a teacher of such a class enjoyed much support in the community. With locally-supplied materials the class was able in a short while "to sell enough baskets, book ends, magazine racks, bird houses, and Christmas decorations to keep our workshop in operation."

According to the teacher her most fulfilling moment came when the class started a wildlife project with the assistance of the North Carolina Wildlife Commission. Game wardens came and instructed the class in game laws. The *North Carolina Wildlife Magazine* featured them "in a centerfold article on our wildlife project, with pictures of our class in action."

The most noticeable handicap for a child is being crippled, and retired teachers remembered, with satisfaction and pride, experiences with crippled children.

A veteran teacher of twenty-five years in an orthopedic hospital described the "many happy days as a teacher in the hospital."

In addition to academic work a highlight of the year was a Christmas party, given by a large department store.

> This had been the custom for over forty years. As many as forty ambulances from the city and surrounding areas, and many, many automobiles were needed to take the one hundred and forty children to the party. The sirens were blowing now and then to give the children a thrill they were never to forget.

There were also trips to concerts and the circus made possible by a local civic club.

Teaching at the hospital, the teacher said, enabled her to see how children blossomed out during their hospital stays, emerging from shy introverts to outgoing persons interested in themselves as well as in those around them.

In remembering their experiences teachers of the handicapped frequently cited examples of youngsters who inspired them by their courage and resourcefulness.

Such was the first class for crippled children in one county in 1954. After taking special training for the work, the teacher contacted the parents of about twelve children who were unable to attend classes in school. All of the parents were willing for their children to attend a special class.

The class began with eight girls and four boys. Ages ranged from seven to fifteen in grades one through seven. The handicaps consisted of cerebral palsy, congenital deformities, heart deficiencies, hardness of hearing, and muscular distrophy. They used crutches, tripods, and wheel chairs. There were beds in the room for the heart patients who needed a great deal of rest.

Among the students "was a little boy seven years old whose legs had not developed. . . . The first day of school he told me he was there to learn. He knew he would have to earn a living when he grew up, and it would have to be with his head." Both legs had to be amputated later, but the boy kept learning, went on to college and was successful after college.

The boy with muscular distrophy had perfect attendance for three years. His father had to carry him to school and place him in a wheel chair in which he was strapped to keep him from falling out. "He never complained, laughed a lot, and was a great favorite with the other children."

A forty-one year veteran teacher and principal remembered with utmost admiration a girl paralyzed from her head down with polio. In spite of her handicaps, the girl wished to continue her education. The mother agreed to do her writing for her, and to place books on a rack for her to keep up her regular assignments. Faculty members agreed to give an hour any day they were assigned to give her individual instruction, sometimes during school hours, before school, after school or on Saturday.

When she graduated from high school, she held one of the three top grade averages for her four years in high school. She went on to college and graduated from a university.

A retired teacher paid tribute to the classmates of a spastic child. As a result of classroom experiences and the respect and help of other children, the spastic lost her fears and no longer jumped and jerked at unusual sounds, enjoyed association with other children and held her own with her normal classmates.

Since 1845 provisions have been made for institutions for the deaf. By an act of 1973 the General Assembly placed the three deaf schools under the jurisdiction of the Department of Human Resources. The three North Carolina schools for the deaf are the Eastern School in Wilson, the Central School in Greensboro, and the North Carolina School in Morganton. The Eastern and Central Schools are elementary only, with graduates going to Morganton to complete their work. In addition there are twenty-three Pre-School Satellite Centers throughout the state where parents and pupils alike can go for guidance.

The state has had institutions for the blind since 1848; however, until recently there were no provisions for the partially blind. This responsibility was left to individual community initiative.

> For about fifteen years (1945–1960) there were two classes for the partially-seeing child in a public school of a major city—a class for the blacks and one for the whites. The classes were located in the public elementary schools and were a normal part of the system's plans. The teachers were employed on a regular basis and received their regular scheduled salaries with a supplement from the North Carolina Commission for the Blind. A local civic club was quite prominent in establishing the classes.

They awarded scholarships for the special teacher training, and provided equipment and decoration for the classrooms.

Eligibility for membership in the classes depended upon three factors:
1. Vision: A score of between 20/70 and 20/200 on the Snellen E chart in the better eye after all treatment and refraction.
2. Recommendation by an ophthalmologist.
3. Normal intelligence.

One child in every 500 school population is the norm for the incidence of partially-seeing children.

There were also temporary members of the class. These included children recovering from eye operations, those receiving treatment (unless contagious) and those who needed special care in the re-use of eyes.

A former teacher of the sight-saving class described the procedures and curriculum in this manner:

> Since precious vision is to be saved as much as possible, the tool subjects (reading, arithmetic, spelling, and writing) were required, and normal grade procedure and progress were expected. History, geography, art, and music were listening subjects and were as often as possible participated in by each student in the partially-sighted group going into the classroom of his grade level, listening to the discussion and explanations, bringing the assignment back to his home room and doing them under optimum conditions. The program was both individual and cooperative. This unique plan gave the child opportunities to participate in classes of his own age group, to become a part of the whole school, and to assume responsibilities and roles in the total environment.

One group of children whose special needs have often gone unrecognized is the gifted. North Carolina was a leader in research and development of programs for the gifted and in providing an educational program that would fit their needs. In 1961 the General Assembly allocated funds for this work.

An elementary teacher of the gifted explains that . . .

> Identification became crucial. It was found that the talented child could be anyone's child, and that he may live under any circumstances. That generally he is highly verbal, individualistic, critical, independent, able to think abstractly, to conceptualize, and to extrapolate. He is a child of keen sensitivity and intense awareness, is often shy, modest, and may have a poor opinion of himself. He is culturally orientated, and if given opportunity can perform well in such areas as music, art, drama, dance, and creative writing.

> Their potential does not alter the fact that they generally develop physically as other children and must be so accepted. Because of this, in North Carolina, the program for these children is not one of acculturation generally, but one of depth and enrichment. The basic subject matter is the same as that of the regular curriculum. However, students are given extra supplementary materials. "They quickly learn resource skills," and they "sort, analyze, record and communicate their findings, then further refine them at sophisti-

cated levels." His freedom to pursue his individual interest is all the motivation needed. The learning process becomes an exciting one and recurrently the child must be brought back to the level of his skills. His ability to conceptualize and to think abstractly are above his grade level.

This teacher feels that the future of mankind lies with the gifted children, for it is "their God-given abilities which will, when mature, search for the solutions to the problems of tomorrow as tirelessly as their fertile minds search for the lesser problems in their classrooms today."

In another elementary school system a teacher told how special attention to two gifted children resulted in a research project on "Pioneer Life in America," which the gifted researchers freely shared with the other children.

> I found, that the outstanding characteristic of gifted children is the number and variety of their hobbies with educational value. Some of their hobbies were crop growing, athletics, animal raising, bird study, butterfly collection.
>
> The two children were anxious to work with me as helpers. For fifteen minutes daily, they worked with the slow-learners with one phase of their reading under my supervision.

In the summer of 1963 the first session of the summer school for the academically and artistically-talented high school students opened in Winston-Salem on the Salem College campus. It was called the Governor's School because it was one of many new educational projects supported by Governor Terry Sanford.

In the beginning years funds were provided by a $225,000 grant from the Carnegie Foundation and another $225,000 from individuals and foundations. Since that time the General Assembly has provided funds.

The students were carefully chosen—first at the high school level and then were subject to further screening and auditions before committees before acceptance. IQ's generally ranged from 130 to 160. The school's enrollment was—and is—limited to 400. In later years the student body has been required to reflect racial balance.

The academically-gifted studies in five fields: English, foreign language, mathematics, natural sciences, and social science. The artistically-talented also participate in five fields: art, drama, dance, choral music, and instrumental music. The study experience was a plus, not a repeat. Each faculty member planned his course, subject to the approval of the director.

One of the first teachers at the Governor's School gives this account:

> The students, both academic and artistically-talented, concentrated on their respective areas for three hours each morning, Monday through Friday, with extensive work in a field outside their principal interest in the afternoons. In addition they were exposed to seminars, speeches, and discussions cutting across the lines of the academic and artistic disciplines. Distinguished persons from all parts of the nation (and occasionally from abroad) came to speak with the students. Many of them stayed on the campus for several days, visited classes, and mingled and talked with the students.

The students had an elected student government, published a weekly newspaper and "enjoyed a wide-ranging sports program under excellent supervision, as well as a well planned social program." Local colleges, industries and civic agencies also offered activities.

A former coordinator for the program at the Governor's School stated that the purpose of the school was to "Open Windows onto the Future" by emphasizing three areas: 1. The area of special aptitude development; 2. The area of general intellectual development; and 3. The area of personal and social development.

Like the elementary teacher of the gifted, the coordinator of the Governor's School saw the gifted students as our leaders for the future and planned activities with this in mind. As he put it:

> The Governor's School seeks to open windows onto the future for the State's most gifted youngsters, seeking thus to prepare them for the productive roles they will be playing in the 20th Century Revolution, which is fast snow-balling toward the fantastic future of the 21st Century.

Teachers were indeed concerned for the special needs of the mentally and physically handicapped and the need for broad enrichment programs for the gifted—the so-called "exceptional" children; but teachers knew that every child is an exceptional child. They testified that in working with standard curricula, they strove for flexibility and broad exposure to individual interests; and in developing methods, they aimed at providing opportunities for individual assignments and projects.

One teacher stated that it was hard to remember any general conversation among teachers in which no teacher failed to express regret that, working with children with unusual needs in large classes, kept them from giving as much individual attention to the "average" child as they wished to give.

> I remember the day the guidance counselor asked me about Tommy. I had taught him in United States history three years before. At the moment I could not recall him; later I remembered. Tommy was the frail boy with the eager blue eyes, who never asked a question or volunteered a contribution but was always prepared, always respectful, and always cooperative. He never needed extra help nor indicated a desire for special attention; but the eager blue eyes and the consistently efficient preparation indicated a deep interest in learning, and suggested a mind teeming with latent ambition—cautious, but none the less intense. I often remember Tommy and wonder what he discovered about himself as his personality evolved.
>
> I remember also the children who had so much in common with one another that they were able to work together harmoniously, accept regulations in good faith, and enjoy sports and social events with zest and assurance. These were the "average" students whose actions will give society stability or disorder; whose support or nonsupport will justify or thwart the efforts of the gifted; whose high percentage of votes will determine the quality of our governments; whose interpretation of our values and our institutions will ultimately determine the future of America.
>
> To fail the handicapped child is inhuman; to fail the gifted child is a tragedy; to fail the "average" child is societal suicide.

Thus, whether dealing with the special needs of the physically-handicapped, the emotionally-disturbed, the mentally-handicapped, or the typical, average child, teachers everywhere were impressed with the sensitivity of *every* child. They learned that the exceptional child tended to be responsive, and thrived on achievements as a result of opportunities geared to his abilities and his needs. They also learned that other children, parents, and the community were aware and eager to open for all exceptional children "Windows Onto the Future."

But teachers did not forget that *every* child is an exceptional child, and every child needs help and assurance in opening these windows.

GET ATTENTION FIRST

Children can sometimes be more logical than adults. One day our first grade was seated in the lunch room when the second grade came in. Tom jumped up, waved his hand and shouted, "Hey Jack!"

Very quietly I said to him, "Tom, you may wave to your friend, but don't shout."

Tom looked disgusted and said, "How's he going to know I'm here if I don't holler at him?"

A BACKSET

In a rural area, twin brothers were in the same classroom. Their cousin was in this room also. During the year the cousin had the mumps. One morning the teacher asked the twins how their cousin was. "He ain't doing good," they said. "He's real sick. Something is wrong with his back now." "What?" she asked. "We don't know. All we know is Mamma said he was worse off. She said he had a 'backset'."

XII ✺ Remembering Students

As They Were and as They Are

A teacher works by faith—faith to believe that what he teaches will be justified in the experiences of his students. Yet in remembering our experiences we find that while we were teaching they were also teaching us, and what they taught us not only enriched our experiences, but also opened vistas of meaning that we had not seen before.

Early in the teaching career of every teacher appears a strong determination not only to strive for high academic standards, but also to teach our students to think, to appreciate the truths of life as reflected in writing, and to enjoy developing their own powers of self expression.

Here is a very good example of such self expression given by a retired teacher from a nearby county:

When My Class Got Out of Hand

There was that afternoon in a high-school American history class when, according to my interpretation, the class got completely "out of hand." I was teaching in the late 60's in a school that had had severe integration problems. I do not remember the subject of the history lesson nor how we drifted into a discussion of the basic problems of integrating student bodies. Suddenly, I realized that the members in my class of racially mixed students were pouring forth their feelings about what they thought the real problems were and what means they thought should be used to solve integration problems.

The discussion was spirited, but not angry; personal, but not vindictive; open, but not prejudiced. Ideas came rapidly and each one seemed to release an idea in the mind of another student; yet not once did a student interrupt another, and never once did a student antagonize another.

For that class period they were apparently unaware that I existed. As enthusiasm arose and voices became stronger, I vainly tried to calm the interchange, fearing interference with other classes because of the "loudness" in my room. But the students were too caught up in their own discovery of common emotions and convictions to be influenced by me; and I myself soon became fascinated by the marvelous demonstration of freedom of ideas in action.

When the bell rang, my young philosophers mechanically picked up their belongings and kept on talking as they left the room. One boy was already in the hall when he looked back and declared, "Best class we ever had!"

Looking back, I realize that my history class that afternoon demonstrated what teaching is all about. We learn facts in order to gain meanings beyond facts, and experience emotions to discover emotions deeper than those of everyday experience.

There comes some pride and also some joy as one sees in the lives of past pupils fulfillment of plans and ambitions stirred in those days. Some, of course, were ambitious and eager for the best that life had to offer; some were mediocre in so far as desire for book knowledge; however each had his own potential for an important self.

As retired teachers, if we had one tiny part in starting these young people on the road to success and happiness, we ask no greater or more significant reward.

EXCERPTS FROM RECOLLECTIONS

Reflections

My 43 years as a fourth grade teacher were enjoyable and rewarding. I recall one experience in my early days that had a profound and lasting influence on me. I had observed a third grade boy with a noticeably enlarged head, with an eye rolled in. He was a loner, unattractive and rather awkward. I instinctively hoped I would never have him in my classroom. When the time came for promotions, I said, "Lord, don't give this boy to me," but the all-wise Father did just that! Then I prayed, "Lord give me the grace, the courage, the understanding to love this child and help him," and the Lord answered my prayer. I soon felt that Tim was a special charge given to me. My class also accepted the challenge of his needs and Tim's response was evident, in the classroom and on the playground.

I can truthfully and gratefully say that this experience caused me to be more compassionate, patient, understanding and loving with all the students I have been privileged to teach.

A. G.

School had been in session several weeks and I had enrolled some forty first-graders, a bright lively group. One morning before the children arrived the superintendent entered with one of the nice ladies who lived near by, another lady I had never seen, and a small boy dressed a little differently from the other boys, short pants, suspenders, and a shirt of many colors, very clean and neat with a pair of beautiful bright blue eyes. I was introduced to the lady who could only speak broken English, Mrs. G. Her son was seven years old. He had never been to school. They were straight from Latvia.

My superintendent told me not to worry. He knew I had all I could do with the group I already had. Let the boy sit in the room; perhaps he could get something. A. G. could not speak a word of English and I could not speak his language.

Mrs. G——— left my school room with tears in her eyes. She took my hand and said, "A. G. must learn." This was all I could understand that she said. For the rest of the day A———'s eyes followed me. Every time I spoke he watched my lips. Every movement I made he watched. I became self conscious before the day was over. I didn't know how to reach him. Finally, I gave him crayons and art paper. His face fairly beamed. I talked with my hands and nodded my head until I convinced him he was to use the paper and crayons. His hands trembled with delight as he started drawing a concentration camp. I thought he did well, but I realized he had seen things that I had not seen.

When the school day was over and the children said goodbye, A———— touched my hand and gave me a million dollar smile. I said goodbye to him and went home wondering how I could help.

Next morning he and I met as old friends. The group I placed him with welcomed him with outstretched arms. They didn't care whether he could talk to them. They talked to him.

When we started to read from our books, I gave him a marker and I held my book, so he could see how I used it. He watched me and listened to every word. I don't know who helped him the most, the children or I. In an amazingly short time A———— was reading with the best of them. All the children loved him. Two little girls were going to marry him. One told her mother that she and her best friend were going to marry A————. Her mother said, "You can't both marry him." The little girl answered, "Yes we can; we will have a double wedding."

A———— continued to do well with his art. He enjoyed it so much that in a short time he drew pictures of the church he attended and seemed to forget the concentration camps.

Never Give Up

In my school work I would often become discouraged. However, one pupil taught me a lesson. He spent an extra year or two in high school before he was given a diploma. In those days a high school diploma entitled a person to enter college. This boy surprised me when he said that he was going to college and enter the engineering school. Knowing that he had to repeat his mathematics courses, I advised him against it. Nevertheless, he entered the engineering school and failed. For the next year or two he shifted from one school to another until he finally entered the medical school. Then he found himself.

The last I heard of him he was one of the leading surgeons of the South. The lesson he taught me was that I should never give up on anyone.

It Took a Miracle

She was eighteen years old and had never had a bath in a tub or a shower; she had never had a pair of hose. She lived in a sparsely-furnished house in a remote mountain area with her hard-working mother, her blind father and numerous brothers and sisters. In Grade 10 she confided to her school counselor that she wanted more than anything in the world to go to college.

S—— was a senior, almost ready to graduate. Her course of study and her class rank indicated that she would be accepted at any good school. Her counselor advised her to apply to a four-year college well known for its self-help programs, but for weeks S—— delayed sending her application for admission. One day her counselor said, "Is it that you don't have the application fee? Meet me here Monday morning with the form completed and ready to mail. I'll bring the ten dollars."

The local Business and Professional Women's Club heard about S——. They made clothes for her; one member styled her hair. They invited her to a dinner meeting, gave her a shower of personal items, including hose. They gave her a $300 scholarship. That night she was the house guest of a club member and had her first bath in a real bathtub.

Fall, winter, and spring S—— went to college. Every summer she worked. The BPW sent her more scholarship money and she graduated from college. Today she is a poised young woman and a valuable professional member of the staff of a large city hospital.

S—— finds happiness in providing for the welfare of her patients and the comfort of her parents. Every day she is expressing her gratitude that her school and her community have helped her to help someone else.

Lost But Found

One school day I came home unusually late and unusually weary. The telephone was ringing as I came through the door.

The voice spoke angrily,

"Mrs. F———, is my child T———, still at school?"

"Why no, Mrs. J———, everyone has been gone for some time. I just checked the building and locked the gate to the teacher parking lot."

"That teacher kept him in and it's all her fault. He hasn't come home."

"I'm sure Miss B—— didn't keep a third grade boy in this long."

"Well, he hasn't come home and it's all the school's fault for keeping him in."

I was alarmed because it was late. As principal of an elementary school I always felt responsible for a child coming to school and going home from school. I assured the mother that I would come immediately. My elder son was at home so I asked him to come with me. A short distance from the school we found the trailer home without difficulty and a distraught mother, but no sign of T———. We looked and called in the nearby woods and around the trailers. Finally, I told the mother to call the police. They came and looked. I asked Mrs. J—— if the family had relatives T—— may have visited. There was an uncle in an adjoining town. The police called and checked with the uncle—no T———.

At last there seemed nothing we could do but leave the matter in the hands of the police. On the way home my son and I stopped at the Police Station to see if T—— had been found in the few minutes since we left his home.

T—— had been found! The policemen found him safe and sound sitting happily in the lobby of a hospital located directly across the street from the school.

Art Marches On

On the wall of my room here in a Retirement Home hangs an oil painting, very eye-catching and quite a valuable possession of mine. In the corner of this nature painting, "Ducks on a Lake," the autograph says, "G. A.—1963."

I want to contribute this "G. A. story" to this compilation of past experiences.

G. A. was a quiet, conscientious eleven-year-old in my sixth grade.

Social studies notebook illustrations and regular art class work soon indicated to me that among all his other desirable qualities G. had a most unusual ability in art.

In conversation with his parents we discussed this talent and soon he was enrolled in a Saturday morning special art class with a local art teacher. G. was happy and began making tracks!

By the time he reached high school I had had him to do a copy of my coat-of-arms. It was perfect! From that he did other coats-of-arms and told me he was saving all his money he earned to help pay his way through higher education. This was not necessary in his case, but it was an indication of his ambition.

From high school in O——— he went to a university and enrolled in all the art courses offered there. He studied, in addition, history and geography.

He was recommended by the university to study in the European Study Center in Bonn Germany. He visited all the NATO capitals, East Berlin, and Moscow. I feel sure his eyes were on every thing worthwhile, especially works of art.

Following his graduation from the university in commercial art, he became associated with the business world in several large stores.

The Boy with a Smile

He was my sunshine. I never think of him without seeing his ready smile and gleaming white teeth, contrasting sharply with his quite dark skin. C. had the mind of a genius and a charming, endearing personality.

He fastened his roller skates on his well-worn shoes, put his books on his head, and rolled to school. A bicycle was beyond his means, if not his dreams. When he had a nickel, he would stop at the corner store to buy a candy bar, his breakfast. Although he far surpassed his classmates in knowledge, his home held no books. The library had been his palace. He had never owned a dictionary, but his vocabulary was amazingly extensive.

One day C. entered the room, saying, "This is Michelangelo's birthday!" He could have written a volume about the master artist and sculptor.

A large university offered him a scholarship. He accepted it, made an outstanding record, and has continued to bring distinction to his family, his alma mater, and his community. Recently I met the young man on the street and recognized him instantly by that same smile.

Children Are Unpredictable

Once while principal of an elementary school several children had been called to my attention as trouble-makers who should be expelled from school. Such advice was always a challenge to me. They were those who made school work interesting.

At that time the raising and lowering of the American flag by flag boys was of great importance. One day I went with a group on a field trip. The flag boys were among the group and did not return to the school until after sun-down when we found that the gate to the wire fence had been locked by the janitor when he left, and the flag was missing from the flag pole. The flag committee, as well as others, was quite worried until the next morning when the problem was solved. The sixth grade boy—considered one of the worst boys in school—had seen the flag up after everyone had left school; so he had climbed the fence, lowered and folded the flag and had carried it home with him for safe keeping. In he came early the next morning, proudly bringing the flag in time for the flag raising ceremony. This act had meant to him his really first opportunity for service.

From then on S—— was not only a cooperative citizen but his influence for good on his buddies was also unbelievable. On the verge of being a school drop-out in 1920, S—— is now manager of a very profitable wholesale business.

Famous Hands

I shall never forget the time I corrected a first-grader who kept making the same mistake in his work on the chalkboard. After two or three or more times of showing and correcting, his right hand was the victim of a little spanking. However little, he never made the mistake of doing that same thing wrong again while he was in the first grade.

The hand that got that little spanking belonged to one of the greatest and most publicized basketball players in recent years!

Determination

One student whom I will call J——, faced many problems both physical and emotional. His chubby frame and his almost uncontrollable temper kept him from getting along well with his peers. The male image in his family was somewhat repulsive to him; consequently, he had a dislike for any man who taught him or tried to correct his misbehavior. For this reason he was placed in a woman's class.

J—— had an alert mind with a thirst for knowledge, but he constantly needed counseling to keep his temper tantrums from causing him to be suspended from school. Often I would talk to him outside the classroom or during his lunch period about the importance of learning and reading. Thus, keeping his mind well occupied, he was able to forget the unpleasant situations he encountered during the day. After developing a determination to learn, he showed improvement in his work and his conduct.

Today J—— is an English teacher in a large city high school.

Jack ———

Teachers were expected to handle every situation that arose in the classroom.

As usual the children lined up in front of the school and marched into the school room. I knew they were all present—but —*an empty desk*. "What happened to J——?" I asked the class.

"He came in that door and went out that door," said one boy, pointing to the two doors in the room. "He did that all the time last year!"

All the children wanted to talk. I got the picture!

After school, in my Chevrolet, I followed J—— home. J——, his doting mother and I met on the front steps. I spoke to his mother and then said, "Now, J——, will you please tell your Mother and me where you spent the afternoon?" He did! His mother was crushed!

As pleasantly as I could, I said, "This can't happen again. If it does, I'll go directly to your father and tell him everything! Your assignment for tomorrow is ——————."

For months he was a good student. Then the family moved.

Four and a half years passed.

One lovely spring night my husband and I had been to an early movie in a neighboring town and were leisurely walking to our car. Suddenly a joyous noise startled us—ten or more boys on roller skates were coming at break-neck speed, laughter filling the air. Abruptly they stopped beside us. One boy moved out and pointed his finger directly toward me and said, "There she is, boys! If it hadn't been for her, I wouldn't have finished the seventh grade. But, thanks to you, dear teacher, I'll graduate from senior high this June." Then they were gone with the wind. . . .

Perplexed, I looked at my husband and said "J——!"

Regrettable

Not all remembrances are happy ones. . . .

Never shall I forget one boy in my class. He was sixteen years old, had been in a reformatory twice and had often spent time in jail. He spent most of his time wandering around the classroom while the other children were working. I learned not to antagonize him and would often lead him back to his desk.

One day he asked to keep a little piece of iron in my desk drawer until the end of the day.

Through the superintendent's investigation I learned, to my

surprise, that I had housed a pair of hand knuckles for him. Of course he was expelled from school for a few days.

When he returned I asked, "Why do you misbehave? You can be so nice and enjoyable after school. You are a great help to me in placing chairs, watering flowers etc."

His reply was, "I like to be with you so that I won't get into trouble. When I go home I have to fight and that gets me in deep trouble."

A few years later I saw the same boy in a chain gang group working on the highway. What a heart-breaking experience!

Surprised!

How the pupils "turn out" is always interesting to the teacher. And truly one can never tell how or when the desire to pursue learning seriously begins. A shy, sleepy, lazy 10-year-old boy in fourth grade graduated from law school and became a successful lawyer. I am happy that some one along the way ignited the spark!

An Excited Father

The telephone rang. An excited young male voice exclaimed, "I've got me a baby boy." The speaker was a former primary-grade pupil, who now lives in another state. How proud he has made his teachers by accomplishing great humanitarian achievements in spite of his deprived childhood and youth; a college graduate, when that had seemed almost impossible; joining the Peace Corps and going to a foreign country to help natives; and, as he said on one visit, "to eat caterpillars with their Chief" because it was *expected* of him.

Scratching or Writing

The boy was a "holy terror" almost every day the first year at our school. (He had attended another school.) The next year his attitude was better, but his penmanship was terrible. One day I told him his writing was poor. Actually, I told him it looked like a chicken had walked in the mud and then walked on the paper.

He did not say a word, but from that day to this he has improved himself. Today he is a leading merchant in a town and owns his own establishment and hosiery business. He is reported to be quite wealthy.

Music Hath Charms

B—— had always been a problem in school. He began the day calmly, but with some nervousness. By midday he would cry and he would go home "sick."

When he came to my third grade room, he began the year by following the same pattern: semi-calm, nervous, crying, "sick."

I found that the subject which interested him most was music. His mother asked if I would teach him piano after school. To this I agreed.

Soon I noticed that his school performance was undergoing a change. The nervous wiggling disappeared and the daily attacks of illness also disappeared. The shared bond of music seemed to have soothed the small savage breast.

I feel pride whenever I hear that B——, now a Doctor of Music, has been home and has played at his church.

Reflections

One of my happiest memories is that of a timid boy in the seventh grade. He would not take part in a program on North Carolina History. I had him do the devotional in the assembly. This was his first public speech. He was encouraged during the year to take part in simple historical dramatizations.

I have followed his career through high school. He has thanked me many times for getting him up to make his first speech. He hasn't stopped talking. During high school he was very active in political activities. After graduation he went to college and was elected freshman class president. He will be a lawyer or follow a career in political science. He still reminds me that if I hadn't insisted he make that first talk, he probably would be following another career.

Have No Fear

I treasure many memories of my pupils. There was D—— in first grade, who was frightened for me to be out of her sight. She went everywhere with me, holding to my skirt like a shadow. She finally became adjusted and today is a musician with no fear of performing.

There was R—— with one parent, learning difficulties, and little personality. He had to be coaxed to take up a paint brush, didn't want anyone to see his painting, but began to like it. Before the end of the term he was coming to school very early each day, in order to paint a picture. Other children admired his work. This satisfaction made his personality blossom and he gave better performances in other areas of work.

Disappointments

I loved every child with whom I ever worked.

I do not know the whereabouts of many of my children. Of those I do know, there are a doctor, a lawyer, a preacher, a goodly number of teachers, mechanics, farmers, nurses, secretaries and homemakers. However, there is one murderer. He was an excellent student. He was kind and gentle in the first grade. He grew more and more resentful as he became older. Also, I taught one girl who is a prostitute now. She has several children. She is not—and never has been—married. As a child she did not like school. She stopped as soon as she could.

Love versus Discipline

An oversized boy for his age could not get along with classmates. "He said no one loved him and he loved no one." I tried discipline and failed. Then I tried love. He responded graciously. I then asked him to come early next morning to help decorate the room. He came and helped, then he asked to be allowed to care for the floors. After that he was a changed child. Love worked where discipline failed.

As I sat one day in my part-time guidance office watching the boys going to the gym, I noticed one boy in particular because of his beautiful body and the grace with which he strode down the hall. When I looked up his file in the office, I found that he was not performing according to his ability. So the next day at this study hall period, I called him to come for a chat. Finally, we got around to his grades. And when I asked the reason why, his answer was revealing.

"Why should I try to excel? When I finish high school, I'll just get a job in the factory, and that will be it!"

Further conversation revealed that he was one of five boys in a family where the father worked now and then; the mother worked hard at home, cutting corners to make ends meet, and managing somehow to keep her emphasis on good wholesome food and a close relationship with her boys. She sent them to school well-fed and well-clothed (by washing their clothes and pressing them at night after they were asleep) so that they could hold their heads up with the best of their friends the next day.

During several conferences with W—— I learned that he would like very much to go to college and that his choice was one of the most expensive colleges in the state. My first thoughts were, wouldn't he be a misfit there where the cream of our city's society sent their sons? But then I realized that I was dealing with a rare specimen.

Following a conference with the incoming president of the college, W—— was accepted. The president gave three reasons for accepting him:

> 1. He did not apologize for being poor—just put his cards on the table. 2. He was innately courteous. 3. When he put his feet on the footstool in front of him, I saw that the uppers of his shoes were polished beautifully even though they had practically no soles.

To make the story shorter, he graduated from the college of

his choice. At commencement he was given The Sullivan Award as the senior whose influence had meant most to his college during his four years.

Was teaching worthwhile? Figure it out for yourself!

Stuck!

At one of our school athletic events recently during one of my days substituting, a large policeman in a brand new uniform came over to me and asked, "Mrs. R———, do you know me?" As I searched for his name, he quickly added, "I'm R——— R——— C———." Then my mind flashed back to the chubby boy who took a front seat in my classroom years ago, the first day of school. Desks were nailed to the floor and he had wedged himself in. I started arranging the students in seats according to their size. I kept insisting that the larger ones move to the back and let the smaller ones have the front seats. I noticed R——— kept squirming each time I asked. After asking several times, "R——— wouldn't you like to move to the back?" He replied "No, ma'm." I finally had his predicament explained to me by a chirply little girl. "Mrs. R———, he can't, he's stuck!"

With Pride

On a beautiful sunny morning in 1930, a six-year-old lad entered my classroom. He came in seemingly full of energy, enthusiasm and curiosity. Added to those obvious traits, was an air of confidence and aggressiveness as if he had said, "Here I am, and I'm ready for business." This bright and promising young lad was J———, who is the subject of my "Proudly I Taught."

By the end of the first half of his first year he had completed all of the work of the first grade. Such exceptional performance was deserving of encouragement and reward. So a trip to the library (which was frequently made) and the second grade room furnished materials for the second half of the year. At the end of his first school year, J——— was tested on the second grade work and came within a fraction of making a perfect score. It was not suprising, then, that when he finished high school eleven years later, he was the valedictorian of his class.

After high school he entered a university, where he was awarded a Bachelor of Science Degree in electrical engineering. Following this success, he entered law school and earned the degree of Doctor of Jurisprudence.

The Supreme Gift

In 1953 I began teaching at White Church School. Mrs. M—— had had B—— G—— the previous year in the first grade. He was large for his age, and she said he was a good pupil. Principal H—— K—— asked me if I would take him in my third grade class, and give him a trial. That I did and he was as good, if not better than, most of the others in this grade. He was active in athletics through elementary school, and when he entered high school he was a star football player, and also in college. After graduation from high school, he joined the ROTC and graduated from college in 1968 with honors. Later he was sent to Vietnam where he lost his life on August 15, 1970. I am proud that I had a small part in his short life.

A school in connection with an orphanage has had some interesting students whose home life was interrupted.

Three Little Boys

Three little boys were sent to an orphanage because they had lost their mother. Their ages were seven, nine and eleven years old. They were polite, intelligent and showed that they had been well-trained at home. The oldest boy would come by the office each day after school to see what he could do to help me. That little boy, now a brilliant young man, heads one of the departments at a University.

✓ ✓ ✓

Values

There were two brothers, both over-age for the grade placement. They were boys who wanted to learn. Both worked hard in school.

One constantly remained after school and asked his teachers for help. His brother finished high school and college. He is now a high school teacher and has what he always wanted, a nice home and family. His home is valued at $50,000.00. The older brother finally finished high school. He attended a technical institute where he could learn a trade. Today he is an engineer in the school system of another state. He owns a home valued at $75,000.00.

✓ ✓ ✓

Effect of Environment

J———, at the age of five, was left to live with her grandparents. They were sharecroppers and very poor. J——— had the ability but because of her physical condition—improper clothing and malnutrition—was unable to express this ability. When asked by her teacher what she wanted to become in life she remarked, "Somebody." Today her dream has come true. J——— completed four years of college in June. She has been accepted in another university to study toward her Masters Degree in Education.

Among the children from whom we hear, we have every trade and many professions included. The children often come back to the orphanage to visit the only place that they could call home—then. When they visit they express thanks and appreciation for the help given them.

He Gave

Many years ago when I was very young and teaching in an affluent section of a rural area of North Carolina I received a great gift.

An undernourished, bashful, poorly-clad boy of eleven or twelve years of age walked to my desk and with a faint, shy, smile handed me a package wrapped in dirty worn newspaper and tied with coarse black sewing thread.

When asked by teacher and pupils what it was, he told us, "It's for the teacher."

The children knew that I didn't like to handle bugs and worms. The boy's eyes assured me I need not be frightened.

Slowly I opened the package. Inside I found a small dingy handkerchief that I later learned had been washed and ironed and neatly folded into a square by this lad.

All eyes were upon me, as I sincerely thanked the boy for his thoughtfulness. The children seemed to understand. Such a long moment!

Years passed, then one day during World War II news came that the same lad had given his life in service for his and my country.

I give thanks and take great pride in being a part of people who have dedicated their lives in service as citizens of this land—Our America!

I Remember . . . . .

I remember . . . I remember many whom I taught, and who taught me. But I especially remember M——. M——, a football player, had only one ambition in life: to play professional football, and "passing" my class in English was a means to that end. It was a tug-of-war between the two of us as to who would outwit the other in making this a meaningful experience: his meaning, to play football and get by English to do it; my meaning to find some way to make his mother tongue a proud form of expression of ideas. About mid-way through the football season, our unit of study was poetry, a delight to me, a waste of time in M——'s book. Poetry was "sissy" stuff, and he wanted nothing to do with it. Hard put to it to find where *his* starting point was, I sent him on a scouting tour of the poetry section of our library, and he came back to class with Edward Lear's limericks. He thought these were excruciatingly funny, and he was rather intrigued at the form and climactic "suprise" always in the last line. Without telling me he decided to try writing a limerick of his own. He left it hidden under many other papers on my desk, and I did not find it until late that afternoon. It was not only a surprise to me to find that he had actually written a limerick; it was also a surprise that it was good! Without understanding form he had uniquely written "The Moonshiner and His Still" with a rhythm, a sense of humor, and a terrific climax!

A few days later, when we were studying paraphrasing as a prelude to style, M—— got permission from the coach to leave football practice for a few minutes and brought up to me in my classroom what he had told his teammates was "an old theme he had to do for English," but which was his voluntary paraphasing of a poem he had read and couldn't get out of his head. M——— was "hooked!" He laid the paper down in front of me, and, embarrassed, said that he had decided to try for extra credit by paraphrasing Sidney Lanier's poem, "The Marshes of Glynn." There was no "extra credit," but M——— saved face by letting this expression say for him that Lanier had said something to him, and he wanted to know if he had heard Lanier in what he had said.

I read M———'s paraphrasing—and it was Lanier coming through loud and clear, but coming through to M——— in his own words and feelings, and it was beautiful. This experience could be the end of the story, and it would be a gamble as to what permanent impression remained. But there is another chapter to M———. It was that spring that M———, like many other young men, enlisted in the Air Force. He became a member of a bombing mission over Germany; his plane was shot down in the English Channel, and he was rescued. But he lost a leg as a result of his injuries. One day his mother came to school to bring me a note which had been enclosed in a letter to her, and it was a note to me. It went like this:

Dear Teach:

A nurse is writing this for me. I am lying here, looking down at where my leg used to be, knowing that everything I ever planned and wanted can never be, and I keep asking why? why? why? And you'll get a laugh of this, Teach—Do you know what is holding me firm in the boat? It is something I keep saying over and over—I learned it in your English class. Remember when I took Sidney Lanier's poem and paraphrased it? I didn't even know I'd learned any of it, but these lines keep going on and on in my mind. . . . "As the marsh-hen secretly builds on the watery sod, Behold I will build me a nest on the greatness of God: By so many roots as the marsh-grass sends in the sod I will heartily lay me a-hold on the greatness of God: . . ." I remember how foolish it seemed to me at the time that the marsh hen would build a nest on the watery sod of that marsh, but I know what she was doing . . . she was trusting. . . . Teach, I never have been very religious, and I can't pray very well, but . . . if the marsh hen could *lay a-hold* . . . so can I . . . And, Teach I am *laying hold!*

It would not be fair to close this chapter without sharing some of the amusing experiences and sayings of our former students:

✓ ✓ ✓

One teacher used to have charge of commencement. Seeing her with seniors apparently caused two freshman girls to connect her with seniors only. These two were sitting on graduation night behind a friend of the teacher who related the incident to her. One freshman said to the other, "You can say what you please about old lady S——, but she learned me all the English I ever knowed!"

✓ ✓ ✓

A teacher received a beautiful Bible as a gift from her students on Valentine's Day. She noted the big print and remarked: "What beautiful print. Now I can read this when I get old." One little boy said to another, "When she *gets* old!"

The following note was found on the teacher's desk the day after one of her birthdays:

Dear Miss P,
We did not have a noff money yesterday, so we will give it to you today far your birthday.
from R. B.

✓ ✓ ✓

Miss G—— was having some visiting teachers when she asked the question, "What do you like best about Christmas?" Several children had given excellent answers and with teacher's confidence restored, she called on a certain little boy to tell what he liked best about Christmas. Looking forlorn and with a quivering voice he answered, "Miss G——, I forgot what you told me to say."

✓ ✓ ✓

After Christmas one year a new student moved into Miss M——'s school. All day he just looked at her without doing any work. Miss H—— kept telling him to get busy, but he never did. Finally she asked, "J——, why do you keep looking at me?" He answered, "Miss H—— I was just thinking how much prettier my teacher was before Christmas."

Miss X's co-workers enjoyed the comments she made on the cumulative folders. One such comment was, "He doesn't know what I would like for him to know, but he is better prepared going than he was coming."

During the opening of school in the fall, Mrs. C____ sat busily greeting and enrolling students. Looking up she saw J_____ looking angry as usual because he had been retained, due to poor attendance and under-achievement, "What! You here again?" He replied, "Yes, I'm here! What's so funny about that? You're still here aren't you?"

Being driven to desperation the teacher called the superintendent's office and asked, "Is it permissible to expel a first grader?" The reply, "Never heard of it in my life!" Well, "One of us is going! You guess who."

Wise Sayings and Doings

Several years ago I visited a kindergarten to observe one of my student teachers. One little boy, dressed in a smock and an artist's tam, was standing, deep in thought, in front of an easel. I watched him paint four heavy black lines to make a square, pause, consider, then draw in a door and a chimney, sigh deeply, frown in concentration, paint in a step in front of the door, then step back from his work. Satisfied, he laid down his brush, cleaned his hands, and took off his smock. I was waiting for him to fill in the windows, but he was finished. As he turned away, I asked him, "Where are the windows?" He looked at me in genuine surprise, and I got an immediate impression that I dropped pretty low in his estimation. "They're on the other side of the house," he said, pitying my stupidity.

Working with a pre-schooler one day, I watched for a long time as she concentrated on colored advertisements, and finally brought them over for me to see. She had only one "O" in "Goose" and I pointed this out to her. She looked at me rather strangely for a moment and then said, condescendingly, "When they're both alike, you don't need but one."

✔ ✔ ✔

One little boy was named W_____ but was called Bull by everyone, even his parents. I said to him one day, "Don't you answer when anyone calls you Bull because that is not your name." That same day his mother called him to bring her some wood: W_____ did not answer; His mother picked up a stick to whip him. He ran off a little ways and said, Miss S____ said for me not to answer when people call me Bull." His mother had to laugh, but said, "I will whip you and Miss S____."

✔ ✔ ✔

I had taught M____'s mother, S____, several years before, and had seen her daddy, G__, at my father-in-law's. M____ on her first day of school introduced herself thus: "I'm S____'s youngen and G__ is my daddy."

✔ ✔ ✔

T__ was a nice little boy with a good family environment and intelligent parents. To him school was just something that interfered with his education. At the end of the year I asked the children to write a paragraph about school, cautioning them to be honest and say what they really thought. T__ wrote the following paragraph: "I do not like school. I do not like reading. I do not like arithmetic. I do not like spelling. I do not like music. I like Mrs. _____ a little bit." Needless to say, I felt quite flattered.

T__ gave no trouble but could not do a single thing in school subjects. His one accomplishment was the ability to sing. So I would occasionally let him get up in front of the class and sing. One day when there were a few extra minutes, I told him he might sing. He sang several verses, ending each with the words, "crazy fool, crazy fool."

I wasn't paying much attention to the words until this caught my attention:

> "Went home early one night,
> My wife wasn't expecting me.

On the pillow was another man's head
Where my head ought to be."
"Crazy fool, crazy fool."

It didn't mean anything to the children, but I was certainly glad that none of my supervisors happened by my door as these words were bursting forth.

✔ ✔ ✔

One day some workmen were replacing part of the roof on the school building. Near the walkway that led to our playground, they set down some of their rubber roofing and buckets of tar (or something that looked like tar).

That afternoon I took my grade out on the playground. I noticed one of my little boys had stopped near a bucket of tar; he was smiling. Just as I came near him, he said to me, "Watch out, don't get any more *tar on you heels.*"

✔ ✔ ✔

The year 1947–48, I was teaching a fourth grade. One of my pupils (a boy) was having some difficulties learning to spell satisfactorily the words required for the fourth grade. One day, as I was trying to give him a little special help on the words on our spelling list, he looked up at me and said, "I am going to buy me a typewriter that can spell these words."

✔ ✔ ✔

In 1955–56 I was teaching a fifth grade in a local school. One of my pupils (a boy) was a very poor reader. I gave him an unsatisfactory grade on his reading.

When he returned his report card his mother had enclosed a note. She expressed an unsatisfied feeling about her son's poor grade on reading. One of the sentences that she included in her note was the following . . . "S—— can read better than his father." Well, I had never met his father!

Human Resources

The teachers of our country have certainly made tremendous contributions to America, although we may sometimes question their value. Yet when we recall some of our former pupils and see them today as successful bankers, lawyers, physicians, news commentators, athletic stars, legislators, congressmen, national, state and local leaders—we swell with pride and realize *we taught them, everyone*!

GEORGE WASHINGTON

A teacher was reading the story of George Washington to a group of first-graders. When the story was finished, they started talking about it. One small boy waved his hand to get attention, and when the teacher called on him, he said, "I met George Washington." The teacher, a little surprised, said, "But, Tommy, George Washington lived 200 years ago. How could you have met him?" "I met him up there before I came down here."

GETTING OLDER

A retired teacher told me this story. One of my first graders lived in her community and some of the neighbors were quizzing him about his new teacher; was she old or young, pretty or homely?

The boy studied a bit and answered, "Well she is not so old, but she is getting older."

The retired teacher said, "As I retire, I feel, 'I'm not so old but getting older'."

A TEACHER

Miss "X":

Roses are red
Violets are blue,
You have been a Teacher
And a Mother, too.

XIII ✌ Remembering Teachers

Tributes and Rewards

"You may boast of your age and your ivied walls
Your great endowments, your noble halls,
And all your modern features,
Your vast curriculum's scope and reach,
The multivarious things you teach—
But what about your teachers?

No printed word nor spoken plea
Can teach young hearts what men should be;
Not all the books on all the shelves,
But what the teachers are themselves—"

Proudly, indeed, have the majority of North Carolina's retirees taught in every section of the state. They have "held" classes in one-room school houses as well as in big buildings in the large cities. There have been lean years when salary checks got smaller and smaller. There have been better years when the state could afford an increase in those salary checks—but in most cases the monetary values have not been recalled by the hundreds who voiced their greatest rewards of teaching.

Gleanings from notes scribbled by those who stayed in the classroom 20, 30, 40 and more years have revealed that a simple "thank-you" and other kind words have meant more than silver trays, silver bowls, and receptions.

The reason for sharing these expressions is to prove that recognition received at the end of a career far surpasses the monetary end-of-the-month compensations.

The fringe benefits that I now receive cannot be translated into dollars and cents. They come from my former students of the past 42 years. The slap on the back and the firm handshake from "my boys," the affectionate hug from the girls, the smiles from my fellow teachers and the cheerful hello from those who pass my way—These speak more loudly than silver and gold.

However, all who have taught are human and both love and deserve a little flattery and praise. The following statements are worth preserving in this volume:

If it had not been for your love and understanding, I would not be the man I am today.

✓ ✓ ✓

I wrote a theme in college on *My Most Unforgettable Teacher*, and received an "A"; that teacher happened to be you.

✓ ✓ ✓

I am standing here looking at a picture of you and you have your arm around me. I was one of your first graders in 1925. My wife and I are coming soon to take you out to dinner.

✓ ✓ ✓

I think you are largely responsible for my being where I am today. You found the comic books I had always kept in my text books which I read instead of studying. You took them from me and started me reading worthwhile things.

✓ ✓ ✓

I always wanted to be a teacher just like you. You could always laugh and have fun. Yet, you had the students' respect and got the best from them.

✓ ✓ ✓

Johnny certainly has improved in his books and he likes to go to school—all because of you.

✓ ✓ ✓

You were never afraid to laugh *with* a child, but you never thought of laughing *at* him.

✓ ✓ ✓

You are a teacher who always knows what's going on, especially when someone has on new shoes.

✓ ✓ ✓

You make school for a child a place of learning that is fun.

✓ ✓ ✓

You have taught me to love poetry. To me you are not only a teacher, but also a friend.

✓ ✓ ✓

I remember to this day the qualities of fairness, balance, serenity, common sense, judgment and level headedness which you brought to all your students.

✓ ✓ ✓

More than any other teacher, you have done more to teach children love of country.

✓ ✓ ✓

Personally, I am utterly thrilled to confess to you in writing that your influence had a lot to do with my not becoming a high school drop-out.

✓ ✓ ✓

Thank you for the little things I disliked so much then, but were the little extras needed, such as: "Class begins at 1 p.m. not 1:05," (punctuality). "Stay out of the halls," (responsibility).

✓ ✓ ✓

You don't know me, but I remember you, for you were my first grade teacher. It has been a long time but I will not forget you or my first year in school!

✓ ✓ ✓

You don't look a day older than you did when you taught me. (That was 42 years ago!)

But flattery will not really take the place of the deep feeling and concern of those teachers who gave "so much of themselves to so many." Perhaps, it is said best by some who have "graduated" from the classroom—

> Our greatest reward is knowing that many of our students have been helped. They have made and are still making contributions to their communities and to society in general. Many have become teachers, ministers, skilled mechanics, good housewives, nurses, dietitians, personnel directors, state and governmental workers.

Too, a memory flashback still recalls the pleasures of teaching to those "who could see little children's eyes and faces light up as they experienced success. They continued to grow and progress from one level to another, learning more and more as they went along until they became fine men and women."

And, then, there was that problem-child whose "background was seemingly good—a well-to-do-professional home with parents extremely interested in their children." But something was wrong. Maybe it was too much regimentation and strictness or too much expectation on the part of one parent. Jack, for example, was a problem to each of his teachers and the school.

> At the end of his third year of school, his family left for another state. Before leaving he wrote his last teacher: "You are the best teacher I have ever had. You have helped me do better. You gave a thing for me to do all my life. I thank you very much for helping me."
>
> > Love, Jack.

The retired teacher realizes, of course, that the greatest tribute paid to her is the progress made by her students, thus she can look back with pride and say, "How glad I am that I had a part in their lives." The following experiences can be applied to many classes:

> The student landed (was 'assigned' to) in my creative writing class in high school because she had thrown a book at another teacher, cut the teacher's eye, and was sent from that class to the principal. Since she had repeatedly been "kicked out" of other classes for very serious behavior, she literally had nowhere else to go. But I have to admit that I resented having such a problem assigned to my class. However, as the months went by, something was quietly happening to this student. She discovered the chance to write as she really felt.
>
> One day I found a moving, heartbreaking piece of writing among her papers entitled "The Unimportant Things" and the paper began as follows:
>
> > "Had I but one day left
> > To do the things that I'd fill a lifetime with,
> > To say and think the things that must live on;
> > If all the years I've planned to fill with work and play
> > And just the joy of life were gone,
> > To gather all the beauty life affords
> > And know that all that matters most was done;

Had I but one day left to put it all into,
What would I do from rise to set of sun?"

Then she lists many things that had never happened to her—just ordinary things like someone's leaving a note in a book for someone else but she would read it as if it were meant for her, since no one had ever written her a note like that.

But really the tribute to the teacher came in the following verses:

"At last I've found a few things about her
that I like,
Although it's taken me awhile to do it—
And three things about her that I do not like-
Miss _____, I'm counting on your being honest
In return for my courage in telling you my
feelings!
You see, Miss _____, you're a *teacher*,
and Teachers never have seen me as I really, truly
am
Miss _____, one thing I do not like about you is
the way
You play with your beads so much. . . .
I find myself watching so intently to see them
break someday
That I can't listen to what is going on.
Why *do* you twist and turn the beads so much?
Are you uncomfortable with us? You really ought
to find out *why* you do it.
I wish you wouldn't trust us all so much, for
that makes it easy
To take advantage of you, and then we feel
guilty.
You see, we're not all at the same point of
taking responsibility,
And when you leave the room, some of us, still
as infants,
Abuse that trust. Please try to understand
That we must grow in taking on responsibility
By gradual steps. Don't help us to destroy our-
selves
By forcing us too fast too soon.
And why is it teachers think they have to analyze

Shakespeare for us?
If the Bard of Avon is half as good as he's
cracked up to be,
He ought to be able to get through to us
With less effort!
Why don't you let us just *enjoy* him—
Not understand every single word!
He's great enough to speak to us – just let him
do it!"

This same retiree records that this student:

Wrote a one-act play which won "Best Play of the Festival" in the annual Carolina Dramatic Association Drama Festival, defeating even my own play. I was never *happier* in my life when this student, unbelieving, went to the stage to receive her award.

Then there is the teacher who can remember with pride the "little boy who was not able to pay for his workbook." She put the money in for him and then fifteen years later that boy—now a grown man—came to her door with the words, "I came to pay you what I owe you. I owe you for that workbook you bought for me in the fourth grade." He quoted an amount due. The teacher could not even recall the incident, much less the cost. But the teacher took the money, saying that if he felt so deeply about it she would accept it. She determined to purchase something tangible with the money, for this was indeed a high spot in her career. For years a small milk-glass hen on her nest has had a prominent place in her living room as a constant reminder of one little boy's appreciation.

Another teacher said it well in the following statements:

We can be thankful that we were given the strength, the insight and love for students that enabled us to function as a worthwhile teacher.

We can be thankful, too, that all along as we worked we saw enough evidence of pupil growth to encourage us to continue our undertaking.

Though it is entirely possible that one has not received tangible recognition for his work, we ourselves know that we helped the students and this knowledge is all the reward that we really set out to achieve. And so in helping the thousands of students with their preparation for life, we have the added honor of helping America prepare for the celebration of its two hundredth birthday. We have made a great contribution to America's success!

Through the years tributes have been paid not only in verse words, and song, but erected over the Tar Heel State are also many school buildings to remind the on-coming generations that pioneers in the field of education have been there. (Note: Only a few can be listed—but the reader will certainly recall others.)

In one county today there are two schools named for retired school principals of elementary schools. One of these has this to say:

> It will take more than sixteen years of retirement to dampen seriously my interest in elementary schools and their achievements. As I read and talk with teachers today, I soon get lost in the maze of activities which are offered in the open classroom, procedures in the complexity of the measurement of various reading levels, in the confusion of the new math principles and in the rush and hurry and changes in a single day's scheduling.

> I would not suggest that we should return to any very formal methods of teaching and learning; but, after all, reading, writing and arithmetic are still basic parts of the subject areas regardless of how modern and how vast the curriculum materials are. I still believe that children enjoy the process of mastering and using basic skills that enable them to participate on their levels of understanding in the affairs of our society today.

The other school was named for a teacher who taught for more than 60 years in the public schools of her city. At the age of 93, she wrote and published "Historical Sketches of the Public Schools."

A high school in another city is named for one who served as city superintendent for a quarter of a century. Many other counties in the state have honored educators by naming schools for them.

Over the state are many other laboratories, schools, libraries, dormitories, and auditoriums built of wood, brick and stone to honor classroom teachers and administrators who have added to the educational progress of their communities.

However, as effectively as these recognitions give satisfaction and bespeak a well-deserved "Thank You," it can be said that each teacher so honored would say:

> It is not what the World gives me
> In honor, praise or gold;
> It's what I do give the world
> for others to unfold.

It is natural for those who belong to the "yesteryear" group, to have had interesting, amusing and perhaps, sad stories to tell. One teacher sums it up in these words:

Now as I look back upon all those years of teaching, I know that they were rich, full, happy ones. All the unpleasant experiences (and I am sure there were many) fade into insignificance. The pleasant memories—the excitement of the football games, the "junior-senior," the plays and musical performances, "student night," "tapping," overshadow the others entirely. Working so closely with such fine young people—often sharing their heartaches as well as their joys—loom above all else. When I think of the wonderful ways that so many of my students have "kept in touch" with me and the many acts of kindness they have done for me through the years, I know that life is good.

No greater tribute could be given to a teacher than one given here by a student, who has followed in his footsteps:

I came to understand rather suddenly and excitedly that this language of ours was a living force for communication of ideas and communion of feeling. And soon my adolescent imagination was being stirred by the magic of words, by the rhythm of spoken poetry, by analyses of human values inherent in the literary products of men's minds, by the architectural beauty apparent in the structure of sentences, paragraphs, compositions. Rules were "discovered" by us, and, these, rarely disturbed us since we knew the "how" and the "why." Reading, under her tutelage, became a persistent search for the author's meaning, unclouded by personal bias; speech became a systematic development into clarity of oral expression; writing was not only a discipline in research but an exciting adventure into discovering a style of our own; and listening became a shared experience with the speaker. She exacted of each student a high degree of excellence, but, in retrospect, I now know she recognized that there would be varying degrees of perfection. In her discernment she capitalized on these differences, urging each one to appraise his own efforts, to be ever critical of his results, to be ashamed to do less than his best. We were never compared by her with anyone else—only with our own past efforts. She had exacting requirements and great expectations for each of us, and she led us to develop great expectations for ourselves.

Added to this tribute is the philosophy of the state's retirees, here given in the words of one who so proudly taught and passed on to those who dare to continue to teach:

If one teaches she must be willing to turn her hopes, ambitions, energies and creative abilities toward teaching, for teaching is not a 'half-and-half' business. It is a calling. In this calling, there are two resources: "the human being and the accumulated wisdom of the ages. The function of the teacher is to bring these two elements into an electrical contact, watch the charge ignite and then wait for the explosion"—and if this has been the tribute given to the retired, they have not served in vain.

WHAT MONEY CAN'T BUY

My second-grade reading class was having trouble understanding the difference between the meaning of "Miss" and "Mrs." I sounded the pronunciation of each word and explained that "Miss" is a lady who is not married, just as the word they used when speaking to me. At once, someone asked, "Why didn't you get married?" Before I had an answer, a dear little brown-eyed boy sitting beside me in the reading circle looked up into my face and said, "If I 'wush' big enouth, I would 'maaway' you."

XIV ໒⁓ Retiring to New Opportunities

Retired Teachers Speak

"Time's Up! The years in the classroom have passed! Time was never long enough!" Many have said, though, that this fact does not mean "we have quit!" There is still work to be done and there are still those who seek help and counsel. Many continue to enjoy the gleam of success and happiness in a child's eyes when he comes and tells of an achievement.

Teaching is in the blood and when someone asks, "What would you be if you could live life over again?" The answer is still, "A teacher."

The following selected excerpts express our feelings toward retirement:

For months before retirement, I began thinking about all the things I wanted to do after I had given the last grade, made out the final report, cleared out my desk and cabinet for my successor, and closed the door on my many years of teaching. There would be plenty of time to carry out my dreams, many of which had been kept in the back of my mind during the ever busy years.

What an awakening when that day arrived! The abundance of time vanished with my dreams. Unexpected activities suddenly crowded in and left little time for dream ideas. We advocate this philosophy for those looking toward retirement: "If you have things to do, don't wait until retirement! Start now!" No, we have not retired; we have just changed pace and environment. Idle moments? Never!

✓ ✓ ✓

As educators we have been in the forefront, guiding, stimulating, inspiring others. Suddenly, and often without sufficient preparation, we are faced with formal unemployment. This period can be a terrific let-down or the most beautiful part of life. When the classroom door closes, we need an alternative, equally gratifying and enticing, filled with many activities denied the teacher as she gave her entire self to the day-by-day schedule filling the needs of her students. At retirement new opportunities, new joys, and latent talents find an outlet.

After liberation from the daily routine of bells, schedules, and extracurricula duties, one can stretch the mind and imagination and find unusual pleasure in doing many of the little but meaningful things for which one never seemed to have time during the busy career days. Thus is born a new vigor and joy in the newly-acquired freedom, and tomorrow forever holds a new challenge. No intelligent retired teacher in good health can afford to withdraw to a corner and withhold his views or actions on issues which need his concern.

Since one is freed from the everyday necessity of earning a living, these unknown energies and talents often burst into regal splendor and retirement years become rewarding, creative, and purposeful. Trying to fill each day by contributing time, talents, and services to the building of a better world makes retirement a rich experience and a more deeply-satisfying way of life. One can say with Tennyson in the poem *Ulysses*:

> "Come, my friends,
> 'Tis not too late to seek a newer world."

During all those so-called "leisure" hours of retirement, what are we really doing? The answers would fill volumes, as evidenced by the reports of our many interests, activities, and causes in which we are involved. There are voluntary involvements in family, in church and community, in hospitals, in service organizations, and still in the schools. Such voluntary hours, of course, have a monetary value to the community, but the higher worth of this loving, person-to-person service is incalculable. Indeed, we may interpret it as continuing to put service before self.

One reporter says "Our years of experience have resulted in deeper appreciation of the needs and problems of today and the

214

desire to do something about them, and thus the so-called leisure becomes a many-splendored thing."

And where shall we begin? Where we are is the place, our community; it is the place where we have taught those forty years or more. It is where we can work with the greatest cooperation, for is it not where our loyal students of yesteryear live? These are now our doctor, our grocer, our lawyer, our plumber, our mayor and councilmen. These and others who worked in our classrooms are the supporters of our causes and efforts today.

While some few of us may want and wait to be served, the greater number are standing ready to serve others. Many write of the satisfactions they find in serving community institutions. Some turn to hospitals and nursing homes where hours are spent each week performing simple routine services to help relieve the busy staff; or they spend time with patients themselves, reading to them, writing letters for them, or simply visiting to help relieve the lonely, tedious hours. Then there are the shut-ins and the lone ones in their homes. For these we shop for medicines, groceries, or other necessities; we help them make contact with service agencies when necessary, or furnish transportation to the hospital, to the doctor's office, to the shopping center to do their own shopping, or just take them for a ride to give them a change and a bit of outing.

William Lyon Phelps once said, "In my mind teaching is not merely a work, a profession, an occupation, a struggle—it is a passion!" With that passion some of us turn toward the school again where we give many hours of service on a one-to-one basis helping students who have fallen behind in some subject; or we work with kindergarten children, helping in music, storytelling or wherever needed; others work with children aiding them to understand our heritage and encouraging love of country.

Of note is the report of one who carries on voluntary activities for the Freedom Foundation through taking to teachers guidelines on teaching the love of country and the American way of life, and in visiting organizations and business men to encourage them to fly our flag and to speak out for America. She also helped set up the George Washington Carver Library in Valley Forge, the Headquarters for the Freedom Foundation, where are housed six research libraries. For her work there she was honored in 1973 by having her portrait hung in the library.

As retired teachers who have been faithful to our churches during the busy years, we continue to take part in all of their activities. We teach in the church school, conduct study groups, serve on church boards, as librarians, as youth counselors, work in church offices, and in many capacities in the women's and men's organizations of the church.

We also put our shoulders to the wheels for various community drives, as the United Way, Heart, visits of the bloodmobile, registration of voters, or getting out the vote for election. There is no limit to the opportunities available!

More than one retired teacher has been in the center of things helping to work out plans for bicentennial celebrations, serving as coordinators for programs, writing skits to be presented, planning exhibits, and working on costumes. Who is better equipped for such work than the retired teacher?

As we have been preparing for the bicentennial celebrations, there has been a definite revival of the early crafts necessary to the very existence of our early ancestors. One says:

> Today these handicrafts can be evaluated in light of the Machine Age with a fresh perspective and enjoyed as true American Folk Art. Now that we have time, many of us try our hands at those skills and crafts that our forefathers forged to perfection.

Happily many of us turn to these crafts for our hobbies. For some there is sewing, creative stitchery for service and beauty, or designing and tailoring one's own wardrobe as well as gifts for family and friends. Many of us use our spare time making quilts, knitting or crocheting afghans and other valued articles for grandchildren. Heirlooms for the future! One reports:

> I am designing seventeen historical panels for hooking rugs to be used for carpeting on the risers of the stairs in the family summer home, a house built at the turn of the century. The family tells me they are too beautiful to step on but I say to them, "Each time any of

you walk on them may you be reminded of the maker's love of her home, her family, her work, and it will be worth the long hours and the love put into it."

Work in the basement shops many of our group have set up in their homes occupies hours. Here furniture is built for the home, and no doubt many of these pieces will become heirlooms to future generations. Others have taken the work of earlier craftsmen (often neglected and abused pieces) and have transformed them into beautiful pieces of treasured furniture.

Some have turned to other types of art. Oil and water color painting, wood carving, ceramics, and gem collecting and polishing are among those commonly reported. These have had the honor of having their works exhibited, have won prizes and even turned hobbies into profit by selling articles produced.

> The esthetic satisfaction of expressing our own ideas, whether the results be crude or of near genius quality, has its value to our nation today, as well as to our own personal gratification, and often gives us the therapy we need.

A number of those reporting have turned to writing. Several are working on family history; others are doing research on county or area history, involving members of the community who have a wealth of contributions to make to such a project. Plans are for publication of these documents. Still others have attended writing workshops and are now writing feature articles for local papers. One writes and illustrates children's books for publication; another has sold some of her children's plays. Interesting reports of individual activities follow:

> After retirement-new opportunites! Animated Story Telling on the Uncle Paul Show of Channel 5, WRAL, Raleigh, has brought a most rewarding and exciting experience for me. Old Classic fairy tales are being redrawn with visual aids across the screen. . . . Twenty classic tales were televised during the spring and plans are in the making for more to come.

> ✓ ✓ ✓

> I worked with an integrated high school and in 1975 accompanied a group to Washington, D.C., to sing at the eighty-fifth Continental

Congress of the Daughters of the American Revolution. The choir received a standing ovation at the end of the concert. A reception was given for the members of the choir and their sponsors in the North Carolina Room of the Convention Hall. The students were mostly blacks and children from poor rural backgrounds. They had worked to earn money to finance the trip on an activity bus. What a wonderful experience it was for these young people to tour our capital city and to be in the stream of history.

Many of us are still "digging in the dirt" with vegetable and flower gardens. Some exhibit and take prizes in county fairs or in garden club exhibits. Flowers can be raised without considerable cost in labor and money. One says, "I don't raise vegetables but certainly enjoy those my neighbors raise, for they are very generous in sharing with me."

"Travel! My dreams come true" report many. Lack of time and sometimes money, cares, and responsibilities prohibited the earlier fullfillment of such dreams. How often in the past we have said with Robert Louis Stevenson, "I should like to rise and go" . . . to those far off lands of enchantment. Now that some of the prohibitions have been lifted, what joy there has been in travel!

In our own state our travels have taken us from Manteo to Murphy, from Currituck to Cherokee, from the border of Virginia to that of South Carolina, with frequent stops along the way, in Edenton for the annual historic pilgrimage and celebration, to Wilmington for the azalea festival, and another historic tour. Raleigh, our state capital, holds much of interest. Westward we have been to Guilford, of Revolutionary War fame, to Winston-Salem with its background of Moravian history, thence to the far west. There has been much of beauty and interest all along the way. We have visited Asheville with its Biltmore House and beautiful gardens, Old Kentucky Home of Thomas Wolfe fame, the Vance birthplace, and in nearby Flat Rock we found Connemara, home of Carl Sandburg, a recently opened historic shrine.

We have traveled on to Cherokee where we were immersed in the culture of the Cherokee Indians in the reconstructed Indian Village, the museum with its many Cherokee artifacts. We even had a tour through the fabulous seven-million dollar ultra-modern high school built with funds provided by the bureau of Indian Affairs to replace old wooden structures, one of which had been in use for more than three quarters of a century. The tour ended with a performance of "Unto These Hills" in the impressive theater.

Yes, we have found beauty and interest all along the way, but with detours, we could have found much more. From the sands of the coast to the peaks of Roan, Mitchell, and Pisgah, there was much to make us proud of our great state.

Numbers of retirees have criss-crossed our entire country in their travels and express their joy and appreciation in learning more about our land through travel:

> My sister and I have visited every state in the union with Alaska and Hawaii last. We have realized the vastness of our land as we covered the great spaces from east to west, from north to south.

✓ ✓ ✓

> Only through travel through all parts of our country can we get a wide view of our rich heritage. We have realized, too, the vast wealth of our land from its huge industries to its grain and vegetable fields, its mighty forests, its miles of orchards, and its tremendous mineral resources.

We have come to agree with the lecturer who said, "America is like a promise, so big it cannot be believed." With travel to other once far-away lands so rapid and easy today, we have adventured throughout the world. One voices the thoughts of many of us when she says:

> The trips I have taken have brought a fuller comprehension of the world and enabled me to re-live my experiences when I look at the treasures I have collected: the totem pole from Alaska, prints from India, France, Japan, Taiwan, jewelry from Mexico, woodcarvings from Indonesia, Switzerland, and Israel, beautiful glass from Bavaria, and linens from Belgium and Italy. Thus I have come to appreciate more fully the life and culture of many of our world neighbors.

Though someone says, "Reminiscing is something with which we dare not spend too much time," another expresses what we often feel:

> I like to recall the dedicated teachers and administrators who meant so much to me and who live in my memory. It gives me a feeling

of gratification when I recall the students I have taught who have grown into such wonderful men and women and are contributing so much to the world today. It seems an extra bonus for the times we have burned the midnight oil, planning and evaluation, trying our new ideas, working to find the best approach for each child.

Some of us have put our thoughts in rhyme:

For thirty-seven years I heeded the school bell's ring,
I welcomed retirement when I could do my own thing;
Now I live in my house by the side of the road
And watch, with pride, my former pupils shouldering life's load.

✓ ✓ ✓

Forty-seven years of highlights supreme
I recall with very great pleasure;
They're the fulfillment of a childhood dream
Each moment of which I treasure.

The main disappointment I ever did feel
Came when even one failed his potential to reach;
I felt I had failed to make the right appeal—
But I never regretted my choice to teach.

✓ ✓ ✓

A teacher I decided I wanted to be,
A work I could do and really be me;
At last in a room filled with pupils so dear,
I started to work—though not without fear—
At what I hoped was a teaching career.

To tell the truth, I never understood,
Though all made an effort as best they could,
Why Johnny couldn't read and Mary not spell
Though at mathematics they did very well.
Together we worked and we played—and teacher prayed.

As I think on these things and my life's work review,
My faith in mankind is greatly renewed;
So I straighten my shoulders and put on a smile,
Then I say it out loud and say it with pride
"Yes, I am a teacher—a teacher retired."

✓ ✓ ✓

I've done my work, I've sung my song,
This is not the end but a new beginning.
There is more to learn and much to do
As I continue to reach for the stars.

Memories continue to crowd in as we note below:

As we look back over the "bright intervals," isn't it fortunate that the unpleasant fades in the distance and an aura surrounds those we remember. At times, though, "my cup runneth over" with regret and sadness for those students I failed to reach, not from lack of desire but for want of the golden key with which to unlock what was within their hearts.

When I retired, my firm resolve was that everything would end with a period! Teaching first-grade children for twenty-five years can take the starch out of the stiffest backbone! First of all, I would no longer worry about the children; next was to end my school lunches! Never another chili bean or hotdog. Never again would I visit the school like a lost wandering soul to peek in at my successor and gloat that she could not teach as well as I.

One small thing I overlooked, though, was the children. I might leave them but they would not leave me. I found myself listening for running footsteps. Children never walk! They run, hop, skip, dance, trot, gallop, shuffle, skid, prance, race! But there came a day when these footsteps became dim and I realized that my little ghosts had faded into memory.

✓ ✓ ✓

I am glad I retired when I did, when I still think that teaching is the greatest profession in the world. But as teachers and students begin their trek back to the classroom each year, we [who are fortunate or not so fortunate,] the retired, may take time to ponder our past performances. Today the sum total of things we learned, along with our students, nourish our days with pleasant memories and beliefs that our efforts were worthwhile and enduring.

With pride and gratitude teachers mention the honors that were accorded them on retiring and later. How many school buildings across the state have been named in honor of a teacher or administrator who had given scores of years of service and had contributed so much to the life of the school and community.

One retiree reported that the old school bell used so many years in the school where she had taught was placed on the civic grounds of the town as a memorial to her many years of service to the community.

Others remind us:

We may be set on a pedestal on retiring, fellow retired teachers, but may our retirement years continue to be active, rewarding, fulfilling, and abundant with living.

✓ ✓ ✓

John Dryden was right in his thinking that a foundation of good sense and a cultivation of learning are the requirements for an enjoyable retirement; hence we who write here should qualify. We have faced the challenges, endured the frustrations, and tasted the joys that come with kindling the minds and molding the characters of youth. In so doing we have built our own lives and formed our own set of values.

✓ ✓ ✓

Having accepted as our slogan "To serve and not to be served," it seems necessary for us to remain active in retirement. Our associations, on all levels, offer opportunities for concerned, informed leadership which cry out for help retired teachers can give. Not all older Americans have the wisdom—wisdom being a gift from God— that members of our profession possess.

✓ ✓ ✓

In the twenty-seven years I have been a part of the teaching profession I have seen many changes in education, but the most important one, I think, has been the increased opportunities offered to young people to better themselves and to learn more about the world in which we live. I am glad to have had a small part in this endeavor. Teaching has been a good life. It has given me a sense of direction, a realization of my own value in the world, and a feeling of continuing growth. It is more than a way to earn a living—it is a way of life!

Still another report closes this chapter for us:

The Age of Fulfillment

His labors done, his harvest reaped,
The senior citizen retires to his own domain—
Not in a world of petty domesticity
But in a new wide world of fulfillment.
Now he deepens his knowledge of the ways of men,
Expands his horizon of understanding,
Lets his imagination have full play,
Rereads his favorite tales of love, hate, battle, joy, and peace,
Garners himself into the full personality of a lifetime,
Selects his books, not from the best sellers or required lists,
But for his own needs and aspirations—
Marveling the values that life has wrought.

XV 🌿 Professionalism in Retirement

Continuing Identification and Activity

Many requisites for successful living in retirement have been proposed. An article in a recent magazine suggested that one seek mental stimulation, develop a creative hobby, maintain involvement with people, engage in physical activity, and seek cultural and intellectual activities. Undergirding these suggestions, though, must be

1. Faith, courage, and determination to eliminate from our retirement boredom, loneliness, and insecurity, whenever possible.
2. Provision for financial resources sufficient to maintain a respectable independence.

Two organizations through which retired teachers can continue their professional involvement are the National Retired Teachers Association (NRTA) and the North Carolina Retired School Personnel (NCRSP), Division of the North Carolina Association of Educators (NCAE).

The National Retired Teachers Association, organized in 1947 by Dr. Ethel Percy Andrus, has become very active in improving the welfare of retired teachers through making provision for a drug service, insurance programs, travel agencies, legislative programs and other services especially for the elderly.

HISTORICAL BRIEF I

THE DEPARTMENT OF NORTH CAROLINA RETIRED TEACHERS

Mr. Thomas L. Looper, a retired teacher in North Carolina, inspired by the programs of NRTA, became very much interested in an organization of retired teachers in the state, whose members might work to achieve advantages for its members. Although, earlier the North Carolina Education Association (NCEA) had authorized a department of retired teachers, it was not until February 1961 that Mr. Looper initiated a movement for an organizational meeting of such a group to be held at the time of the state convention of NCEA in Asheville. At that assembly on March 24, 1961, the department was organized and Mr. Looper was elected president for 1961–62. The next four years Dr. Ben Childs, D. C. Mosteller, and D. P. Whitley, respectively, served as president.

In 1963 the NCEA sent a notice to all retired members stating that:

> The Board of Directors of NCEA has changed the membership fee for all of its retired members from the *annual* $2.00 fee to a $10.00 *Life Membership* fee, to be made in one payment, effective beginning with the 1963–64 membership year. This will eliminate the inconvenience of joining NCEA each year. Included in the life membership is a life subscription to *North Carolina Education*.

Mr. Looper was appointed by the National Retired Teachers Association as its state director, thus broadening the possibilities for service to school retirees. In 1965 the Department of Retired Teachers became affiliated with NRTA.

HISTORICAL BRIEF II

THE DIVISION OF NORTH CAROLINA RETIRED SCHOOL PERSONNEL

With the election of Mrs. Lucille Allen as president of Retired Teachers in 1966, there began a decade of intensified activity. Others serving as president during this decade were: Maie Sanders (2 years), W. W. Howell (2 years), Alma Browning (3 years), and Ernest Morgan is currently serving a two-year term, which ends in 1976.

At its annual meeting in 1966 the members of the retired department voted to request the NCEA to grant that group the status of a Division. This request was granted. Following this change, a constitution and by-laws were adopted and the name was changed to the North Carolina Retired School Personnel, a Division of the North Carolina Education Association. From its inception the NCEA has given its wholehearted cooperation and support to the division. NCEA gave financial help in getting started, and ever since has aided in legislative, research, and consultant services by members of the staff.

By 1966 there had been built up a deep realization of the unresolved inequities in the Retirement System and a growing number of division members felt keenly that something should be done about the situation. Also until 1970 the division had depended on voluntary dues or contributions to finance its activities. This arrangement resulted in a very limited budget. A survey of its Retired Life Members of the NCEA in 1969 showed that 96% of the 600 responding to a questionnaire were in favor of regular annual division dues. The by-laws adopted at the state convention in 1970 contained a requirement for regular division and district dues. This change enabled both state and district officers to increase their activities in organizing local units, conducting workshops, and attending necessary meetings.

The North Carolina Teachers Association had organized a department for retired teachers as early as 1957 with R. L. Hall as president. Mr. Hall served in that capacity for several years. Mrs. E. M. Kelley was serving as president when the NCEA and the NCTA merged to form the North Carolina Association of Educators. Mrs. Kelley became co-chairman with Mr. Howell for the Division of Retired School Personnel in the newly-formed NCAE, for the year 1969–70.

Following Mr. Looper's retirement as state director of NRTA in 1969, Maie Sanders was appointed state director and Fred

Brummitt became assistant director. Later Mr. Brummitt became state director when Miss Sanders was appointed vice-president for Area III of NRTA. Both have worked untiringly for NRTA as well as for NCRSP.

The following statistics are indicative of the effort on the part of many persons in the NCRSP to promote increases in membership in NCAE and NRTA, as well as in the division:

	1965	1970	1975
NCAE Life Members	243	2,100	6,125
NCRSP Members	N/A	1,550	3,600
NRTA Members	2,250	4,116	11,072

This disparity between NCRSP membership and NRTA/NCAE membership carries both positive and negative implications. On the positive side there are some 3,600 retirees who are *involved*. Not only are these members of the parent organization, the NCAE, but most are members of NRTA. It is to those 3,600 that major credit must go for the benefits being enjoyed by many non-members. On the negative side, it is obvious that several thousand retirees are not sharing the satisfaction of their peers in these cooperative efforts.

Since economic independence is so basic to a good retirement, the following are some of the policies and actions of NCRSP with respect to legislation for the decade now ending. Throughout this period it has been the policy of NCRSP to have one or more members present to observe, answer questions, and speak for retired teachers when any retirement legislation is being considered. This policy has included meetings of the NCAE Legislative Committee, Trustees meetings of the State Retirement System, Retirement Study Commission, and Legislative Committees in the House and the Senate. While we have recommended and supported other legislation for the elderly, the following are some of the significant retirement legislative measures enacted since 1966:

7/1/67 Percentage increases for those receiving benefits before 7/1/67 of 5% (minimum increase $10.00 monthly) up to 29% for those retired in 1942.

7/1/69   3% cost-of-living increase commencing 7/1/70 provided cost-of-living increased at least 3% if funds were available. This was increased to 4% beginning in 1971.

7/1/71   20% increase for those who commenced receiving benefits prior to 7/1/63.

1973   An amended homestead tax exemption bill was enacted which gave homeowners age 65 or older with limited incomes, a homestead exemption, which compares favorably with that of other states.

7/1/75   Persons who retired July 1, 1974, or earlier, were given an 8% cost-of-living increase in benefits instead of the originally scheduled 4%. On July 1, 1976, another 8% increase is scheduled.

As a retired educator, you are a recipient of state retirement and, to this extent, at least, NCRSP IS IN YOUR RETIREMENT!

If you are a retired educator and not a member of NCRSP, shouldn't you be?

RETIRED—RETARDED

It was the very next day after the PTA had honored the oldest member of the faculty with a lovely reception and presented her with the traditional silver Revere bowl, all inscribed with her name and years of service, as a retirement gift.

One little girl came in sobbing uncontrollably after a short break. All she could say was, "They, They—," She really did not know just what had been done to her. "What happened to L____," I asked. No response. After urging, one girl said, "She wasn't talking very nice."

L____ found her voice and began talking very fast. "I didn't say nothin' 'cept what you said yourself. I jes' told my cousin that Mrs. M____ was goin' to stop teaching, 'cause she was RETARDED an' you all started on me."

XVI ᷓ Looking Back and Ahead

Into Our Third Century

Educators should always look back to get a better perspective for looking ahead. A distillation of their findings in looking both ways should lead to the best wisdom. The inevitability of change will surely be an ingredient of this wisdom, but change should not overshadow the conclusions. In commenting on her philosophy of education, one teacher sees it this way:

> Today's challenge in a changing world has opened avenues hitherto unknown. Parents, plus community, plus teachers are capable of meeting the problems if they work together. Much depends on the teacher. She is the "Potter who molds the clay many hours during the day." Her influence, her attitude toward and her devotion to her profession teach the child the true values of life which determine success and security. The genuine teacher teaches more than the "Three Rs." She teaches her pupils how to meet problems and how to solve them. They learn to feel secure and become aware of things that count.
>
> Years ago I taught with the "Three A's" as my guide: Acceptance; Adjustment; and Achievement. What a help and a blessing a good teacher can be who realizes *life's values* and how to build a strong structure for education tomorrow.

When educators look at how well they have measured up to their opportunities and possibilities and try to assess their measure of success, they are far from unanimous in their conclusions. Experienced teachers write:

> I have talked to many teachers and a few principals in North Carolina. Secretly they admit that our children are not getting what

228

they should from our schools. I just can't bring myself to approve of the New One-room School House where all learning must be pleasurable and the children (all ages) on the floor instead of in seats.

✓ ✓ ✓

Education of all children is suffering from lack of discipline. Discipline begins in the most sacred place in the world—the home. Too many parents have let the bars down. It's a sure thing that parents and teachers will never be able to discipline until they can discipline themselves. Children deserve responsible parents and teachers. This discipline excludes alcohol, drugs, family squabbles and vile language. Most children want to do right, especially if they are loved and the right is expected of them.

✓ ✓ ✓

I know a high school boy who said to a friend, after being told he must go home, "My parents don't care when I go home. I wish they did." What is clear is that parents and teachers are *behind this notion.* As long as children are allowed to do as they please, they won't obey social or moral or civic powers.

✓ ✓ ✓

However, what a child is in school does not always indicate what he may be as a man. The success of many of our greatest men has proved that. I would like to add that every teacher has had some disappointments in the students he/she has taught. Gladly, I can say that mine have been very few considering my 35 years as a teacher. There have been so many outstanding persons produced in North Carolina, who have contributed so much to their community, our state, and our nation that I am confident, with all our weaknesses, that we are and have been second to none in the nation in the field of education.

A teacher interviewed in her wheel chair commented:

From this beginning in education, in later years I had the thrill and opportunity, as a supervisor, to plan with the teachers and architects a most modern educational facility that was student-centered. This modern, up-to-the-minute facility still did not make the program, as education must depend upon inter-action of students and teachers.

It was an inspiration to see the teachers plan and initiate new ideas that enhanced the program for today's teenagers who are interested in both academics as well as vocational programs.

Education in North Carolina has many accomplishments to its credit. It has come out of the one-room school into tremendous modern structures with ample aids and equipment, with programs and even schools to fit the needs of the student. Great progress has been made in educating teachers, in planning programs and in supervising the whole educational process. Upon looking back, the vast results of modern day education can scarcely be comprehended.

One teacher has recommended an article written by Ada F. Marsh and published in the *Marshville Home*, Marshville, North Carolina, May 2, 1973, as a summary of some of the nation's accomplishments in the early years of the twentieth century. The following are edited excerpts from this article:

> Lets examine the facts and name some of the accomplishments and some things not yet accomplished and also some of the prospects that lie ahead:
>
> Four times we have been involved in foreign wars and have battled against aggression, injustice and tyranny without grabbing one inch of another's land or seizing any uncompensated wealth for our nation. We have helped bind up the wounds of the vanquished and given our wealth to impoverished nations.
>
> In this one generation we have learned to control the ravages of diphtheria, polio, measles, smallpox, typhoid, tuberculosis, and pneumonia.
>
> We have built more schools, colleges, hospitals, and libraries than since the beginning of recorded time. We have trained more scientists, doctors, surgeons, dentists, lawyers, teachers, engineers, and physicists than did our ancestors for over a thousand years.
>
> We now have a standard of living and luxuries that were beyond the dreams of kings and the wealthiest a generation ago. We introduced the automobile, radio, telephone, airplane, television, and antibiotics within the life of people living today.
>
> We have taxed ourselves to bring health to the sick and poor and the aged in need. We have made personal gifts to private charities more than the cost of our government a generation ago. We have given equality and self-respect and opportunity to all minority groups greater than has ever been done since the beginning of recorded history. Today the average black in our nation is more

likely to go to college than white or black in England, Germany, Belgium, Denmark, Italy, or Spain.

Yet, there are still many challenges to be met. There are many goals to be attained. Time will never come when there will be no problems to solve by willing minds and hands. If it should arrive it would be Utopia.

Here are some of the goals that must be met and solved, which must be a challenge to our youth. They are the ones who will be in a position to meet them. Our youth can solve our social problems in this melting pot of America. They can find the ways to grow more food for our people and help prevent famine. They can become doctors, nurses, surgeons, dentists, lawyers, teachers, engineers, physicists, farmers, plumbers, carpenters, brick masons and perform many other services too numerous to name. Youth can become the heroes in finding the many cures we so badly need. Youth, with their better educational opportunities, has a head start over the past generation to deal with problems such as drugs and alcohol. Alcohol has been a problem ever since the days of Noah. Can there be a greater challenge?

Our youth will be better equipped to find new inventions and to improve on the inventions of the past. They can find new avenues of energy and new adventures overcoming gravity. They can help us undertake greater exploration of the beds of the oceans and seas, and learn to farm the seas for food.

According to a noted writer, "There is still work to be done. There are still goals to be attained." They will not be attained by some of the off-beat activities that some of our young engage in. They'll be attained by unsung heroes of every generation—the workers who can dream and the doers who can hope. They'll be attained by the men and women who honor the Ten Commandments, respect the Bill of Rights, and have faith in the American system, men and women who believe in a better tomorrow and are willing to work to that end.

SOME ASPIRATIONS AND INSPIRATIONS

I saw tomorrow marching by
On little children's feet,
Within their forms and faces read
Her prophecy complete

I saw tomorrow look at me
From little children's eyes,
And thought, how carefully we'd teach
If we were wise.

Author Unknown

In review it can be seen that even though there have been changes in every area of teaching, the one thing that seems to have remained is the desire of many dedicated individuals to teach to make a better world for the citizens of the future.

In the excerpts given below, teachers reveal that their concern is for children, for that is what education is all about:

My aim was to teach them impartially with respect to race, creed or their aptitude and in accordance with their needs.

✓ ✓ ✓

Frightened! For I realized that I could teach them little; but I strove to encourage them to reach out, search, examine. My aim was to inspire them to make "mansions of their minds" regardless of their ability.

✓ ✓ ✓

I realize that I grow as I live with others; that *myself* has to be built through my interaction with others as I strive to keep alive my profound sense of responsibility; I must be able to render a greater service in making the school a more effective agency for preserving and fulfilling the ideas and promise of American Democracy.

✓ ✓ ✓

As I have been recalling the many programs which were presented in the old auditorium, I can't help feeling nostalgic. How many hundreds of boys and girls had perhaps their few moments of glory there.

✓ ✓ ✓

If I were advising a young teacher, I would say, "Let the children know that you love them. Help them to learn how to study, and teach them the joy of reading. If you can create in them the desire to continue to learn, and to help others, you have given them something that will make their entire lives fuller and happier."

✓ ✓ ✓

Please, teachers, give every child a chance. There is hidden talent and there are learning abilities in each child whether he be angel or demon. We must take "the high road" and help each child climb his own ladder. *Know* the child *and* his parents if possible.

✓ ✓ ✓

My advice to new teachers; save notes from parents, pictures the children draw, and keep a note book handy for their cute sayings. Also, note some of the amazing things they do, like putting their shoes on the wrong feet after nap time and wearing the teacher's galoshes home.

✓ ✓ ✓

My sincere desire is to continue to broaden and deepen my concept of organized education in America; to keep alive my profound sense of social responsibility; to be able to render a greater service in making the school a more effective agency for preserving and fulfilling the ideas and promises of American Democracy.

Horizons

As teachers come to summarize their "Pride in America Project" and look into the horizons, every red-blooded retiree is challenged to heed its slogan and work "Toward a More Perfect Union."

So while they glory in their American Heritage and pay tribute to those who have shown the way, their attention and God-given energies must be centered on those areas of American Life which call for change and for which they may hope.

These areas may include a relationship with world neighbors strong enough to resolve international differences and eliminate the need for expanding armament. They could also include a hope for a broad-based economy in which the pride of ownership could be enjoyed by every citizen.

233

Others, among retired educators, looked deeply also. Their thoughts are summarized editorially in the following excerpts:

In our concern for education of the future we must look deeply into the horizons for some vision of the future. We know that, since the school is society's only formal agent for educating a people—and thus for perpetuating its value system in a democracy—it plays a particularly significant role.

A basic question thus arises: "Education for what?" Shall we focus on pragmatic education? Shall we define the goals in terms of "quality" education?

Is education for the exceptional child to be accorded priority? If so, isn't every child exceptional in some unique way? Aren't we all exceptional in different situations in some way or other? Must not democracy teach each child who is talented to live compassionately with the slow learner and to put a high value on the slow learner as a person whose contributions are valuable to our social well being? Our education would, by inference, afford the experiences by which the slow learner and the talented would each in his own way, participate constructively and uniquely for the common good.

Suppose it is education for the "average?" Average being a statistical concept, can education for a democratic society afford to label 66% of its learners by a depersonalized, dehumanizing term, forgetting that "average" represents two-thirds of our citizens, each unique in his or her own capabilities? Must we not remember that in a democracy it is the average person who furnishes our first line of defense and the bulk of our citizenship?

Our process of education must not stifle initiative, discourage questioning, neglect creative expression, demand stereotyped answers, test for product rather than process.

Let uniqueness be our goal. Let me be judged by my own progress. Let me, as a citizen, experience the education that citizenship in a free society demands. Education is social as well as academic, and for the vision of our forefathers to become reality, qualities of the spirit as well as of the mind are fundamentals.

Democracy is a way of life, a way of behaving, and the school room must be the testing ground where the learners practice and evaluate the attitudes which will create a society wherein the differences that exist become valuable assets for enriching our heritage, rather than separating one person from another.

LOOKING DEEPER INTO THE HORIZONS

In this bicentennial year, a prominent retired educator looks at the past, the present, the future, and contributes for this collection of aspirations:

We who have spent from 20 to 40 or more years actively engaged in our educational process are now having time for deeper reflections. We look out and see that the training of the young goes on and must go on. Our secret wish is to go on with them. In fact we will go on in our concerns and by our endeavors be supportive of those who continue the active role.

For us in this bicentennial year Robert Frost has pictured our genuine and continuing challenge in a poem containing these lines: "For I have promises to keep . . . and miles to go before I sleep." We do, indeed, as a free people, have promises to keep, and, because we *are* free, we welcome the "miles" we must travel to bring our promises into the rich fulfillment which our freedom permits.

We have a past which teaches us lessons of fortitude, sacrifice, loyalty, belief in our purposes, and a dedication to the concept of earnest and honest work to reach those purposes.

We have a present—and the present moment is all that we do have—which raises new and, often, frightening issues. If we continue to try to use old solutions which, in many cases brought us to these troublesome issues, we lose sight of the challenge of our freedom—the freedom to search, to study, to read widely, to imagine, to dream, and in these processes, to face the inescapable fact that, through dissent only, do we weed out error and arrive at a wiser solution to a problem.

We have a future, and, with our future may well rest the future of all free peoples everywhere, for in our "great experiment" with self-government through the consent of the governed, we have set before the world the only way of life in which men make their own decisions both for themselves and for others. This freedom is a blessing, but it is also a potential danger if, with it, we do not join responsible behavior, both in our own self-discipline to sacrifice individual and selfish interests for our common good, and in our management of our behavior as a unified people. Unity does not mean uniformity, and to perfect our union certain self-imposed limits must be imposed upon "liberty" to prevent its becoming "license."

And so, in the school rooms of this nation our heritage must be lived in every sense of the word, not simply talked about or read about. The basic principles safeguarding human rights and personal dignity must become our practice, as well as the subject of discourse, for it is only in our individual greatness that there is a total common greatness. And greatness we have if we re-examine our stated beliefs.

In the tributes paid to teachers in this book it is clear to see that students listen, not so much to what these teachers have *said* as to what these teachers *were* and *are*. In the lives of these students, it has been the teacher's "quality," the personal integrity, the dedication, the genuine concern for the student, the "authenticity" of the teacher as a person of honor and integrity as well as of scholarship, which have remained in the memory and affectionate regard of those whose lives have been influenced in the classrooms where important lessons have been taught and learned.

"Civilization is a race between education and catastrophe," and it has been the privilege of the teacher to be a participant in that race. "Your young men shall see visions and your old men shall dream dreams". . . We have dreamed many dreams and have made some of them come true. Now, it is time for the dreams to become visions—visions of faith in ourselves as a nation of unlimited resources, both material and human; of a people committed to compassion and trust in the inherent goodness of our fellow Americans and of other world citizens; of individuals, purposefully urged on to appraise their own best efforts and to use these efforts, not only for selfish gain, but also to enrich and enhance the heritage already theirs, a heritage which needs the differences as well as the likenesses among them to utilize all the talent available to bring this nation to its greatest period of leadership—leadership in finding peaceful means for living together; leadership in creating a more human and just world. And for ourselves, visions of reaching beyond the grasp to seek the ultimate desire of our forefathers—a "nation indivisible, with liberty and justice for all."

MILES TO GO

And so Tar Heel teachers have herein spoken. Here are their dreams . . . and may their dreams grow ever in dimension until there is a vision, and the vision becomes a reality:—a heritage which in all of its aspects will come ever nearer that ideal implicit in the words of the documents which undergird the rights as persons, possessed of worth and dignity.

A Promise . . . Miles to go . . . What a heritage!

LOGICAL

Having just completed a farm unit, the children were at their seats illustrating the story they had read about "The Farm Animals in the Barnyard."

One boy had drawn a big white barn with a fence around the barnyard. A heavy shower of rain was falling everywhere. He was asked by one of the students, "Where are all the farm animals?"

"It is raining and they've gone into the barn."

✒ List of Contributors

Abernathy, Rufus Henry
Abrams, W. Amos
Adcock, Lillian F.
Albright, Lesta
Alderman, Hilda
Alexander, Flora
Alexander, Jessie
Alexander, Rachel
Alexander, Wynola Spencer
Allen, Estelle L.
Allen, Lucille Kirby
Allgood, Mary
Allison, Daintry
Amick, Pomona J.
Anderson, Mamie Willette Rush
Anderson, Margaret C.
Andrews, Madoline Cathey
Archbell, Martha Pat
Armstrong, Rosina Pittman
Arndt, Grace Yoder
Arndt, Harry M.
Arrington, Alethea
Atkins, Lula M.
Auman, Treva

Badger, Esther
Bailey, Mrs. R. G.
Baird, Iris Woods
Baker, Elizabeth

Baker, Meta
Banner, Estelle Mauney
Barber, Lunette
Barker, Charlie Mae
Barker, Esther T.
Barker, Vascelia Spencer
Barnes, B. N.
Barnes, Hallie S.
Barnhill, Pearl Cook
Barrier, J. F.
Barrier, Verney M.
Barringer, Margie E.
Bault, Pauline B.
Beam, Charlotte
Beason, Gertrude
Beck, Mary Turner
Bennett, Elizabeth S.
Bennett, T. W.
Berkheimer, Lois
Berry, Eunice G.
Berry, Margaret Neill
Bigelow, Ruby Haynes
Billings, Nellie S.
Bingham, Lois Crouse
Bisher, Ola U.
Bivens, Edna S.
Black, Minnie G.
Blakemore, Elizabeth
Blaylock, Maud

Boggs, Frances Sherrill
Bohnsdahl, Naomi
Boston, Nannie M.
Boswell, Emma K.
Bowe, Stephen A.
Bowers, Lettie G.
Bowles, Garnette
Bowles, M. H.
Boyd, L. B.
Boyette, Frances
Bradshaw, Beulah
Brawley, Frances
Breedlove, Evelyn
Breedlove, La Rue M.
Breedlove, Ruth
Bridges, Ezra A.
Britt, Clarinda A.
Britt, James E.
Broadie, Cornelia H.
Brock, Barbara
Brooks, Wilma Woods
Brown, Evelyn Rumple
Brown, Ila Brady
Brown, Mary T.
Brown, Rachael B.
Brown, T. Carl
Browning, Alma
Bruce, Margaret
Brummitt, Fred G.
Brummitt, Grace
Brummitt, Kate Fleming
Bryan, Mary
Bullock, W. J.
Bulluck, Willie Eliza Forbes
Bumgarner, Cornelia Gilreath
Burchette, Edith
Burke, Althea Williams
Burnette, Ella Lee
Burris, Edgar
Burriss, E. M.
Burrows, Louise H.
Byars, Jenny Woodward

Cannon, Elma B.
Cannon, Elma W.
Capel, Amanda
Cardwell, Alma H.
Carmichael, Dorothy T.
Carr, Woodrow W.
Carroll, Ruby G.
Carson, J. W.
Carswell, Mada Franklin
Carter, Fannie Lee
Carter, Jennie
Cates, Thelma
Cathey, Aurelia
Causey, Mozelle
Chandler, Lizzie Gray
Chandler, Minnie
Cheek, Nellie R.
Childers, Elizabeth Gwaltney
Chiltosky, Mary
Christy, Jean
Clapp, Edna R.
Clodfelter, Selma Crews
Cloud, Eunice
Cobb, Virginia S.
Coble, Lelia W.
Coble, Lois
Coble, Mrs. M. A.
Collins, Alline T.
Collins, Fannie T.
Coltrane, Pattie J.
Cooke, Frances Furr
Cooper, Bertha
Cooper, Elizabeth Scott
Cooper, Gertrude W.
Cooper, Rosalie McEachin
Cooper, S. A.
Corbett, Dora
Covington, Macie L.
Craig, Carrie Rickert
Craven, Florence Boyette
Crawford, Dorothy R.
Crews, Josephine M.

Cromartie, Minnie H.
Cromartie, William K.
Crotts, Gertrude S.
Crotts, Luther O.
Crowell, Carolyn
Cureton, M. T.
Curl, Mary P.
Currin, Ila D.
Curtis, Mary S.

Dagenhart, Carl D.
Dale, Mertie
Daniely, Rena Maude Iseley
Danner, Edna
Danner, Susie
Daughtry, Angerola M.
Davenport, Mellie R.
Davis, B. L.
Davis, Virgie Jones
Dean, Loleta
Deans, Mary Benoy
DeVane, Cato C., Sr.
Dickens, Roslyn
Diffee, Bertie
Dillard, Margaret
Douglas, Clara
Dowdy, Dora G.
Draughan, E. W.

Eagle, Mrs. John K.
Ebersole, Wilma
Edwards, Ema W.
Elledge, Everette I., Sr.
Eller, C. B.
Elliott, Eugenia L.
Ennis, Carolyn G.
Eury, Miriam
Evans, Evalee

Fain, Missouri C.
Farrior, Beulah C.

Farrior, Elizabeth B.
Faucette, Maude
Faulkner, Marian Black
Felts, Lula Belle
Fennell, Cornelia E.
Fennell, Mary A.
Feree, Ruth
Flowers, Annie
Fogleman, Gwendolyn Patton
Ford, E. Alberta
Formy Duval, Frances
Foster, Betty N.
Foushee, Helen Peare
Foust, Marcia Elizabeth
Fox, Ruth C.
Freeman, Merline D.
Fryar, Lucie Hayes
Fuller, Mildred Harris

Gallimore, Mrs. J. Frank
Gamble, Elizabeth McGill
Gardner, Mae B.
Gardner, Ruth
Garrett, Audrey W.
Gathings, Jewel B.
Gattis, Hassie V.
Gillon, Laura
Gilreath, Sallie
Gleaves, Mary Lee
Glenn, Enola S.
Glenn, Katie B.
Gooden, Mae Gwaltney
Goranto, Pauline
Gore, Jonnie
Graham, Kara
Greene, Mrs. Roy B.
Greer, Manie Taylor
Griffin, R. B.
Griffin, Wilma
Gulledge, Eddie Lee
Guthrie, Ola Bradshaw

Hall, Henry R.
Hall, Kathleen
Hall, Mary W.
Hall, Ruth B.
Hamilton, Louise
Hamilton, Marie H.
Hamilton, Mary Lou McK.
Hammond, Leah
Hammond, Tiny
Hammonds, Albert
Harbison, Bedie
Hardister, Nora Scarboro
Harrell, Kate
Harriman, Cecile James
Harris, Allie Nooe
Harris, Catherine L.
Harris, Essie
Harris, Julia Wyatt
Harris, Sallie E.
Harris, Winnie B.
Hartsell, Annie Parker
Hauser, Orressa Harris
Hayer, Nelle Jolly
Hayes, Pauline Neal
Heavner, Ilease F.
Hedrick, Ethel Merritt
Herring, Lucy S.
Hester, Hattie
Hildebran, Abbie Seals
Hildebran, Eleanor G.
Hill, Beulah W.
Hill, Irene D.
Hines, Jessie Pauline
Hinson, Thelma Stone
Hobson, Mary Ellen
Hoffner, Thettis
Holbrook, Beatrice
Holderby, Alene Clayton
Holland, Irma Ragan
Hollingsworth, Maggie
Holmes, Ralph W.
Hood, Louise E.

Hopkins, Mary H.
Horne, Lillie
Horton, Lela G.
Howell, W. W.
Hudson, Erma P.
Huff, Flora G.
Huffman, Leona W.
Hughes, Christine A.
Humphries, Ruth
Hunt, Elsie Brame
Hunter, Hortense Honeycutt

Ingold, Maude Pierce
Ingram, Laura Jane Mullen
Ipock, Janie
Ivanoff, Josephine Buck

Jackson, Della Hayden
Jackson, Kathleen S.
Jackson, Lena T.
Jackson, Louise B.
Jacoby, Carlotta
James, Estelle H.
Jamieson, Eleanor
Jarvis, Ada L.
Jarvis, Mona W.
Jeffers, T.
Jeffryes, Bernice G.
Jenkins, Sadie Richardson
Jeter, Nan
Jetton, Lula
Johnson, Annie W.
Johnson, Evelyn Adelaide
Johnson, Frances F.
Johnson, Roberta B.
Jones, Mary

Keck, Fostena E.
Keever, Homer M.
Kennedy, Florene
King, Adelaide S.

King, George R.
King, Louise Willis
King, Rena
Kinney, Mae Patterson
Kinsland, Gladys
Kirk, Faedene R.
Kiser, F. D.
Knight, Watha
Knott, Rosa Jane
Knox, J. H.
Knox, Katherine Nooe
Kreimeier, Anne

Lackey, Adline Sharpe
Lackey, Edith
Langdon, Maude B.
Lanier, Fannie K.
Lanier, Jesse J.
Lanier, Sallie D.
Laws, Thelma
Leatherwood, Lawrence
Leggette, Marguerite Barnes
Lemmond, Thelma
Lenon, Lola
Lentz, Fred W.
Leslie, Mary Ann
Lewallen, Inez
Lewis, H. Michael
Lewis, Thelma
Ligon, Sallie Mae
Little, Virginia
Littlejohn, William
Loflin, Donna Lee
Logan, Mary
London, Martha Hood
Lovett, Lucy Leigh
Lowry, Calvin
Lowry, Docter F.
Lowry, Phelia E.
Loy, Leona F.
Loy, Mrs. W. L.

Lyon, Lillian T.
Lyon, Mattie M.

McBane, Mrs. T. W.
McBee, Helen
McCoy, Mae
McDade, Kathrine Nicks
McDermott, Margaret B.
McDuffie, Alice W.
McEwen, Celeste White
McFadyen, Pauline
McGhee, Mrs. C. H.
McKay, Vera
McKinley, Johnsie L.
McManns, Ednir H.
McMurren, Lurania E.
McMurren, Mattie
McPherson, Bertha Isley
McPherson, Beulah T.
McPherson, Eunice M.

Mabe, Coy E.
Madison, Mrs. R. B.
Mann, G. O.
Mann, Ione Mebane
Manning, Dorothy
Manning, Irene
Marsh, Ada F.
Martin, Ann R.
Masemore, Ann Little
Meadows, Madge Millsaps
Meekins, Milah P.
Melton, Edna
Miller, Geneva Burke
Miller, Lillian
Milstead, Vona Gryder Thomas
Minor, Lillian Patrick
Minor, Vauda Merrell
Mitchell, Lillian Looper
Mixon, Ina
Morgan, Claudia I.
Morgan, Ernest W.

Morgan, Ethelene C.
Morgan, Margaret H.
Morrison, Jettie D.
Morrison, Mary N.
Morrison, Mary Woodside
Morrow, Adelaide
Morrow, Narvie W.
Morrow, Nellie Hendrix
Morton, Sadie
Morton, Shannon
Moseley, Blanche Harper
Moseley, Martha
Murrain, Della M.
Murray, Mary Deese
Murray, W. A.
Musgrove, Christine Reaves
Myrick, Lillian S.

Neal, Helen G.
Neece, Marietta
Neil, J. Berge
Neill, Gertrude
Neill, Lillian Washburn
Newell, Blanche Harris
Newlin, Pearle K.
Newman, Sallie B.
Nichols, Mildred S.
Nicholson, Thelma B.
Noble, Edoth
Noell, Emma A.
Norwood, Lillian D.

Oaks, Maude R.
Odom, Lena M.
Oliver, Sarah B.
Owen, Carrie Pierce

Padgett, C. C.
Pagaent, Lillian
Pagaent, Mae
Page, Anne T.
Palmer, Mary

Parker, Mrs. B. C.
Parker, Marie
Parsons, June H.
Patterson, Nannie T.
Pattillo, Eugenia K.
Patton, R. L.
Payne, Ruth H.
Pearson, Phairlever
Pemberton, Amanda
Pender, Irene Oliver
Penn, Juanita Smith
Perkins, Eugenia E.
Person, Thelma P.
Phelps, Eloise Ward
Phillips, Naomi
Phillips, Sue S.
Pickard, Elizabeth F.
Pittman, Cora H.
Plonk, May
Poole, Mabel Harden
Pope, Helen M.
Potts, Sophia H.
Powers, Margaret Haywood
Prevatte, Amanda Ruth
Pritchard, Annie
Pritchett, Lois Albright
Proctor, Reba
Pruitt, Fannie Lee
Pugh, Mrs. Robert L.
Purkey, Hazel

Radford, Maude
Ragland, Carl
Ramos, Pearle R.
Ready, I. Epps
Rector, Gillie S.
Reid, Daisy Hines Hairston
Reinhardt, Bertha
Reitzel, Blanche
Reynolds, Dora Z.
Rhu, Beatrice Evans
Rhyne, Myra Lutz

Rhyne, R. L.
Riddle, Fannie J.
Robbins, Bessie Holmes
Roberts, Ida H.
Robertson, Emma A.
Rogers, Annie P.
Rogers, Mattie Belle
Rose, Elna Connelly
Roseman, Forney
Royal, Leah S.
Royster, Kathryn B.
Rudisill, Bessie Leona

Sadler, Vera P.
Sampson, Estelle H.
Sanders, Maie
Satterfield, Hilda Hayes Fountain
Satterwhite, Gladys S.
Schooler, Frances W.
Schooler, J. M.
Scott, E. Merle
Seals, Carrie Kincaid
Seay, Esther
Seay, Mrs. Russell M.
Shamburger, Mary Ina
Shamburger, Pearl Gordon
Sharpe, Elizabeth Allen
Sharpe, Willard
Shavender, Mary S.
Shaw, Margaret
Shepherd, Anna Keever
Shepherd, H. S.
Sherrill, Angelita Harrilson
Sherrill, Lumicia
Shoulars, Leta W.
Shoulars, Philip Edison
Simkins, Virginia
Sims, Edna B.
Singleton, Mamye Sullivan
Sink, Pauline G.
Sitton, Lucy G.
Sloan, Inez K.

Smith, Charles C.
Smith, Eugene R.
Smith, Gloria
Smith, Mrs. L. G.
Smith, Mary Livas
Smith, Ned R.
Snead, Nell
Sparkman, Anne W.
Spencer, Elizabeth Masemore
Spencer, Mary S.
Sproles, Charlie Mae
Stanley, Morgan G.
Starnes, Ethel
Stem, Frances
Stephenson, W. C.
Stewart, Estelle W.
Stockman, Ava Rudisill
Stockman, Waldo W.
Stovall, Annie Hart
Stovall, Thornton
Strawn, Lila Faircloth
Stuart, Lyndon E.
Summers, Mary
Swaim, Francine Holt
Swann, Nellie R.

Talbert, Marie E.
Tallant, Vadah McMurray
Tatum, Helen Adams
Taylor, Mae White
Taylor, Mary
Teachey, Guy B.
Teague, Dessie Brown
Teague, Gay
Telfair, Katie Burnett
Terrell, Elizabeth Yokley
Tester, Mildred
Thacker, Eulalia C.
Thomas, Evelyn
Thompson, Elizabeth
Thompson, Hattie M.
Thompson, Mrs. Kermit

Thornberg, Nancy
Thrower, Irene D.
Tomlinson, Pearl Miller
Truitt, Adelia
Tull, Rowena H.
Twiford, C. W.
Twiford, Ethel W.

Underwood, Mozelle Jackson

Vannoy, Belva Burleson
Venters, Carrie
Villines, Lottie M.
Villines, Sudie F.

Walker, Alvin A.
Walker, Gatsey B.
Walker, Ruie H.
Wall, Anne Lee
Walsh, Virginia
Ward, Dean A.
Ward, Glenn
Ware, Jessie H.
Warner, Montie
Warren, Marion
Watkins, Lou P.
Wehlitz, Lou Rogers
Weir, Josephine Ellerbe
Weir, S. S.
Welch, Elizabeth
Wellman, Lela
Wells, Mrs. Hugh M.
Wells, Louise H.
West, Edwin A.
West, Ruby Reynolds
White, Frances Whitted
White, Jeanette
White, Mary Shaw
White, Viola J.
Whitefield, Esther Wilson
Whitehead, Cora

Whitted, Grace M.
Wilder, Myrtle Wilson
Wiley, Mary
Wilhelm, Blanche
Williams, Catherine Brinkley
Williams, Frankie J.
Williams, Lena Merritt
Williams, Mary C.
Wilson, Beatrice
Wilson, Bettina S.
Wilson, E. D.
Wilson, Eugenia G.
Wilson, Janie
Wilson, Margaret W.
Wilson, Mary Horne
Wilson, Mary R. Stallings
Wilson, Mittie J.
Wilson, Myrtle F.
Witty, Ruth H.
Wolff, Mary
Wood, Elizabeth
Wood, Lillian C.
Wood, Loyd
Wood, Monta Clark
Wood, Vida M.
Wooten, Mary Louise
Worsley, Mary Lee
Worsley, Rosa A.
Wyke, Thelma Kerley

Yarborough, Mary Belle
Yarborough, Virginia
Yeargin, Effie M.
Yoder, Sarah
York, Elizabeth
Young, Annie Lee
Young, Ethel
Young, Madge Cline
Yow, Nancy Burrows

Zimmerman, Blanche